Jacob Roemer

Reminiscences of the War of the Rebellion

1861-1865

Jacob Roemer

Reminiscences of the War of the Rebellion
1861-1865

ISBN/EAN: 9783337116446

Printed in Europe, USA, Canada, Australia, Japan

Cover: Foto ©ninafisch / pixelio.de

More available books at **www.hansebooks.com**

REMINISCENCES

— OF THE —

WAR OF THE REBELLION

1861 — 1865.

— BY —

BVT.-MAJ. JACOB ROEMER,

BATTERY L. SECOND N. Y. ARTILLERY, and
THIRTY-FOURTH N. Y. V. V. IND. LT. BATTERY.

Edited by

L. A. FURNEY,

Late Capt. Forty-fifth U. S. C. T.

Published by the
ESTATE OF JACOB ROEMER,
Flushing, N. Y.

1897

Copyrighted 1897
By Estate of Jacob Roemer.
[All rights reserved]

PRESS OF THE FLUSHING JOURNAL.
FLUSHING, L. I.

CONTENTS.

	PAGE
LIFE OF MAJOR ROEMER BEFORE AND SINCE THE WAR	5
INTRODUCTION	9

CHAPTER I.
ORGANIZATION.   LIFE AT CAMP BARRY. 11

CHAPTER II.
REORGANIZATION.   CEDAR MOUNTAIN. 28

CHAPTER III.
SECOND BATTLE OF BULL RUN. 57

CHAPTER IV.
ANTIETAM.   FREDERICKSBURG. 85

CHAPTER V.
FREDERICKSBURG TO VICKSBURG. 104

CHAPTER VI.
HAYNES'S BLUFF, JACKSON AND VICKSBURG. 117

CHAPTER VII.
VICKSBURG TO KNOXVILLE. 135

CHAPTER VIII.
THE TENNESSEE CAMPAIGN.   CAMPBELL'S STATION. 149

CHAPTER IX.
THE TENNESSEE CAMPAIGN.   SIEGE OF KNOXVILLE. 165

CONTENTS.

CHAPTER X.
CLOSE OF TENNESSEE CAMPAIGN. RE-ENLISTMENT. VETERAN FURLOUGH. ... 175

CHAPTER XI.
RETURN FROM VETERAN FURLOUGH. THE WILDERNESS. SPOTTSYLVANIA COURT HOUSE. ... 192

CHAPTER XII.
NORTH ANNA RIVER. COLD HARBOR. FORT FLETCHER. BEGINNING OF SIEGE OF PETERSBURG. ... 210

CHAPTER XIII.
SIEGE OF PETERSBURG CONTINUED. THE HARE HOUSE. FORT WILLCOX OR BATTERY XVI. ... 223

CHAPTER XIV.
SIEGE OF PETERSBURG CONTINUED. BATTLE OF THE PETERSBURG CRATER. ... 241

CHAPTER XV.
SIEGE OF PETERSBURG CONTINUED. AUGUST 1st, 1864 TO DECEMBER 31ST, 1864. ... 251

CHAPTER XVI.
SIEGE OF PETERSBURG CONCLUDED. CAPTURE AND RECAPTURE OF FORT STEDMAN. SURRENDER OF PETERSBURG. ... 260

CHAPTER XVII.
RETURN FROM PETERSBURG TO WASHINGTON. THE GRAND REVIEW. ... 278

CHAPTER XVIII.
HOMEWARD BOUND. THE BATTERY MUSTERED OUT. ... 297

APPENDIX. REGISTER OF NAMES. ... 309

A BRIEF SKETCH

—— OF THE ——

LIFE OF JACOB ROEMER.

JACOB ROEMER, BREVET MAJOR, U. S. V., the author of this volume was born April 3, 1818, in the village of Wahlheim, Greiz Alzey, Hessen Darmstadt. His father died in August the same year, and his mother followed her husband in March, 1822, when her son was scarcely four years old. During the year succeeding her death, the young boy was cared for by friends of the family, and was then taken by his uncle, Peter Roemer, to live with him. This uncle was a well-to-do farmer, living in the village of Dandenheim, Greiz Alzey. When the boy was fifteen years old, he was, as his uncle used to say, well instructed in all the rudiments of farming. He also had become acquainted with the principles of bee-keeping, the budding and grafting of trees, and of the proper care and management of horses and cattle. He had also learned how to use all the tools and implements used by farmers.

It was now decided that he must learn some trade, and that of shoemaking was adopted as being the least expensive. Accordingly he was apprenticed to the village shoemaker, so that his aunt could see to his washing and mending, and also that his share of the interest money derived from his father's estate could be saved up against the time

he should become of age. He was apprenticed for two and
one-half years to this shoemaker, under strictly drawn in-
dentures and a guarantee for good behavior. For his services he was to receive 75 gulden cash, and whatever else
might be necessary to pay for his clothing, washing, mending, etc.

Having served his apprenticeship, he went to the city of
Worms, where he worked at his trade until he was twenty.
He then entered the army as a recruit. He was well fitted
physically to become a first-class cavalryman. Being fond
of horses and having been promised speedy promotion to
the rank of corporal, he was highly elated over his prospects. But his sister Anna Maria, two years older than
himself, did not like the idea of her brother's becoming a
soldier, and, with the assistance of a friend, bought his discharge before he was 21 years old.

As soon as he was released from military service, he
planned going on a six years' tour. After completing all
necessary arrangements, he started in May, 1839, with
about $300 in his pocket, on a trip down the Rhine, visit-
ing all places of note on the river. Thence he went to Rot-
terdam, then to London, and finally to New York, where
he went to work again at his trade. He was married in
New York in 1840, and moved to Flushing in 1842, and
established himself in business. The failure of Dr. Hawkes
in April, 1843, was a terrible blow to Mr. Roemer, for by it
he lost $3,500, and was left almost penniless. However,
with 75 cents in the house, he determined to continue his
business. Realizing that rigid economy must now be his
watchword, during the years 1843, 1844 and 1845 he often
walked to New York, starting at three or four o'clock in the
morning so as to be able to buy his stock and take Benj.
Byrd's stage for Flushing, which left Franklin Square at
nine o'clock in the morning.

In 1845 he received some $800 from Germany, and by the advice of his wife, went at once to New York and paid all his debts. He returned to Flushing with $43, of which he gave his wife $23. He now went on with his business clear and unencumbered, and with good credit both in Flushing and New York. By the end of the year his business had increased considerably.

At that time there were very few English-speaking Germans in Flushing, and Mr. Roemer was very often called to court to act as interpreter. One day, being very busy, he refused to go when Judge Silliman sent for him, and then the judge sent an officer with a bench-warrant with $25 fine attached. Of course he obeyed this summons, but as soon as the court adjourned he went down to the armory of the Light Horse Artillery and enlisted. This was on September 11th, 1845. His certificate of membership is now in the possession of one of his children.

From this time on until the breaking out of the War of the Rebellion, Mr. Roemer continued to prosper in business and enjoyed the esteem and confidence of his fellow-citizens of Flushing. The story of his life from 1861 to 1865 is recorded in this volume. At the close of the War the Generals under whom he had served wished him to join the regular army, and a captain's commission in it was offered to him, but he declined, saying that he did not wish to play soldier on the drill ground, for he preferred active service in the field, yet he thanked them heartily for the compliment. He then resumed his place in his shoe store among his clerks and workmen after his four long years of active service in the field.

Major Roemer joined Geo. Huntsman Post, No. 50, Dept. N. Y., Grand Army of the Republic, Dec. 11th, 1872, and became its Commander in 1878, and was re-elected in 1879. In the latter year he lost his devoted wife, Sept. 13th,

1882, he left the Post on transfer, but rejoined it Sept. 8th, 1883. In 1884 he was elected Post Surgeon, to which position he was regularly re-elected until 1889. In 1890 he was elected Post Quartermaster, and was annually re-elected until 1894. He was also annually elected a member of the Post Council of Administration from 1884 and appointed a member of the Bureau of Employment and Relief from 1887 up to the time of his death.

When money was to be raised to erect the Soldiers' Monument now standing in the Park, Major Roemer was one of the Committee appointed to solicit subscriptions, and was one of the most active members of the Committee. He was also a member of the Water Commission elected by the Village of Flushing to introduce the present system of supplying the Village with water. Twice he was elected Town Trustee of Flushing Township.

In 1889 he was attacked with Bright's disease, but he rallied so greatly that it was thought he would fully recover, but as time went on successive relapses occurred. It was not, however, until late in 1895 that he was obliged to take to his bed. He rallied several times, and on different occasions regained sufficient strength to go to his store and attend to business. About the 1st of July, 1896, the Major was stricken down by an unusually severe attack, and despite all the efforts of his physicians, he grew steadily worse, and died peacefully and calmly Wednesday evening, July 15th, 1896.

Major Roemer was always glad to give aid to needy comrades of the Grand Army, and to extend a helping hand to the poor. So he lived and so he died, a noble, self-sacrificing man. Justice was the law that governed him in all things.

INTRODUCTION.

For a number of years it has been the intention of the author of the following pages, Major Jacob Roemer, to write out his recollections of the Civil War in which he took part during four long years, but it was not until the spring of 1895 that he actually began to carry out this intention.

As he had been repeatedly asked how the "Flushing Battery" came to be organized, it seemed to him but proper that a brief history of the organization which eventually became the Flushing Battery should be prepared. The material for this was obtained partly from the Major's own recollections and partly from a "History of Flushing" published about the time of the beginning of the War and now long out of print.

The "Flushing Guard," the earliest uniformed military organization in Flushing, was mustered into the New York State Militia, November 1st, 1839, as Light Infantry, and was attached to the 93d Regiment, N. Y. S. M., as a flank company. It made its first public parade with twenty-six uniformed men January 16th, 1840. In February, 1843, the company was changed from infantry to artillery, and in 1845 it was again changed to Light Horse Artillery and attached to Storm's famous First Brigade, L. H. A., in which it became the leading organization. At that time it was commanded by Captain William A. Mitchell, and was attached to the 3d Regiment, N. Y. L. H. A., Lieutenant-Colonel Charles A. Hamilton commanding.

Mr. Roemer enlisted as a private in this Battery September 11th, 1845, and was promoted corporal in 1846. At the breaking out of the Mexican War its services were tendered to the United States Government, but they were not accepted. By 1848 this Battery had attained a state-wide reputation in Light Horse Artillery evolutions. Its parades called together the most celebrated tacticians in the army, who styled it the "incomparable" and gave it the name of "Bragg's Battery," after the hero of Buena Vista.

In 1849 Corporal Roemer was promoted to Sergeant, and in 1851 was made First Sergeant. He was promoted First Lieutenant July 26th, 1859. The Battery was at that time commanded by Captain Thomas L. Robinson, and was attached to the 15th Regiment, 6th Brigade, Second Division, New York State Militia. This organization continued until it was superseded by the Flushing Battery in 1861. At this point Major Roemer begins his story, and if it shall seem to the reader that he is too egotistic, it should be borne in mind that the Major is not writing a history of the Civil War, but simply relating his own and the Flushing Battery's experiences during their four years of service.

CHAPTER I.

ORGANIZATION. LIFE AT CAMP TODD AND CAMP BARRY.

When President Lincoln issued his call for 75,000 men for three months on the 15th of April, 1861, the day after the surrender of Fort Sumter, the 15th Regiment, N. Y. S. M., considered the matter of offering their services for that period, but they delayed so long in making preparations for it that before they were ready to go the enlistment of troops for three months was stopped, and all further enlistments were ordered to be for three years, or during the war. This was a decided change. Many would have gone readily enough for the shorter period, thinking it would be simply a pleasant little vacation, but when the longer period was determined upon and the stern realities of war loomed up before them with all its possibilities, the less enthusiastic backed out.

Over $8,000 had already been spent in purchasing clothing, blankets, equipments, etc., for the regiment. This sum had been laid on the table in cash at a meeting of the citizens of Flushing, held April 20th, 1861, in the old Flushing Pavilion, at the corner of Lawrence avenue and Broadway. At the same meeting a further sum of $20,000 had been subscribed to be used, if necessary, in equipping the regiment for active service in the field.

Those were times to stir men's souls, and the patriotism displayed at that meeting by Flushing's citizens will never be forgotten by those who were present.

After receiving the War Department's order relating to enlistments, etc., the 15th Regiment was broken up and all those belonging to the infantry companies who were willing to go for three years enlisted in various organizations. The greater number of these went to Staten Island and joined Sickles's Brigade. The 15th had consisted of five companies of infantry and one of artillery. It had had the right to elect a colonel, a right it would not have secured if the Battery had not been the sixth company.

A deputation was sent from Staten Island to Flushing to try to induce the Battery to join Sickles's Brigade, but the Battery, influenced chiefly by myself, would not consent to do so unless General Sickles should give it a written guarantee or agreement that it should not be changed to any other arm, as we wished to remain, what we already were, Light Artillery. I had myself already served sixteen years in the Light Artillery and did not care to begin learning other tactics. The required agreement was not made, and with this ended all communication with Sickles's Brigade.

At this time a number of the prominent citizens of Flushing met and organized a "Committee of Arrangements," as it was called. This Committee included, so far as I can remember, the following-named gentlemen: Luther C. Carter, Captain George B. Roe, R. C. Embree, Garret Van Sicklen, Edw. E. Mitchell, Colonel Charles Hamilton, Judge MacDonald, Rev. Dr. J. Carpenter Smith, E. A. Fairchild, Captain William Prince, G. R. Garretson and Henry Clement. The latter was elected Treasurer of the Committee.

This Committee met the officers of the Battery (then called the "Hamilton Light Artillery"), Captain Thomas L. Robinson and myself, then First Lieutenant of the Battery, and made the following proposition, viz.: That they enlist with the men of the Battery for "three years or during the war," as the President's proclamation read. The Committee promised us that, if we would organize for service in the field, they would equip us, furnish us with everything necessary—money, clothing, and rations—and assist us by all the means in their power to raise an organization to represent Flushing in the field. The Battery officers accepted the proposition at once, and the Battery was then and there named the "Flushing Battery," to be so called until it was formally accepted by the Government, when, of course, some number or letter would be assigned to it and by which it would be known in the field.

A formal petition, signed by Captain Thomas L. Robinson and Lieutenant J. Roemer, requesting permission to raise a battery of artillery in Flushing, was at once sent to the Secretary of War. The required permission was granted by the Secretary in a letter dated July 25th, 1861, and reading as follows:

WAR DEPARTMENT,
WASHINGTON, D. C., July 25, 1861.

Captain Thomas L. Robinson, Flushing, L. I., N. Y.:

SIR—The company of Light Artillery which you offer is accepted for three years or during the war, provided you have it ready for marching orders in thirty days.

This acceptance is with the distinct understanding that this Department will revoke the commissions of all officers who may be found incompetent for the proper discharge of their duties.

You will promptly advise Adjutant-General Thomas at Washington of the date at which your men will be ready for mustering and he will detail an officer for that purpose.

By Order of the Secretary of War.

[SIGNED.] JAMES LESLEY, JR.,
Chief Clerk of War Department.

As soon as the above was received the work of organizing was begun in earnest. The Committee, in accordance with their promise, furnished each man with a fatigue suit of gray clothes, shoes, a blanket, and other necessary articles. All who had relatives dependent upon them for support were to receive two months' pay in advance. Captain Robinson and I each received as a present, a fine horse, together with a saddle and a bridle, the whole costing over six hundred dollars. All this expense was met by loyal and patriotic citizens of Flushing.

Ground for a camp was selected on an elevation north of Myrtle avenue, between Farrington street and Congress avenue, in Flushing, on property owned by Thomas Leggett and rented by Adam Todd for a pasture. The camp was named Camp Todd in honor of the latter. This matter being settled, we began the work of recruiting.

Requisition was made upon the proper officers of the New York Militia, at the State Arsenal in New York City, for camp and garrison equipage. These soon arrived, and when the tents were pitched the camp ground assumed the appearance of a real camp, and soon became the wonder of the surrounding country.

Recruits came to us from all parts of Long Island, and on August 27th, 1861, the first body of recruits was mustered into the United States service. After this date recruits came in more slowly, as most of the young men who had caught the war fever had already joined other organizations.[*]

We had in camp two pieces of artillery obtained from our old command, and with these we drilled the men in such

---

[*] In the preceding May, when the gallant 15th Regiment made its triumphal march around Long Island, there were 185 names on the Battery roll, but, as the men had not been sworn in by a magistrate, they could not be held to service, and, at the breaking up of the regiment, they left for other places and we were left without men. In like manner the blankets and the cloth for uniforms that had been procured for the 15th Regiment vanished; in fact, as Charles R. Lincoln remarked in the Flushing Journal, of which he was editor at the time, "everything pertaining to the 15th Regiment went up like a rocket and came down like a stick."

portions of the artillery drill as were practicable every day and always in the presence of numerous spectators from the village. To perfect myself in all the details of the drill, I purchased a miniature battery, and in company with Lieutenant Rawolle, each alternating in command, went through the various maneuvers repeatedly. It did not take us long to become very familiar with all the technicalities of artillery drill.

The people of Flushing did not allow their soldiers to suffer. Farmers frequently brought them loads of vegetables, the residents of the village sent them delicacies of all kinds; in fact, everybody thought it a duty to take care of them, and right royally was the duty performed. The Fair of the Queens County Agricultural Society was held on our camp ground while we were still there, and the Battery furnished guards for it night and day. When the Fair closed all the prize pumpkins, potatoes, and other vegetables were left to the "Boys in Blue," and for many days they lived in clover. One day, I especially remember, there arrived in camp, sent by Mrs. William Hamilton, mother of Charles A. Hamilton, with her compliments, two huge washbaskets filled with apple dumplings. That day there were a number of visitors in camp. After having served the 150 members of the Battery with all the dumplings they wanted, we found there were some left, and with these we regaled our visitors. There were many other times when the men were remembered by friends of the Battery in a similar way.

The men were provided in this way not only with eatables, but with other things as well, such as towels, combs, brushes, needle-cases fitted up with all necessaries, Bibles, prayer-books and other books and pocket-books, besides many other small but useful articles. Some of these donations I have found recorded in my diary. Mrs. Abraham

Bloodgood and Mrs. Edw. E. Mitchell each gave fifty towels. Other names are those of Mrs. Henry Clement, Mrs. William Murray and Mrs. E. A. Macdonald. All these and many others, whose names I cannot now recall, most certainly had the welfare of the soldiers at heart and tried to make camp life pleasant and comfortable.

During the whole of our stay at Camp Todd, drill with the guns and in marching went on without cessation. This unaccustomed labor so told on me in the beginning that in the first twelve days I lost ten pounds in weight. Our daily routine was as follows: Reveille at daybreak; drill from 5 to 7 A. M.; breakfast at 8; drill, 9–11; dinner, 12 M.; drill, 2–4; supper, 6; tattoo, 8; and taps, 9. The result of all this drill was that, when the order came to report in Washington, the members of the Battery were well grounded in their duties as artillerymen. At last the long-expected order came.

GENERAL HEADQUARTERS, STATE OF NEW YORK,
ADJUTANT-GENERAL'S OFFICE,
ALBANY. N. Y., Nov. 26th, 1861.

Special Orders, No. 514:

The organization heretofore known as the "Hamilton Artillery" is consolidated with and will compose Company "I"* of the Second Regiment New York Volunteer Artillery. The following persons are appointed officers of the company:

   Captain—Thomas L. Robinson.

   First Lieutenant—Jacob Roemer.

   Second Lieutenants—William Hamilton and Henry J. Standish.†

   Captain Robinson will proceed with his command to Washington on Friday, November 29th, 1861, and on his arrival will report for duty to the General-in-Chief and to Colonel Palmer, commanding his regiment.

---

*Afterwards named "Battery L."

†Lieutenant Standish was a First Lieutenant and William C. Rawolle was the other Second Lieutenant after December 4, 1861.

Captain Robinson will cause timely requisitions to be made for arms, uniforms, and all other supplies, as well as for transportation and subsistence on the route.

Brigadier-General Yates is charged with the execution of this order.

By Order of the Commander-in-Chief.

E. D. MORGAN.

Official: ──────────────
Adjutant-General State of New York.

The Battery left Flushing December 2d, 1861, and arrived in Washington on the 3rd. After its arrival had been reported in accordance with the foregoing order, it was ordered into camp on Capitol Hill, near the Bladensburg Gate. It then numbered five commissioned officers, 150 enlisted men and one laundress.

Soon orders were received from Artillery Brigade Headquarters for all officers to attend "school," as it were, in order to prepare for an examination that would be held later to ascertain the fitness of the officers for the several positions held by them. Recitations were held three times a week and instruction was given in the maneuvers of a mounted battery in the field. These continued until the 25th of February, 1862, on which date the examination was held at Headquarters. This over, the officers of Battery I. thought no more of it, and as the papers relating to it were not returned from Albany until May 23d, 1862, they were, until that date, wholly in the dark concerning the result of it.

In the meantime the Battery was engaged in drilling as before. We three lieutenants noticed, however, from day to day that our maneuvers differed somewhat from those of the regular batteries stationed near us, and as our Captain scarcely ever went out to drill the Battery, we began to mistrust that matters were not conducted exactly as regulations required.

Knowing that "practice makes perfect," and that it was wrong to spend valuable time in doing things in the wrong way, especially when we considered that the time for us to take the field was drawing nearer day by day, we strove diligently with all our nerve and energy, to ascertain what was wrong and then to correct it, to bring men and horses up to the mark of obeying promptly and strictly every order given in maneuvering the Battery, and also to perfect ourselves to such a degree that each lieutenant should be able to handle the Battery in any manner required on the battlefield. All three of us were in perfect accord in this matter.

Our captain, however, paid little or no attention to our repeated requests for "battery drills" and exercises in "field maneuvers." It soon became apparent to us that to drill as he wished would compel us to face the enemy in battle with divided commands, for the captain was not at all in harmony with us as to the Battery's maneuvers on the drill ground. We knew, furthermore, that if the new tactics were not put in force, and the men and horses well drilled in them, our Battery would most likely be routed in its first engagement, and we had no thought, as "Flushing Boys," of letting the enemy get the best of us at the start. We felt that if we lost the first advantage in battle the result might be, for the army, the loss of the battle, and for us, the loss of the guns and the capture of the men. To gain the first advantage quickness of movement is always essential and often decides the day. We believed, furthermore, that if men and horses were well drilled to obey the right commands and our shots were well aimed, we could hold our own against odds.

All this happened thirty-four years ago, yet I can now recall the resolution I then formed. My study of the accounts of many different battles had led me to believe— and experience on many battle-fields has confirmed me in this belief—that if the first shots are not well directed the enemy gains courage at once. I, therefore, resolved, if I should be in command when we went into action, to make it my first care to have the first and second shots tell, and thus mark the dividing line between the opposing forces with absolute certainty.

To have the enemy say (as they have said many a time) of my command, "Look out for that d—d Yankee battery or they'll give us h—ll," suited me far better than to have my guns spiked and my men taken prisoners. This resolution of which I have spoken was ever uppermost in my mind, while the "Flushing Battery" boys were becoming more and more efficient in drill on Capitol Hill. They had not experienced as yet the stern realities of actual warfare, but they were soon to do so.

By the end of March, 1862, the men had become quite proficient in "section drill." I was well pleased with my brother lieutenants, Standish and Rawolle, but not with our captain, for he neither appeared on the drill ground, nor showed any concern about the Battery's proficiency in drill. I spoke to him one day upon this subject, saying the Battery was making good progress in drill, and then asked him to come out and drill with us, taking my section first, and then each of the others in turn, and thus he would become familiar with his command by sections. He said he would come out that very day, but would have a battery drill. I begged him not to do so, for the sections had not yet made sufficient progress to go through it with success. The protest was of no avail. I then told him Gen. Barry was always out on the ground watching the drills of the twenty-three batteries belonging to his command, the Artillery Brigade. This remark had no effect. A mounted battery drill he would have, and we, as good soldiers, had to obey.

The Battery marched out in column of pieces. When it had arrived near the drill ground, Capt. Robinson rode up to me and said, "Lieut. Roemer, the first movement will be 'Battery front into line.'" "All right, captain," I answered. He then rode to a point opposite the middle of the column and gave this order: "Forward into line! march!" The command being incorrect, I raised my sabre and commanded "Halt." The captain rode up to me and asked: "Lieut. Roemer, what is the matter?" "Captain," I replied, "you did not give the right command for the execution of the maneuver you wish to have performed." "Well," said he, "I will give it again." He then gave exactly the same command, omitting as before, the phrase "Right (or left) oblique." Consequently, I again raised my sabre and halted the column. The captain said no more, but turned and rode back to camp. Lieuts. Rawolle and Standish rode up then and asked: "What shall we do now?" "Lieutenants," I replied, "we are all right. Gen. Barry and Col. Bailey have not as yet noticed the blunder. Take your respective stations and we will see if we cannot perform the maneuver. 'Battery, front into line,' but be careful to give the right commands to your sergeants." I then rode to the left, raised my sabre, and gave the command: "Column forward, march." When the column was in motion I gave the command: "Column forward into line, left oblique, march." It was like magic; the Battery came forward into line like veterans. I then gave the command: "Halt. Right dress. Front." I rode out in front of the line and said: "Officers and men, that was well done." The lieutenants now wanted to know what the next maneuver would be. "Recollect," said I, "this is now 'Battery front.' The next command will be 'Battery forward.'" I now gave the commands: "Attention. Battery forward, march. Right section, right wheel, Left section, left wheel, Center section, forward, march. Each lieutenant will take command of his own section and drill it in section drill."

That day we had one of the best mounted drills we had ever had. Both men and horses behaved unusually well. Just as we were about to leave the ground, Colonel Bailey rode over to us, congratulated us on our splendid drill, and then asked where the captain was. I told him the captain had come out with us, but had gone back to camp soon after. "Well, Lieutenants," said he, "you have had a very fine drill. General Barry was very much pleased with it, and wished me to present you with his compliments and congratulate you on your efficiency." He then bowed and rode off. We were justly proud of this and left the ground in high glee at being complimented by the Chief of Artillery of Camp Barry.

Upon reaching camp I went to the captain's tent and told how General Barry had honored the Battery by sending Colonel Bailey with his compliments to express his pleasure with our splendid drill and to ask where the captain was. This seemed to be too much for him, for he addressed me thus: "Lieutenant Roemer, I want you to understand I am captain of this Battery and not you." "I am well aware of that," said I, "but you will recollect that from the first organization of the Battery up to the present moment my pocketbook and my services have been acting captain. But in future Lieutenant Roemer will attend to only such duties as he may be ordered to by his captain." This ended all confidences between us.

Lieutenant Rawolle and I held a consultation to consider the state of affairs as between the captain and the Battery. We came to the conclusion that the captain was no drillmaster, although entitled to our respect as our superior officer. I was, naturally, greatly put out by his conduct, for I had, from the time the Battery was first organized, been advancing money, and had given my time to the recruiting service. Before leaving Flushing I had paid all bills owed by the Battery, for I had promised to be responsible for them. Of course the Government paid me back the greater portion of it (some $1,300), yet quite a sum came out of my own pocket. These annoyances and my mistrust of the captain after what had occurred, greatly discouraged me, especially as he did not give me a single chance to explain or defend myself.

About the end of March my wife and my young son, George, six years old, visited me in camp. After they had been with me about two weeks my son was taken very sick. I called in the two camp surgeons who at once pronounced the sickness to be camp fever. They positively forbade our moving him under penalty of his life, for he was in a very dangerous condition and must have the best of care to insure his recovery. After seven weeks' careful nursing he recovered and was soon able to travel. I must here express my sincere gratitude to the boys of the Battery and all in our camp for their devotion to my son during his sickness.

As affairs in the Battery had not improved during this dismal time, I now made up my mind to resign and return home with my wife and son. Lieutenant Rawolle also determined to resign. We wrote out our resignations and sent them to Colonel Bailey, Chief of Staff to General Barry, commanding Camp Barry. Colonel Bailey took the papers to General Barry and they held a consultation regarding the matter.

The next day Colonel Bailey came over with the papers to meet Lieutenant Rawolle and myself. He said: "Gentlemen, General Barry and I have had a talk about these papers. We know who are the workers in this Battery. I came to return these papers, but now I will hold them until there are some further developments relating to the affairs of your Battery, and they will, most likely, come soon." We also learned from Colonel Bailey that Captain Robinson had not, as we supposed he had, reported the Battery ready for the field.

The Battery had now its full complement of horses, 110 in number, and twelve mules for the baggage wagons. Lieutenant Rawolle and I had spent some thirty dollars in putting everything in trim and in good working order, thinking every morning the order to march out would come that day. The Battery was now in fine order, and if anybody ever was proud, the officers and men of Battery L were whenever they went out on the drill ground. But the Battery's pride was humbled when, about the 1st of April, 1862, an order came from Headquarters to turn over to a captain who had reported ready for the field, sixty horses that he needed to fill up his complement. Sixty of the Battery's best horses had to be turned over, and great was the dissatisfaction and disgust that reigned that day in the camp of Battery L. Men that had had fine horses and had taken great pride in them were wild, and bitterly denounced the captain for not having reported the Battery ready. Some went so far as to steal their horses from the stable where they had been put, take them out on the Bladensburg Road, and remain out all that day. Others drowned their sorrows in the flowing bowl, supposing they could "get even" with the captain in that way. It was, certainly for us officers, a most unpleasant time, and yet we could not, in a measure, blame these men who had bestowed such love and care on their horses that the latter seemed really a part of themselves.

Things were going on as usual when one morning, just before my wife and son were to start for home, she called me to her and asked me if it were true that Lieutenant Rawolle and I had handed in our resignations. I said it was and we were waiting for their acceptance by General Barry. Turning to me she said: "I don't want you to resign. What would the people of Flushing say if you should desert the Battery here? No! I would rather have your dead body brought to me from the battle-field than have this happen just now. It was a struggle for me in the first place to give my consent to your going into the army, but now that you have undertaken this work, and have promised the wives of most of the men to stand by their husbands, I will make all sacrifices for your honor, and will gladly care for our children if you shall fall in so just a cause."

This was an inspiration, and turning to her I said: "I will heed your words, my dear wife, and, as Heaven is my witness, I will stand by the Battery amid shot and shell. You are the woman who has taught a soldier his duty to his country."

After that I felt like a new man, and no longer cared what unpleasantness might be brought to bear upon me. I went to work with renewed energy. Fresh horses were drawn to make up our complement. They were a sorry looking lot compared with those just lost. It took two weeks to get them broken to harness and accustomed to the drill. Many were the bitter words uttered by the men, who had to break in these green horses. "If our captain had only reported the Battery ready," they would say, "we would now be with 'Burnside's Expedition' on the way to New Bern."

But all complaining went for naught; we had the work to do, and do it we must if we expected ever to make any progress. We got along very well. Mounted drills were held daily and target practice was also frequently held in addition to the drills. One day, shortly after receiving our new 3-inch rifles, we went down to the Potomac, where we had a target placed, and had our first trial of these guns which, with a powder charge of one pound, could send a ten-pound shot three and one-half miles. There were also frequent evening recitations by the non-commissioned officers in the instructions given them by the lieutenants.

While we were stationed at Camp Barry, the 15th Regiment New York Engineers, attached to Sickles's Brigade, arrived and encamped near the Bladensburg Gate, Capitol Hill. When we heard of this, a number of us, officers and men, knowing there were many Flushing and Whitestone boys in the regiment, went over to see them. I can remember now meeting Captain Dermody of Company H, Sergeant G. O. Fowler of Company F, William Smith, Frederick Smith and Ezra Fowler, all also of Company F, besides many others whose names I cannot now recall. We went through the camp and visited many of the tents. As one after another greeted us, it seemed good to be there. We talked of home and home-folks, and then, after smoking the pipe of peace, we bade them "good-bye," and left them not knowing on which side of the "great divide," we should meet again. There must have been as many as two hundred Long Islanders in Sickles's Brigade.

At another time we visited Brickel's Brigade of five batteries, a fine organization, and witnessed their drills and field maneuvers. A mounted artillery drill is, I think, the most exciting drill to be seen in the military service. We also visited Captain Best's United States Battery of Napoleons. He had a fine body of men and the battery officers were unusually social and pleasant. Being volunteers we, of course, had great reverence for United States regular troops and courtesies received from them were highly valued by us green hands.

While my wife was with me, Captain Best invited us one day to spend the evening with him. As such hospitalities are seldom extended to ladies, I accepted the invitation with pleasure and we went over that same evening. Captain Best gave us a hearty welcome and said he was glad he had had his tent carpeted for the better entertainment of the lady. When he opened his tent, we saw that good, clean, rye straw had been spread on the ground. We were soon engaged in a friendly chat and spent a very pleasant evening. (I will here note that at the Battle of Cedar Mountain he was chief of artillery). Captain Best's rye straw carpet gave me a valuable hint, and afterwards we carpeted our tents with the same material. We found it very comfortable for our feet. It was quite cold in camp, and the rye straw kept the March and April winds to a considerable extent from singing through the tents.

Camp Barry was, at that time, a mud hole (if any one who knew what it was then should visit Capitol Hill now, he would hardly believe it was the same place,) and every Saturday there was taken from beside the tent door a whole load of dirt we had brought there on our boots. Washington itself was a sorry looking place; there was scarcely a decent street in it. I have seen loads of hay drawn through the streets on wagons whose wheels seemed to be solid because of the mud packed between the spokes. The whole winter was cold and unpleasant. The horses suffered greatly from diseases of the feet; hoof-rot was sure to set in if the hoofs were not washed and cleansed every day. Dismounted drills were attended with much discomfort and often had to be omitted. We Long Islanders were not used to such mud and such poor roadways. We had often heard of Jersey mud, but Washington and Virginia mud beats it, I am sure. But that is now a thing of the past; the Washington of to-day is a marvel for fine roadways.

How many old soldiers remember the huge blocks of stone and massive timbers lying about the Capitol grounds and around the unfinished Capitol? Who will not say that Abraham Lincoln was a tireless worker as well as an able President? In four short years, aided by more than two millions of men, and at a cost of hundreds of millions of dollars a year, he carried on, to a successful termination, the most gigantic war known in American history, and yet he found time to complete the building of the Capitol. Another such man is unknown to history.

The first of May came, but the situation remained unchanged. Drilling was carried on incessantly that the Battery might be thoroughly prepared in every detail of our arm of the service and ready to do its work perfectly whenever it should be ordered into the field. The men were made accustomed to perform all maneuvers at full speed, mounting and dismounting the whole battery, mounting and dismounting the pieces, charging at a gallop, etc. Mounted drills are not only exciting but also dangerous, unless the greatest care is exercised.

The batteries and regiments that had been for months encamped around us were now leaving daily, and farewells were said for, perhaps, the last time, yet the men of Battery L were anxious to be ordered into the field. They had made many friends during their stay at Camp Barry, and would, no doubt, meet them again on bloody battle-fields. We all had devoted our lives to our country's cause and there should be no hanging back when duty called. For my part, I did not believe there would be any flinching in Battery L. All we wanted was a chance to prove our devotion and our loyalty to our country.

CHAPTER II.

REORGANIZATION. CEDAR MOUNTAIN.

At last, on the 23d of May, 1862, the fog which had been hovering over Light Battery L, Second New York Volunteer Artillery, since the 25th of February, 1862, was lifted. It was then learned that all the officers of the Battery, except Captain T. L. Robinson, had passed their examination creditably. The latter was now dismissed from the United States service. On the same day Lieutenant Roemer received the following order:

HEADQUARTERS LIGHT ARTILLERY DEPOT, CAMP BARRY,
WASHINGTON, D. C., May 23d, 1862.

Orders No. 47:

Pursuant to "S. O. No. 49, Headquarters Army of the Potomac," Captain Thomas L. Robinson, having been discharged from the service of the United States, will turn over all the public property, ordnance and quartermaster's stores in his possession to First Lieutenant Jacob Roemer, Co. L, 2d N. Y. Art., and Lieutenant Roemer will receipt to him for the same.

By order of Major Keefer.

ANGELL MATTHEWSON, Post Adjutant.

Lieutenant Roemer was ordered to take formal charge of Battery L, and Captain Robinson was ordered to report to Governor Morgan at Albany, N. Y.

As soon as Captain Robinson left camp to report to Governor Morgan, Colonel Bailey came over from Headquarters, called the lieutenants together, and said, "Gentlemen, this is the reason why I asked two of you to withhold your resignations. After the examination of February 25th I knew what must happen in the Battery, but I was not permitted to explain matters until we had heard from Governor Morgan. The papers just received and presented to Captain Robinson have been under way three months. Now, gentlemen, work together and see how soon the Battery can be made ready for active service in the field."

Now we were all in great excitement. After a careful examination of all stores on hand in the Battery wagon, forge, etc., requisitions were at once made for all stores found to be needed, ammunition, clothing, etc.

On this same May 23d Lieutenant Jacob Roemer was promoted to Captain of Battery L, 2d N. Y. Art. to rank as such from March 4th, 1862, by a commission signed by Governor E. D. Morgan. Second Lieutenant H. J. Standish had already been promoted to Junior First Lieutenant and Sergeant Jerome Van Nostrand to Junior Second Lieutenant, vice Standish promoted, January 16, 1862, but these promotions were not made effective by commissions until May 23d. On this same date Second Lieutenant William C. Rawolle was promoted Senior First Lieutenant, vice Roemer promoted Captain, and First Sergeant William Cooper was promoted Junior Second Lieutenant, vice Rawolle promoted.

By S. O. No. 87, Headquarters Mil. Dist. of Washington, dated May 26, 1862, and G. O. No. 1, Headquarters Sturgis's Brigade, dated May 27, 1862, Battery L was assigned, with other troops, to Sturgis's Brigade. By S. O. No. 91, Headquarters Mil. Dist. of Washington, the assignment was greatly changed, but Battery L's assignment was not affected. On May 29th, 1862, Third Sergeant Moses E. Brush was promoted First Sergeant. The same day the Battery was reported ready for the field, whereupon it received orders to march at once to Camp Waagner, near Tenallytown, D. C., ten miles distant. The Battery arrived the same day and reported to Colonel Waagner, commanding 2d N. Y. Art., the regiment to which Battery L belonged.

That the connection of Battery L with the 2d N. Y. Art. may be understood, the plan of the organization of that regiment is here presented. This regiment of artillery consisted of twelve companies or batteries. Each company was composed of 150 enlisted men and five commissioned officers, viz.: one captain, two first lieutenants and two second lieutenants. The field and staff consisted of a colonel, a lieutenant-colonel, three majors, an adjutant, a quartermaster, a surgeon and one or two assistant surgeons—making in all a maximum number of 1,870 officers and men.

There are two classes of artillery—heavy and light. Heavy artillery companies are drilled as infantry with muskets, and are also trained in the management of heavy guns—siege guns—that are mounted in forts, etc., but not in the use of field pieces. Light artillery companies, usually termed light batteries or field artillery, because their duties are chiefly performed in the field, are drilled very differently. All officers, commissioned and non-commissioned, are mounted. The drivers of gun and caisson teams ride one of the horses they drive, while the cannoneers ride on the limber and caisson chests which carry the ammunition when on the march. Battery L was a light battery, and because, at that time, it was the rule for all light batteries to be attached to regiments of heavy artillery, Battery L was attached to the 2d N. Y. Art. merely formally. Colonel Waagner seemed to be much pleased with it. He witnessed a mounted drill of the Battery on May 30th, and gave it credit for accuracy of movement.

By G. O. No. 7, Headquarters Sturgis's Brigade, dated June 3, 1862, Lieutenant Rawolle was detailed Acting Aide-de-Camp on General Sturgis's staff, and this detail was made permanent by G. O., No. 15, dated June 14, and by G. O., No. 16, of the same date, he was made Acting Insp.-Gen. of the Brigade. I was very sorry that Battery L should lose the services of so efficient an officer.

In consequence of the dismissal of Captain Robinson, some twenty-seven men who were in sympathy with him deserted the Battery within five days after our arrival at Camp Waagner. Before Captain Robinson left the Battery he had given these men to understand that they had a right to leave because they had enlisted to serve under him and not under his successor. They were not well posted in Army Regulations. Five of the poor fellows were caught, brought back, court-martialed, and sentenced to the Rip-Raps. I asked the president of the court for permission to make a statement regarding the matter. Permission was granted. I then told the court that these men were not to blame for deserting, and then asked the men to tell the court what Captain Robinson had said to them. One of them acted as spokesman for all. He stated that Captain Robinson left camp May 23d, 1862, but before going he had told them they could go home because they had enlisted to serve under him and not under Captain Roemer. This enabled them to escape punishment for desertion. Later one of the five deserted again, but this time there was no intercession in his behalf. He knew well what he was doing and had to pay the penalty.

These desertions left the Battery short of its necessary complement of men. To perform the routine work of a battery without overworking the men or neglecting any duty, it should have its full number of men. A detail of thirty men from the heavy artillery was sent to help the light battery men.

June 6th, 1862, I was ordered to New York to recruit as many men as possible within twenty-five days. I returned to camp July 1st with eight men, but others had been sent on ahead.

During my absence in New York the Battery had gone to Fairfax Seminary, Va., in accordance with G. O., No. 3, Headquarters Reserve Army Corps, dated June 26, 1862, and joined the 2d Brigade of the Corps, commanded by Colonel Z. R. Bliss, 10th R. I. Vols. The Battery now had six pieces of artillery and 115 horses, and numbered 133 enlisted men, five officers, three officers' servants and one laundress. (The possession of a laundress was a luxury of which few organizations could boast. This one was the wife of one of the men and had insisted on going with us. I may here say she went through the war with us, and at the final review in Washington in 1865 rode on a limber chest with the men.) The battery received the following orders July 5th, 1862:

HEADQUARTERS RESERVE ARMY CORPS,
ALEXANDRIA, July 5th, 1862.

Special Order, No. 25:

Battery L, 2d N. Y. Art., Captain Roemer; the 2nd Excelsior Battery, Captain Bruen; the 16th Indiana Battery, Captain Naylor, and the six companies of cavalry of General Banks's command now in Washington, will report at once to Lieutenant-Colonel Copeland, 1st Mich. Cav., at quarters east of the Capitol, Washington, for marching orders.

By Order of Brigadier-General Sturgis.

WM. C. RAWOLLE, Captain and A. D. C.

HEADQUARTERS DETACHMENT,
WASHINGTON, D. C., July 5th, 1862.

S. O., No. 1:

The companies of this command will be in readiness to march to-morrow at 10 A. M. with five days' rations and as much forage as they have transportation for. The command will proceed under the immediate direction of Captain Hourigan to Alexandria or Bailey's Cross Roads, as hereafter may be determined, where it will be joined by three batteries of artillery and 200 wagons, the whole to proceed to Manassas in the following order: one company cavalry, two companies artillery, two companies cavalry, 100 wagons, one company artillery, two companies cavalry, the balance of the wagons and rear guard, one company cavalry.

By Order of Lieutenant-Colonel Copeland, commanding.
Lieutenant F. H. ROGERS, Adjutant.

As the men had not been paid, and the paymaster was expected at any moment, the above order was modified.

July 6th, 1862.

Captain Roemer, you will join the cavalry at Accotink to-morrow morning (July 7th) as soon as possible.

By Order of Lieutenant-Colonel I. T. Copeland, commanding.
Lieutenant F. H. ROGERS, Adjutant.

By 1 P. M., July 6th, the payment of the Battery was finished and the order to march was given. It soon reached Fairfax Court House, where it joined General Banks's 2d Corps, Army of Virginia. We remained in camp over night with our new friends, and I became somewhat acquainted with our new commander, General D. N. Couch.

During the 9th the Battery marched through Centreville, crossed Bull Run, passed Manassas, and arrived at Catlett's Station, near which it encamped for the night. On the 10th it marched to and through Warrenton and encamped two miles beyond the village. On the 11th orders came not to move. Here we learned that the 9th N. Y. Vol. was in camp about three miles east. I immediately told my orderly to saddle five horses and then with him and the horses started out to bring some of the Flushing boys in the 9th back to our camp. We brought back with us William Prince, Thomas Cassady, Isaac P. Jones, Thomas Howard and Hicks to see their fellow townsmen in Battery L. Many others of the 9th sent messages to their friends in the battery.

That night the Warrenton woods were lighted by a huge camp fire, around which gathered a gay party composed of our guests from the 9th, the boys of the Battery and many officers and men from the regiments and batteries in camp near by. It was not until the "wee sma' hours" of the morning that the camp fire was deserted. As the Battery had an extra wall tent, we could make our guests from the 9th comfortable for the night. I may say that they did not answer at roll-call the next morning; in fact, it was fully eight o'clock before any signs of life were manifest in the tent. At that hour I looked in. Prince and Howard were sitting up and looking around, and just as I stepped inside I heard Prince say: "Tom, where are we? In the guardhouse again, by God!" And, as he espied me, continued: "And there is the devil that put us in." I hustled them all out to breakfast and then said: "I will send you back to your camp and you will surely get into the guard-house, for I noticed that your captain was not inclined to be sociable, but as I have your colonel on my side, I guess you will be all right. He could not refuse me when I asked him for the pleasure of your company for twenty-four hours. He knew well what a pleasure it would be for fellow-townsmen under the circumstances." That the boys of the 9th enjoyed the visit, and that it was appreciated by the battery boys, goes without saying.

On the 14th the Battery was formally assigned by S. O. to Gen Crawford's brigade of the 2d Corps. The next day the Battery paraded mounted, and was inspected by General Crawford. On the 16th orders came at 11:30 A. M. to be ready to march at 12 M. to go to the Rappahannock River, and after crossing it, to bivouac on the hill just beyond. The next day the Battery marched to Blue Mountain, near Little Washington. I reported to General Crawford on the 18th that the roads leading to our position were so heavy that it was almost impossible to bring up our heavily loaded ammunition wagons, and asked permission to change the Battery's position. The request was granted, and the Battery was removed to higher ground out of the mud. Here also was found fine grass for the horses, which soon put them in fine condition.

Here the Battery remained until 3:30 A. M. on the 22d, at which hour it marched out to Sperryville. Passing this place it went on, and then, after passing Sigel's 1st Corps at 8:30 P. M., went into camp near Woodville, having marched thirty miles, the longest march yet made in one day. On the 23d the Battery moved to Culpeper Court House and encamped six miles east of the town. The next day was spent in making some necessary repairs to harness and other equipments. Orders came on the 25th to drill five hours every day, to keep everything in readiness to march at any moment, night or day, and to have the six pieces, when not used in drill, so stationed as to command the roads approaching the town, and especially the one from Orange Court House, on which two pieces must be placed.

At 2:30 A. M. on the 29th an order came to be ready for action at once. This was the first time the Battery ever received such an order, and all felt rather queer. The second section was ordered to go out with the cavalry on the road towards Orange Court House.

On the 31st the Battery went out for target practice to a point two miles south of Culpeper, in the direction of Cedar Mountain. Thirteen shells were fired at 735 and 1,795 yards. The ammunition was found to be unreliable for the shells burst before reaching the targets. This was reported to General Crawford, and it was arranged to have another trial of target practice sometime before the 7th of August.

August 1st an order was received announcing the death of ex-President Martin Van Buren, and as Battery L was on picket duty, that is, out on the advanced line, to it was accorded the honor of firing a salute in honor of the ex-President, of thirty-four guns, one gun for each State that was in the Union during his Presidency. At 6 P. M. the firing began, one gun every minute. No sooner was the second gun fired than the town of Culpeper was aroused. The inhabitants thought the Yankees had opened fire on the town. The darkies, especially, went running about for dear life in every direction, hallooing and screaming at the top of their voices. We held a commanding position and could see the whole affair before us. It was for our troops a highly amusing sight, but, doubtless, it was not so for the people in Culpeper, startled as they were by the unexpected firing.

The battery was supported in this advanced position by General Bayard's cavalry. The cavalry have the advantage over all other troops in one respect, at least, for if there are chickens, pigs, cows, oxen or anything else in the way of live stock in their way, they can easily clear these obstacles out of it.

In consequence of their superiority in this respect, the night of July 31st, 1862, will always be a memorable one, at least for the boys of Battery L, for they were invited that night by the cavalry to a supper just in rear of the Battery's position as near as I could find out afterwards. There must certainly have been 250 men who partook of the feast. As the place where the supper was spread was so near our camp, and as the men had been invited, I could scarcely blame them for participating in the feast, and no doubt they had a good time.

The Battery boys now wished to return the compliment, but not being so good at foraging as the cavalry were, they were obliged to adopt a different plan. They went out into a field belonging to a Mr. Smith, where a yoke of oxen were eating their noonday meal, and finding the driver absent, unyoked one of the oxen, killed it, and prepared a grand supper, to which they invited their cavalry friends, and, doubtless, everything "went merry as a marriage bell." As I was on duty that day as Officer of the Day, inspecting the camps of all the organizations in the Brigade, I was out from 8 A. M. to 9 P. M., and so they had everything their own way. On my return to camp I found an order from Gen. Bayard to report at his headquarters as soon as possible. I asked Lieut. Standish, who was in charge of the camp, what it all meant. He told me that eight men were under arrest for killing an ox belonging to Farmer Smith. I rode over to headquarters and asked for General Bayard. He came to me, but his manner was cool and distant and his remarks were very curt. I told him if he would give me a chance I thought I could explain matters. Finally, to cut the matter short, I said: "General, I must tell you that your men initiated mine into this business." This seemed to anger him and he exclaimed: "I can send every one of those eight men to the Rip-Raps!" "What I say, General," I replied, "I can prove, for I have seen the thing with my own eyes. If you will go with me through the camps, among your own men, you will see what I meant by my remark." "Well, Captain," said he, "report here to-morrow morning at 8 o'clock." "All right," I replied, and galloped off, but not back to camp.

I rode over to Farmer Smith's (it was now 10 P. M.) and made myself known to him. I then said I had heard that some of my men had killed an ox belonging to him. "Now," said I, "I have come to your house as a friend and not as an enemy, and if you will kindly listen to me, we may be able to settle the affair. This ox belonged to you and I am willing to settle with you for it, for I do not want General Bayard to have anything to do with it. I will give you another ox or pay you the money value of the one killed, just as you say. If that suits you and you will agree to go to General Bayard to-morrow before 8 A. M. and tell him you have settled the ox case, our bargain is made. I do not consider it a small matter for either of us. If these eight men are taken from the Battery and, as General Bayard says, sent to the Rip-Raps, I would not give a snap of my finger for all you have on your farm." This seemed to scare him, and he said he would do almost anything to settle the matter. He then proposed that I should pay $130 for the ox, and to this I agreed. Leaving him, I rode over to our Quartermaster and arranged with him to let Mr. Smith have $130 for his ox. Thus everything was settled before I went to bed that night.

The next morning I rode over to General Bayard's Headquarters and found Mr. Smith there. He said he had been into Headquarters, and then told me, to my surprise, that General Bayard had been called off with his cavalry. He had, however, seen General Crawford and talked with him. I went to the General's tent. General Crawford told me Mr. Smith was well satisfied with my offer and then said I should settle with him. For his part he considered it a very liberal offer. "Captain Roemer," he continued, "you are a gentleman, and I have nothing further to demand of you." This, of course, gave us back the eight men and got Battery L out of its first trouble of this kind. After Mr. Smith had received his money from the Quartermaster he came to me and said he bore no malice towards the Battery, and at any time when the boys passed the house, they could have all the milk they wanted.

During the afternoon of August 3 the cavalry brought in forty prisoners, including a colonel, two captains and several other officers. My curiosity was aroused, and I rode into Culpeper to see them. On the 5th Lieutenant-Colonel

Johnston, Captain Deisfield and Lieutenant Joseph of the 5th Conn. Vols. brought in fifty-five prisoners captured near Orange Court House. Things were now becoming quite warlike.

On the 6th all drills were on foot, for the pieces had to be kept in position to defend the approaches. The men now began to think that actual fighting would soon occur. The Battery went out on the 7th for target practice. Twenty-eight shots were fired at the same ranges as on July 31st with very satisfactory results.

The next day, 8th, orders came to be ready to march at 1 P. M. Within thirty minutes after that hour the Battery was marching out on the road to Culpeper, through which it passed, and arrived at Cedar Mountain Run at 5 P. M. Four pieces were put in position, while the remaining section was sent to Captain Knapp, on the left of the line to stay there in position during the night—the night before Battery L's first battle.

How can I describe what I felt that night, knowing what was before us? What a responsibility rested upon me! I felt that the lives of my men were in my hands and that I must give account of them. All night long the minutes seemed like hours. I thought of everything—of my family at home and of the possibility that I might not see the morrow's night. If I should not, what then? The thought was agonizing. It seemed as though I could not endure it, but endure I must, whatever my feelings might be, for I knew the enemy were right in front of us and we had been told to hold ourselves in readiness for any emergency that might arise during the night. By 10 P. M. everything in the Battery was quiet; all seemed to be at rest and asleep, but I could not sleep. Then I walked through the camp. The men were all lying down, wrapped in their blankets, resting peacefully. As I looked at them

I thought, "How many of you will be sleeping the eternal sleep at the setting of to-morrow's sun?" I returned to my tent, but to sleep was still impossible. My mind was oppressed by a indefinable dread of the dangers that awaited us on the morrow. Who is there that has ever been in the service that has not had the same feeling on the eve of battle? Some call it fear, but I do not think it is actually fear, for I have always found men who had such feelings to be brave in the presence of real danger. The man who boasts of having no fear is often the first to abandon the post of duty when he is most needed. The man upon whom one can depend to obey implicitly all commands, whatever they may be, no matter how near shot and shell may be flying, is a noble soul and is worthy of the high honor of being a United States soldier. I had absolute confidence in the men of my command, and they proved themselves worthy of it throughout all our campaigns.

About 12:30 A. M. on the 9th, I went out again down toward Cedar Mountain Run, some two hundred yards away in rear of our camp, and sat down on its bank. Thoughts of all kinds passed rapidly through my mind as I viewed the scene before me. The water, illumined by the bright moonlight, was as clear as crystal, and I could see the little fishes swimming over the white pebbles at the bottom. Impelled by something, I know not what, I knelt down and offered up my humble prayer to God, that if it should be my lot to die on the morrow, I might be ready to sacrifice my life for my adopted country; but, if it might be His will, to spare me to my family, and be with me amid all the dangers before me. Strengthened in every nerve, I returned to camp, where I found the officer changing the guards. I spoke with him about the beauty of the night, and then walked around the camp. Finding all posts well guarded, I returned to my tent, to secure, if possible, an hour's sleep, at least, but found it to be in vain. I then strolled around to pass the remaining hours of the night.

At 4 A. M., I ordered the sergeant of the guard to summon the men to reveille roll-call, without sounding the bugle, by passing the word from man to man. At the roll-call every man was present. Breakfast was ordered to be ready at 5, and the horses to be watered at the same hour. I then walked out westward as far as the level top of the hill extended. I saw our cavalry some 250 yards in front, near some woods.

A group of officers were standing a little distance away, and they called to me to come over. I went, and Gen. Crawford, our Brigade commander, saluted me as I approached with, "Good morning, Captain; have you had your breakfast?" "Not this morning, General," I replied. Thereupon he called out to his cook, "Bring the captain a chop." The cook brought it on one of the first forks ever made with five prongs. The general at the same time handed me a musket cartridge, saying, "Captain Roemer, we have no salt this morning, and as you will have to smell powder to-day, you may as well eat some this morning. They say it is very encouraging before a battle, even better than whiskey; it fires the blood, but does not stupefy as whiskey does." I had several of these chops, broiled on the hot coals and eaten on the spot with the seasoning given me by Gen. Crawford. I defy any epicure to prepare anything finer.

Then the general asked how near ready the Battery was. It was now 4:35 by his watch. I then told him I could have the Battery ready to march by a quarter to five. "That will do," he said, "although they are close in our front. It is best to be ready in case of need. I do not think, however, they will advance before 9 or 10 o'clock."

After telling the general he could call on the Battery at any time after 5 o'clock, I left him and returned to camp. Everything was in order, and the Battery was ready to march at a moment's notice.

My young son Louis, eleven years old, had been staying with me in camp, but now at the moment when real dangers were confronting us, I thought it best to send him to the rear with the baggage trains. I called him to me, and, taking from my pocket a twenty-dollar gold piece, handed it to him and said: "My son, we may soon be exposed to a deadly fire and I do not wish you to risk your life here. Now, take this gold piece and go to the baggage train, and if I am killed go home to mother, using this money for your expenses." After a loving embrace and a promise from him to do as I bade him, we parted.

At about 5:30 A. M., the Battery took position on a hill about 500 yards in front of our camp and awaited developments. At 12, noon, a strong attack was made on our left wing. The first shot against the enemy's line was fired by Battery L. This attack was of short duration, but we could see the enemy's troops marching, countermarching and changing position. At 1 P. M. the attack on our left was repeated with a larger force. At 2 P. M. the Battery was ordered to move from the right of the road to the left of it and take position on higher ground. The Battery opened fire at once from this position, and for several minutes the scene was an exciting one. At 2:30 P. M., by order of Gen. Banks, the Battery went into position in a cornfield six or eight hundred yards farther to the left, and about the same distance farther in front, and immediately opened fire. At the same moment, I saw that two of the enemy's batteries were directly in our front, and a third on Cedar Mountain. The latter opened a very heavy cross-fire on Battery L which replied with vigor. By this time all three of the

Brigade's batteries were in position actively engaged. Capt. Best's Battery F, 4th U. S., was about 500 yards to the right of Battery L and Capt. Knapp's Battery E, Penn. Vol. Art., with one section of Battery L about 800 yards to the left.

The battle was now raging furiously. Shot and shell were flying all around us. I was not pleased with our position, but we had taken it under orders from Gen. Banks, brought by one of his aides. The position was on a hill on the side toward the enemy, whereas, if it could have taken position 300 yards farther back with the hill in front of it, men and horses would have had better protection, and the Battery could have had as good a range on the enemy's lines. As good luck would have it, however, the enemy fired too high, and four out of every five shots passed over us and struck about a mile in our rear, but for this, the rebels would have had the best of the Battery in its first battle— its "baptism of fire."

As soon as I saw how things were going, I sent three of our ammunition wagons back over the hill, the better to protect the horses, and charged 1st Sergeant Brush to look after the fourth ; and, as soon as it was unloaded, to send it back and bring up another loaded wagon. Matters had now become very lively ; shot and shell of various kinds and sizes were flying around us thick and fast. I now dismounted and sent my groom with my horse to seek shelter under a lovely forest tree some fifty yards to the left, there to stay until called for ; and, strange to say, the groom was glad to get away.

Now the enemy prepared to make a heavy cavalry charge on the center of our lines. I ordered the pieces turned in the direction of the advancing column, and aimed at the horses' breasts and legs. I took charge of the right gun myself. As the advancing column came on at full gallop, the guns were fired by battery. The cavalry broke and retreated to their lines. There they reformed and, with Gen. Winder at their head, made another dash. When we saw the maddened crowd of horses and riders coming nearer and nearer, tearing and plunging with such force that the earth trembled beneath them, we knew what they intended to do—to destroy Battery L. if possible. Though greatly excited, I gave the same command as before. The command was scarcely given before it was executed, so promptly did the men obey. Some of the horses jumped four and five feet into the air as the shrapnel burst among them. At the fourth "battery fire," they showed us their backs, and we gave them two shots more, to make sure they would go home. In this last charge, Gen. Winder was killed. Men and horses strewed the field across which the cavalry had charged.

Due west of us was a rebel battery called the "White Horse Battery." This battery now opened a tremendous fire from its six rifled pieces upon Battery L, to demolish it, in revenge, as we believed, for the havoc it had made among the cavalry, or at least give it so much work to do that it would be compelled to leave the cavalry alone. The rebel battery soon became satisfied, however, that it was best to leave Battery L. alone. One of their shots, though, struck the ground some eight feet in front of where I was standing and about two feet lower down and plowed through the earth directly under my feet, thus upsetting me. I fell on my hands and knees near Private D. S. Johnston, cannoneer No. 3, whose duty it was to hold his thumb on the vent while Nos. 1 and 2 were loading the piece. One would naturally suppose he would have asked me, "Captain, are you hurt?" Not he. With the serenity of a veteran he called out, "Captain, get up off your knees. There's no time to pray now!" I looked at him as I arose and could not but remark his coolness. If this boy only seventeen years old can display such coolness and courage in the midst of such a bloody conflict, I thought what splendid soldiers my men will make and how I can depend upon them in the most trying times.

Just in the midst of all this, one of the officers called my attention and said, "Captain, your son Louis is out there right behind the Battery." I looked around and there Louis was, sitting on his horse and looking around coolly and collectedly. I called out to him, asking: "My son, what are you doing here? This no place for you. If a stray shot or shell should hit you, how can I console your mother?" "Oh, papa," he replied, "don't, don't send me back where I was, for several horses have been killed and wounded there, and I see you have not lost a man or a horse. Do let me stay here with you and the men. I feel happier here." "Well," said I, "if you feel happier here, dismount and give your horse to the groom, who will put her with mine under the tree. You can make yourself useful among the men, and we will trust God to keep you safe."

When the main charge was made on our center, at the same time Capt. Best and Capt. Knapp were both severely attacked by the enemy's artillery, and a tremendous artillery duel raged from three to five P. M. During all this time the infantry had been in rear of the artillery. The 5th Conn. Vols. was the Battery's support. At about five P. M. this regiment was ordered to pass to the front of the Battery, and while passing they all greeted the Battery with loud hurrahs. Very many of the poor fellows lost their lives in the charge on the enemy. The officers especially suffered; out of forty officers who went to the front that day not one-half returned uninjured. The others were either killed or wounded. Who of those now living that lived in those days can look back and think, without tears in their eyes, of the brave, willing souls that gave up their lives for their country, of the homes made sad and desolate by the loss of loved ones that went forth from them never to return.

The Battery was now ordered to move to a point a little to the right and rear on higher ground, to cover the advance of our infantry against the enemy's lines by firing over their their heads. As soon as it reached this new position, it opened fire, but the fire was only of short duration. Nothing could then be heard but the rattle of musketry. By thousands our troops charged the enemy's lines and were driven back in turn by countercharges. These attacks and counter attacks continued with great severity for a full hour. The Battery was now ordered back to the east bank of Cedar Mountain Run. Three pieces only could be used, the fourth having become disabled by the rapid firing during the cavalry charge. The gun had become so hot that the bore became too small to permit a shot being sent home to the bridge, and a shot had stuck fast half way home. This could not be moved either way until the gun became cool. This was done a day or two after.

When the three guns was in position as ordered, one was at the foot of the hill, a second, 150 yards higher up, and the third, 150 yards higher still. As soon as the pieces were in position, a second order was received to the effect that the Battery commander would be held responsible for the protection and support of the troops in the woods at all hazards, even if the Battery had to be sacrificed. I called my two lieutenants, Standish and Van Nostrand, and told them to meet me at the lowest piece, where I would explain to them what this order meant. I then told my groom to bring me my flask out of my saddle-bag. When we met again at the lowest piece, I asked my lieutenants to stand on the other side of the gun, thinking it would make a good altar for our last communion. Then I said, "Gentlemen, you have asked me several times for a drink of whiskey, and each time, I told you I had none for the purpose for which you wanted it. I have some in this flask, but it is no longer to be regarded as whiskey ; it is the blood of Christ and we take it together as such, not knowing to how severe a test we shall be subjected before the day closes." I passed the flask to Lieut. Van Nostrand, then to Lieut. Standish, after which I drank some myself. By this act, we placed ourselves unreservedly then and there in the hands of God. Lieut. Standish then came to me, fell on my neck, kissed me, and said, "Capt. Roemer I thought I knew you, but this is beyond anything I ever expected. I will not let you take charge of this gun, for this is my place." "No," I replied, "the orders have been given, and you must obey. This gun I reserved for myself. All I ask of you is, if it should come to the worst and I should fall, ask the men to stand by you and defend our infantry against the enemy to the last." We then separated, each one going to the post assigned him.

The latter raged hotly for an hour or more. Infantry charges were repeatedly made by both sides, and the rattle of musketry was deafening. We of the artillery being just now in the rear, were, for the most part, simply spectators, and could only once in a while, find a chance to fire a shot, which we did whenever opportunity offered, and then we tried to make every shot tell.

On the west side of tha creek, there was a wood, then a clear field about 400 yards wide, and beyond this was another wood. Our commanding position afforded us a perfect view of this exciting moving panorama. Our infantry would drive the rebels clear across the open field to the edge of the farther woods, and then would be pressed back to the bank of the creek. At such times, we would be enabled to send a shrapnel or two into the midst of the rebels with good effect.

At about 7 p. m., there was a cessation of the musketry fire, and our troops were holding the outer works. The Battery's position was not so hazardous as I had, at first, expected it would be. Our infantry held their own better than the generals had calculated, fortunately for us and our three pieces on the eastern bank of the creek. At 7.30 p. m., Capt. Best informed me that the troops were to be withdrawn from the field. He instructed me to hold my position until the last regiment, which was to follow my battery, should come up.

When our time came, we went through the woods to a sunken road, across which we were to go into a cleared field. Beyond this field, rose a hill on which was a battery in position. The rest of the troops had already entered this field by the time the Battery and the following regiment came up, and the entrance to the field was choked with troops. My orders had been to make my way to Capt. Best's position, and I was using the utmost diligence to accomplish this. We had gone into the field just about 300 yards from the entrance, when an officer galloped up and said, "I want you to halt this battery." I replied that I could not as I was under orders to report it as soon as possible to Capt. Best, Chief of Artillery." "But," said he, "I want you to halt here." Becoming somewhat excited, I said I would not. He replied rather abruptly, "If you don't halt, I will use my saber." "Then," said I drawing my own saber, "we will be quits." I then said, "Now I will tell you this Battery is going to join Capt. Best's Battery. I don't know who you are, but I have had prior orders to yours." "I am on Gen. Sigel's staff," said he. "That may or may not be," I replied, "just as you say, but you must understand you can't bluff me. I am under

Capt. Best's orders and, as his battery is a short distance ahead of me, I shall join him." Just at this moment a cannon shot came rolling through the Battery. A section of a rebel battery had followed the regiment that was following Battery L and had thought to take us by surprise. The battery on the hill, of which I have made mention, opened upon the rebels, but, unfortunately, the first shot killed nine of our own troops, and the second wounded two or three. This created something like a panic, and the troops who had lost the men mentioned, were stampeded like a flock of sheep, and the whole camp was aroused.

After conferring together in Capt. Best's presence, Gen. Banks and Gen. Sigel decided to have the Captain take the position on the hill, but the Captain said his battery had sustained such losses during the day that it was not equal to the task. Then Gen. Sigel and Capt. Best came to me and asked me if I would take the position for the night. I agreed and Battery L, at once, marched up the hill, took position, and, with a dozen well-aimed shots, silenced the rebel artillery. (We found the next morning, that the rebels had vanished and left six dead horses).

This day (August 9th) had been for us an exceedingly busy day. It was 11 P. M., when the last shot of the day was fired, and the men were all tired out having worked very hard all day. After the poor fellows had had something to eat, they all lay down where they had been standing and were soon lost in sleep. Our casualties were two men slightly wounded, six battery horses killed, and two wounded. My own saddle horse, "Joe," was twice wounded, and so badly that I could no longer ride him. This was a great loss to me, for I had so trained him that I could depend upon him at all times. He was the one presented to me at Camp Todd, Flushing. An artillery officer is very dependent upon his horse and it takes considerable time to break one into the work it must perform. The two pieces that had been sent to Capt. Knapp in the morning, rejoined the Battery while on the hill, at 11 P. M., and took its proper position with the other pieces.

After breakfast the next morning (Sunday the 10th) I took a stroll to visit the various regiments that had, in company with the Battery, passed through their baptism of fire, but many of the familiar faces were found to have passed over the river of death. The 5th Conn. Vols. had lost its colonel and many of its captains, besides very many of the rank and file.

The behavior of the officers and men of Battery L during their first battle was far better than I had expected it to be. Lieuts. Standish and Van Nostrand proved themselves worthy of their positions, but Lieut. Wm. Cooper proved himself to be wholly unworthy of being even a private soldier. His behavior was most demoralizing, especially as he had very often boasted of his service in the French army. Naturally more is expected of an officer who claims to have seen service than of one who has not. The battle had not fairly opened, only a few cannon shots had been exchanged, when Lieut. Cooper was seized with the "cannon fever." Trembling from head to foot, he was put into an ambulance and sent off the field. The behavior of such a man could easily have created a panic among the men, with the result that not one would have been fit to hold the post assigned him, and the sooner he was sent off the field, the better. He never appeared in the Battery again. Of the enlisted men, very few faltered in their duties. Boys of sixteen and seventeen fought like heroes throughout the battle.

Battery L was now ordered to go into position at a point farther to the right and on higher ground. The Battery had already limbered to the rear to make this change, but when the proper command had been given to start the movement, a strange thing occurred. Some of the battery horses seemed either to have forgotten what they had learned on the drill-ground or to have become totally deaf. The heavy cannonade of the previous day must have had a bad effect upon them, for they seemed as if they had been paralyzed. The first two pieces started off readily enough, but the third would not start. The driver of the lead team had caught the "cannon fever" and had lost control of his horses. The rebels had by this time noticed our movements, and now greeted us with a shower of shot and shell. Thick and fast the missiles came. I saw at once that the lead driver could do nothing with his team, and that he and the team would certainly be destroyed if he stayed much longer. I ordered him to dismount, and calling the boy, Dan Johnston, whom I have mentioned before, said: "Come, mount this team, its driver is not fit to drive a lead team." Johnston came, but instead of letting him mount by himself, I took him by his jacket collar and the seat of his trousers and threw him into the saddle. Then, taking a whip, I struck the horses to start them off at a full gallop and followed them for several yards, still on foot.

Just then my groom called me and asked me if I did not want my horse.

"Yes, Jimmy," said I, "bring him along. You are a brave boy. But why did you not follow the other pieces as you had a right to do?" "And sure," he replied, "I would not leave my captain without his horse." At the same moment a shot came flying and I had just time enough to get out of its way and mount my horse, or both Jimmy and I would have been stricken down. When Jimmy brought up my horse amid the flying shot and shell, the horse was so uneasy and restless that I had to be, on that account, very quick in mounting, but as soon as I was in the saddle the horse was all right.* I then started off at full gallop across the cornfield in which the cornstalks were some eight or nine feet high. While thus riding on, one of my men ran in front of the horse, and the latter striking the man on the shoulder in front, whirled him around like a spinning top. At the same time I noticed that his coat spread out as he whirled.

As soon as I caught up with the Battery, thinking the man, Igo by name, whom my horse had struck, was wounded, I sent a corporal with two men back on my trail to find him. The corporal found the man, brought him up, and took him to the surgeon to be examined. Igo declared positively that he was wounded, as he knew a ball had struck him in front. On examination a 10-pound shell was found—in his coat pocket, where he had put it himself, having picked it up on the field for some unknown reason. The horse striking him in front as it did, had caused him to spin around, and he thought he had been mortally wounded. It was some time before he could be convinced that he was wholly unhurt. Ever after, the wounding of Igo was a standing jest among the men.

Private Wm. Ludwig, driver of the pole team of one of the pieces which had been sent August 9th under command of Lieut. Howard to support Capt. Knapp on the left of our line of battle, showed himself equal to any emergency. The section to which he belonged was stationed on the left of Capt. Knapp's battery during severe fighting that continued for fully two hours. Capt. Knapp's battery lost heavily

---

* How soon a horse can learn the maneuvers of artillery is shown by the fact that my horse, although but a short time in the service, wanted, when the bugle sounded the command to march, to go to the head of the column if it were possible, and, if he were kept back, would plunge and rear until he was allowed to go to what he seemed to think was his proper place.

in both men and horses from the fire of the enemy on the mountain. This battery was more directly in front of the mountain than Battery L was.

When the order came to withdraw the artillery and advance the infantry, Capt. Knapp's battery was ordered to move first, while Battery L's section was ordered to follow. Just as the movement was about to be executed, a horse belonging to the middle team of Ludwig's piece was killed and fell right on the pole in front of the pole team. The driver of the lead team loosened his horses the quickest way he could and galloped off. The driver of the middle team did the same with his remaining horse. Thus poor Ludwig was left to his fate. He, however, took in the situation at a glance, and proceeded to extricate himself from his trouble in a way that seemed like an inspiration. He backed his horses, as they interfered with freeing the pole from the burden resting upon it, pushed the dead horse from the pole and turned his horses directly eastward to hug the lee of the mountain. Lieut. Howard galloped up to him and ordered him to go right out and cross the plain. But Ludwig replied, "No, Lieutenant, if I do that both horses and piece will be lost. I will hug the mountain until I reach the road, and then I will be all right." He knew that the enemy were close at his heels and he thought that by doing as he did they could not reach him either with cannon or with muskets. Ludwig brought his gun safely to the rear. Gen. Pope saw his maneuvers, and just as Ludwig was passing the general and his staff, the general said to him, "My boy, you are a brave man; to what battery do you belong?" "To Battery L, 2d N. Y., General," replied Ludwig.

My opinion regarding the battle of Cedar Mountain is this:—If Gen. Sigel had not come up just at the time he did, the 2d Army Corps would have suffered a terrible defeat. It could not possibly have held its own. All the trouble arose in consequence of the terrible blunder perpetrated by the battery on our right, in firing on our own men just as they were entering the large clearing near the woods while falling back from the battlefield. The troops fought well that day, yet we stood on the brink of a terrible disaster. We were only about 8,700 against the enemy's 20,000, so one can judge what work we had to do to hold our own. The dead and wounded lay thick around us, yet we could pay no attention to them. They had been our comrades and we felt for them, but we were fighting to save our country and that had to be our first care.

Right here I wish to say that the men who fought in the first battles of the war were wedded, body and soul, to their country's cause, and that it was pure love of country that inspired them to fight and die for its sake. I only wish that my dear friends in Flushing could have stood by gun No. 1 of Battery L on that 9th of August. They would then have been in a position to understand better the terrible nature of that battle. They could have told by the changes of color of the officers' faces how the tide of battle was constantly varying. Our men would charge heavily against the enemy's lines only to be driven back in turn; then the reserves would force the enemy back until they in turn were compelled to give way; then again, after reforming, they would press heavily against the enemy's lines. No matter how many dropped out of the ranks, the remainder, gallant fellows, struggled hard to gain the victory.

After the battle I paid a visit to the field hospital established in an old log house. Operating tables had been put up and about a dozen surgeons were hard at work amputating torn and shattered limbs. So urgent were the demands for the surgeons' services, there was no time to remove the clothes covering the limbs; limb and covering were both removed together, that the work might be completed before the truce came to an end. Just to the right of the operating tables, was a window through which the amputated limbs were thrust. I walked around the hospital on the outside, but one look at that pile of human flesh, mutilated as it was, was enough for me. It was sickening and I was glad to leave, yet I knew this work of amputation had to be done.

In the afternoon, I rode over the whole battlefield, both on the enemy's side and our own. At the place where our infantry had struggled so gallantly against terrible odds, those that had been killed outright had been buried where they fell, if buried it could be called, for, as I rode over the field, I could see here and there a foot or an arm projecting above the ground. It was horrible, but the necessity for burial had been so very great that this could hardly have been avoided.

Now I learned why the enemy's "White Horse Battery" did not stand its ground when the fire of our batteries was directed against it. It must have suffered severely. One trench was marked, "24 men, White Horse Battery." Farther on, I came to a single grave surrounded by a fence made of pickets taken from a fence a short distance away. It was marked, "Captain, White Horse Battery." Close by this, was a ditch containing seven of the infantry support of the battery, and near this ditch, was a tree fully one foot in diameter that had been shot clean off about three feet from the ground. Just to the right of this battery's position, was the place where their cavalry had formed twice for those desperate charges made on our battery to break the center of our lines. Here death and destruction had been rampant. Who can describe such a scene? Most of the dead soldiers had been buried, and the wounded removed, but the field was covered with dead horses that had belonged to the artillery and cavalry. The hot sun pouring down upon them created such a stench that, as a sanitary measure, they were burned as soon as possible. I was glad to leave this sickening sight and ride back to camp, though I fully realized I might have to behold such a scene many times in the future, unless as a soldier I should myself be soon called upon to yield up my own life for my adopted country, a sacrifice I was willing to make.

CHAPTER III.

SECOND BATTLE OF BULL RUN.

On the eleventh of August the Battery was ordered to take position on the left of the Culpeper road, which position it occupied until the 15th. By a Special Order from Hdqrs., 2d Corps, Army of Virginia, dated August 14th, the Battery was assigned to the Reserve Artillery commanded by Maj. Kiefer, 2d N. Y. Art.

On the 15th the Battery went by order to Culpeper to report for future service, and, after repairing damages and drawing 750 rounds of ammunition, to be ready to march at a moment's notice. At 3:30 P. M., August 18th, it was ordered to march at once. Our coffee was almost ready, but we had to leave it. Men and horses had to go without supper, which means much to a soldier. We fell into our place in the column and then halted till nine o'clock the next morning. At that hour an order came to march to the Rappahannock River. That night the whole army bivouacked on the right bank of the river, and crossed it the next day, the 20th. The Battery went into camp in company with the other batteries of the Reserve Artillery.

Two of the Battery's pieces were put in position near the edge of the wood ready for action. They were posted near a water course that had a fence in it following the center line of the channel, to prevent cattle from crossing. As night came on a heavy rain storm set in; it rained harder and harder till, finally, the rain came down in perfect torrents. I thought of the two pieces and of Sergeant Kaufman in command. After supper, the rain having slacked up, I rode over to see how matters stood there.

After looking over the situation, I concluded to remain there for the night. I told the Sergeant to keep a close watch in front, and said I was going to pass the night with him. "I am glad, Captain," he replied, "for this is a nasty place to be attacked in." I told him to charge his cannoneers not only not to undress, but also to keep on their accoutrements and be ready for action at any moment. The Sergeant soon reported everything in order. At 10 P. M. the storm began again, the rain coming down in torrents. Not a man in the section had an overcoat with him, and all were without shelter of any kind. The ground was fast becoming saturated. Sergeant Kaufman had an India rubber talma. This we fastened to the fence rails and under it we huddled together. The water course was fast filling with water. In some places it rose from five to seven feet, and the current soon became so strong that no swimmer could live in it. There we were, with just a few fence rails to support us and a single talma to cover us. But we had to make the best of it. The one thing we were thankful for, was, we were not attacked during the night.

On the 21st, by orders from Hdqrs., Lieut. Standish was sent with two pieces to go out with Gen. Bayard and his cavalry on the advanced line, to ascertain the enemy's position. The next day I was ordered to report with the four remaining pieces and 300 rounds of ammunition to Gen. Sigel. At 10 A. M. orders came to march at 12 M. At that hour the Battery started, and, after marching six miles, joined Gen. Sigel's First Corps just above the bridge. The moment I reported I received orders to take position in a shallow valley near the river. Here our troops were soon engaged in a sharp encounter with the enemy across the river. During this fight, the brave Gen. Bohlen, commanding the 1st Brigade, was killed while leading his men to the attack. After his fall, Gen. Carl Schurz commanding the 3d Div., First Corps, was especially conspicuous on the battlefield. Toward evening, an order came for the Battery to go into position in a rye field nearer the river. I was also ordered to allow no cannoneer to leave his post or his piece during the night, and, as soon as I had any knowledge of an advance by the enemy, to open fire at once. Occasion to obey this order soon came. The enemy advanced, but after we had fired about thirty rounds, they fell back.

At 10 A. M., August 23d, orders came to march to Sulphur Springs. When the troops had gone about four miles the march was suddenly interrupted by the enemy. The Battery was ordered to the front. Arriving there, it opened with shot and canister, and compelled the enemy to retreat to Sulphur Springs, whither our troops followed them. The next day the Battery was ordered to take position on the hill near Sulphur Springs. From this position we opened a terrible fire, to which the enemy replied with a fire about as terrible as our own. Thinking we were in need of railroad iron, they sent us some in pieces about ten inches long from their guns. These pieces were wound with wire to make them fit the bore of their guns, and when they came whizzing through the air, they shrieked as though the "old boy and his grandmother" were coming to visit us. One of these curious missiles struck a gun carriage and smashed it to splinters, leaving nothing but the gun uninjured.

When about half of the advancing column had passed the Battery's position, I left the Battery and galloped on to Sulphur Springs to find a better position. Finding one, I returned and ordered the Battery forward. Just as it started the enemy redoubled their fire, but it went on piece after piece in fine style. Once in a position behind a building in Sulphur Springs, the enemy lost their hold on the Battery, while our troops, protected from the enemy by the Battery's fire from this position, passed in safety. Capt. R. B. Hampton' Battery F, Penn. Art. here joined us as our support, and then we were abundantly able to hold this important position. The Battery was then ordered to advance in the direction of Waterloo Bridge to get on the enemy's flank. Just as it started Lieut. Standish with his two guns reported back from his work with Gen. Bayard's cavalry. It soon reached the position assigned to it. Here it remained until 2 P. M., when I was ordered with four pieces to follow the advance of the 1st Army Corps towards the Bridge. When we had arrived at a point one mile distant from the Bridge, we halted and went into bivouac on the road in company with the advance guard.

On the 25th, Hampton's and Roemer's batteries were ordered to proceed to Waterloo Bridge. Hampton's Battery was alone in action until 2:30 P. M., at which hour Roemer's Battery was ordered forward, for that was the time when the infantry had been ordered to burn the Bridge, under the protection of our guns from the enemy's combined artillery and infantry fire. Gen. Milroy, commanding the Independent Brigade, now ordered the infantry forward to burn the Bridge. This advance of the infantry was a signal for the enemy to make a general attack upon our whole line to prevent the destruction of the Bridge. Gen. Milroy now ordered the Battery to take position with the left wing, but Gens. Sigel and Schurz countermanded the order. We had, therefore, to remain with the right wing to draw the enemy's fire and shelter the infantry. For a considerable time the Battery peppered the Johnnies across the river well ; it had no notion of allowing them to bother the infantry who were trying to execute the order to burn the Bridge. Both

Hampton's and Roemer's batteries were hard at work; they succeeded not only in keeping the infantry, but the artillery as well, from coming near the river. The artillery tried several times to advance their pieces, but after each attempt they retreated to a safer position. These retreats gave us to understand they had respect for us and that our fire was too much for them.

At last, the Bridge was successfully fired by our troops, but we still kept a close watch upon the rebels who did not seem to be satisfied. About 7 P. M., they evidently had a notion to charge on the burning bridge. Their movements were very sly, yet we kept pretty good track of them, and thought to take advantage of them. As soon as we saw them preparing to charge with both infantry and artillery both Hampton's and Roemer's batteries, comprising ten pieces, opened a rapid fire upon them. This soon quieted them, and, and for the remainder of the night all was quiet along their lines. On our side of the Rappahannock, its left bank, everthing had become quiet by 7:30 P. M.

As the Battery boys had not had much time the whole day long for anything but fighting and watching, their stomachs had not been cared for. I asked some of the staff officers if the men could not make coffee. They said, "You can do so at your own risk." A sheltered place, where, it was thought, the light could not be seen, was soon found and a fire started. The coffee was just boiling, when the order came to march at once. The temptation was too great; the men all came running up, cup in hand, dipped the cup into kettle, then ran to their several places each with a cup full of boiling hot coffee. While they were mounting their horses, I heard on all sides, various exclamations; such as, "But this coffee *is* hot!" "How I burned my mouth!" "Whoa, pet, I did not mean to burn you!" I was powerless; I could not order them to throw the coffee away, for I knew what a precious boon it was to those tired and worn men.

At last all were ready, and the Battery went on through the woods. As time went on, the darkness seemed to become denser and denser. Every few moments, some gun-carriage or caisson would bump against a tree, but the coffee had made the men happy and they did not mind the discomforts of the march.

It was at Sulphur Springs, I remember, that we drew our first rations of "hard tack." They deserved the name, for they were hard, yet, I think, they were very nourishing. "Hard tack" with a cup of good hot coffee, every soldier fully appreciated, especially when they could not be had. The men of Battery L saw many such occasions before the war ended. I used to think that a "hard tack" toasted before the fire and eaten hot, was better than the best pastry.

During the whole night, the order given to the artillery was to take the full step, wherever the roads permitted. The Battery reached Warrenton at 4 A. M., August 26th. Both men and horses were used up. For twenty-four hours, they had scarcely anything to eat. They had been marching all night after fighting all day. As soon as the Battery halted, the men began scurrying around to get a cup of coffee and something to eat for themselves and then to get something for their horses. At 8 A. M., all commands were ordered to be ready to march at a moment's notice with one day's cooked rations per man, and, during the march, to allow both men and horses to have as much rest as possible.

The saddle-horse presented to me by the citizens of Flushing, had, as stated before, been twice badly wounded in the left foreleg at Cedar Mountain, August 9th. My young son, Louis H. Roemer, thinking he must and could be saved had tried every means in his power to save poor "Joe." I now saw that he could not be cured, and as he seemed to suffer so much, we sent him into a cornfield near by and had him shot. There poor "Joe" was left. The gun, whose carriage had been smashed at Sulphur Springs by the rebel artillery, was sent from Warrenton to Washington.

At 9 A. M., August 27th, the order came to march at once. The whole of Sigel's First Corps took the main road to Gainesville.

When the army had marched four miles beyond Warrenton, it was quite close to the rebel lines. I was now ordered to have the right section under Lieut. Standish, take position in the woods on the right of the main road, and to have the three remaining pieces under Lieut. Van Nostrand, take position on a hill farther on and on the left of the main road. From this commanding position, it being considerably elevated above the surrounding country which was quite level, I could, with my field glass, see all the movements of the enemy, and also their baggage trains coming up. It seemed as if the whole rebel army were right before us. They saw our troops advancing and fell back. An order now came for me to have the right section, posted on the right of the road, move to the more advanced position on the hill. This brought the Battery together again.

Gen. Sigel now rode up to our position and ordered me to take one of my sections to a hill farther in front and open fire at once. Both Durell's and Roemer's batteries were engaged in several skirmishes by sections during the day, both on the right and the left of the road. While the troops were passing the Gaines' House, some of the staff officers remained behind. The two batteries, Durell's and Roemer's, went on down to lower ground, where we came to a brook. Crossing this we found ourselves again on rising ground. Some of the enemy's cavalry were right behind us. Looking back, we saw some of the officers who had remained behind, enter the Gaines House. They had no sooner entered, than rebel cavalry seemed to spring up all around the house, right, left, and rear. We saw the whole affair from our position, and were ordered to open fire upon the house at once. Durell's battery was on the left of the road and Roemer's on the right. The enemy returned our fire with four guns. I saw at once that they had a dead shot on us, and, finding that the left piece was very much exposed, I had moved it to a point some forty yards to the right of the right piece, behind a clump of cedars, from which position the gunner could make a dead shot every time. Durell suffered greatly, for he lost one of his lieutenants and three men. I then advised him to change his pieces as I had done. It was not long before we had fired the house and silenced the rebel battery with percussion shells. The house was burned to the ground. I now felt better, but I was very sorry for Capt. Durell's misfortune in losing such a fine young officer who was literally torn to pieces. So the day passed. As we advanced, we had to fight now on the right, now on the left. Battery L met with no casualties, and fired some sixty rounds.

The course of events on the 28th was almost the same as that on the preceding day, fighting right and left, as we advanced along the Gainesville road. Once when a section took position in the woods on the right of the road, the rebels, who were close at hand, succeeded in capturing Sergeant Werner. He was an old soldier, and, after his capture, played his part so well that his captors placed considerable confidence in him and allowed him many liberties.

About 5 P. M., Gen. Sigel called for one section of Roemer's battery. I went out with the section, over a corduroy road, through a swamp to the top of a conical hill.

This hill was surrounded for several miles by swamps, which in turn were encircled with woods. Gen. Sigel himself accompanied us to the hill. From this position we were to drive the rebels out of the woods. After forty-six rounds had been fired Gen. Sigel left the place.

The section remained in position until 9 P. M., and then we made our way back as best we could. The corduroy road over which we had gone on our way out, was but eight feet wide. It was light when we went out, but now it was intensely dark; we could scarcely see our hands before us. We had, therefore, to feel our way. I placed men along the edges of the road to prevent cannon-carriages and caissons from going off at the sides. When we reached the end of this road, we were all right. Soon we struck the main road, and started on our way to the battle-ground of the next day. While on the road, whom should we meet, but Sergeant Werner, who, as noted before, had been captured during the day. He told us that, as the intense darkness and the dense woods seemed to favor it, he thought it best to try to escape.

When the Battery halted it was about 12:30 A. M., August 29th, and as the men had not had much to eat for the past four days, and had not had their clothes off for the same time, I ordered coffee to be made that they might have some little refreshment. We ate of what food we still had on hand and then tried to sleep, but an order was now received to the effect that the order of the night before, to be ready to march at a moment's notice, was still in force.

At 4 A. M., August 29th, the Battery was ordered to take position, at once, at a point in front of a wood, about three-quarters of a mile northwest of the Stone House, at Manassas, Va., with the right wing of the army. On the road to our position, we encountered some very peculiar war material, in the shape of feminine paraphernalia seldom found on a battle field—hoop-skirts, under clothing, shawls, blankets, hammocks, books, papers, pillows, and a variety of other knick-knacks, to which the Battery boys took quite a fancy. I myself would have liked one of the hammocks, but as my General was right behind me at the time, I did not have the face to stop and pick it up.

At 6 A. M. we changed position and did some firing, then changed position again, this time to the extreme right. Here, finding the Battery had no infantry support, I sent to Gen. Schurz, our Div. Commander, asking for one. He sent seven companies of infantry, and, in addition, the 6-gun Cohorn "Jackass" Battery, so called because the mortars were carried by mules.

Soon after this, Gen. ——— (I cannot recall the name) came to me and said: "I want you to take that position with your battery," at the same time designating the position. "All right, General," I replied, "but only on your responsibility." "What do you mean by that?" he asked. "I mean, General," I answered, "just what I said." "Then you won't take the position?" said he. "I beg your pardon, General," said I, "I will take the position to which you have assigned me, if not a man or a horse comes from it alive, but only on your responsibility." At the same time, being greatly excited, I shook my finger in his face. (I well knew what our occupation of the designated position would mean for the men and horses). "Don't shake your finger at me!" said he, and then he began to ridicule me. Placing my finger on my shoulder-strap, I said: "General, you have no right to ridicule me before my men. I respect your shoulder-straps, and you must respect mine." Stepping back ten or fifteen paces, he beckoned me to come to him, and then asked: "Captain, what do you mean by saying 'on my responsibility?'" "I mean this," I said, "if this Battery is lost as a consequence of taking that position, it will be your fault and not mine." "Captain," he then asked, "have you looked at any other position?" "General," I answered, "if I had not, I would not have said what I did." "Then I will allow you," he said, "to choose your own position." Judging from the general's actions that a court martial might be the result of this squabble, I called Lieut. Van Nostrand and said, while the general was still standing near, "General, this may mean a court martial for me, therefore, I want my lieutenant as a witness that you have said I could choose my own position." The general replied: "Yes, you can." I thanked the general, and he left with the understanding that I was to select my own position. I at once moved the five pieces farther to the right, near a clump of trees. I posted three pieces just in rear of the clump, and the remaining two on the right of it, thus showing the rebels two only of five pieces in position.

By 8 A. M. the battle was fairly opened, especially in the center of the line. The ground in front of Battery L was a clear field extending out some eight or nine hundred yards to a piece of woods, in a downward slope ; on the right the ground sloped sharply to the east. As the Battery was facing north from this eastern slope, the guns behind the trees could not be seen. I had made up my mind, therefore, if a charge should be made on the Battery, it would be made from the east, on the extreme right flank ; and so it happened.

The enemy evidently thought they would have but two pieces of artillery to contend with. On they came, and when the two visible pieces were fired, they thought there would be no further trouble, and dashed on in the direction of the three concealed pieces. These were all ready for the enemy, each being loaded with a double charge of canister. Now they were fired, one after the other, and when the third was fired, the two other guns in the open, having by this time been reloaded with double canister, were also fired one after the other. This proved to be too much for them, for they turned to the rear, and went back at double-quick to the point whence they had started, but to make them run faster, the contents of the other three pieces, which had now been reloaded, were sent after them.

Their rapid retreat was witnessed by the infantry, and the hurrahs for Battery L that were shouted all along the line were deafening. Even the "Jackass" Battery, our reserve, hurrahed for Battery L. General ——— then came galloping up in our rear to ascertain the cause of the cheering; he was told about the rebel charge and its sudden ending, and then all the troops shouted in chorus: "Roemer's Battery did the work."

The general galloped up to where I was standing, and, extending his hand, said, "Captain, here is my hand; let us be friends as long as the war lasts. I know you now." Since then we have been, indeed, true friends. At a grand reunion of the "Burnside Expedition" and the Ninth Corps, held at the International Hotel, Niagara Falls, a few years after the war, and which I attended with two of my daughters, the general told this story, and he has told it many times since.

Major Kiefer of the Reserve Artillery took to himself all the credit that really belonged to Battery L. Riding around our position, proud as a peacock, he went out to a big stone heap lying some 300 yards north of the knoll on which the Battery was posted, and called to me to come to him. I replied that I had no business out there, and that my proper place was with my Battery. He rode around for some time, and the enemy resumed their fire. The second shot struck his horse which fell, carrying the Major down with him. The Major scrambled out and came running to the Battery. Putting on a serious face, I asked: "Major, what is the matter? Where is your hat?" "Why, didn't you see my horse was shot? I want one of your men to go out and get my saddle and bridle." "Major," I replied, "I never send a man to any place I won't go myself." But I turned to the men and said: "Any one of you men that is willing to go out and get the Major's saddle and bridle may do so, but I will not order you to go. He had no business there, and that is the last of one of our fine battery horses." The Major's horse really belonged to the Battery. No one, however, was willing to take the risk, and so the Major did not recover his saddle and bridle.

By 10 A. M., the fighting point had moved from the center farther to the right. At this time shot reached us from the railroad cut, beyond a belt of woods north of our position. Up to this time we had met with no losses except that of the horse lost by Major Keefer. The Battery's two pieces outside of the woods were still in plain sight of the enemy. The other three were still kept in the woods ready to do any work that occasion might require, and yet were so sheltered that no shot could be aimed directly at them.

Our infantry were brought up to charge upon the railroad cut in our front, both in the center of our lines and towards the left. Soon the rattle of musketry and the booming of artillery increased in severity. This warned us of what might be expected from the enemy on the left, for they were evidently warming up to their work, and, though they had been silent the whole morning, were now smelling powder. Twelve o'clock came, but with it came no signs of dinner, and the appearance of things seemed to warrant the conclusion that no dinner would come.

The center of fighting passed from right to left and back again without cessation. At the railroad cut, especially, the fighting was terrific. Reinforcements were brought up and into the woods they went, but it seemed as if more dead bodies and wounded men were brought out than there had been living men sent in, at least, it seemed so to us. Thus we knew the place was a real slaughter pen. I have positive knowledge of the First Corps' line only, on which line Battery L held the right.

The fighting was still going on at half-past two, when Capt. Schirmer came up to say that Capt. Hampton's Battery F, Pa. Art. would relieve Battery L, which was to go back east of the Stone House, there to refresh men and horses, but to be kept in readiness for any emergency. The Battery went to that place and at once prepared to make coffee, but before this could be accomplished, an aide galloped up and asked what battery it was. "This is Battery L, 2d N. Y.," I replied. "You are ordered to report to Gen. Sigel," continued he. "From whom does this order come?" I asked. "From Gen. Pope," he replied. "Well," said I, "that is strange. I passed Gen. Pope on the hill yonder but ten minutes ago. Capt. Schirmer, our Chief of Artillery, had just then ordered us here." "Well, Captain," said he, "I have given you the order as I was told to give it."

I then told Lieut. Standish to discontinue the coffee making and await further orders. I called my orderly, mounted my horse, and in company with the aide, galloped over to Gen. Pope. Saluting him, I asked if he had given orders for me to report to Gen. Sigel, and he said he had. "Well, General," said I, "allow me to say that Capt. Schirmer has just relieved the Battery. It has been in position since four o'clock this morning." "I am sorry, Captain, but Gen. Sigel wants your battery." "Where can I see Gen. Sigel?" I inquired. "There he goes towards our left," the General answered. I saluted and rode off with my orderly at full gallop and soon caught up with Gen. Sigel. One of the aides, seeing me coming, spoke to Gen. Sigel, who faced about just as I rode up. I said, "General, I have the honor to report Battery L, 2d N. Y." "Capt. Roemer," said he, "I thank you." "Capt. Dahlgren," he continued, speaking to an aide, "you will accompany Capt. Roemer to the left immediately. Capt. Schirmer's Battery has been annihilated, and that position must be held at all hazards." This was said with great emphasis. "But, General," I said, "my men and horses are all used up." "Never mind men or horses," said he; "how many rounds of ammunition have you?" "Five hundred," I answered. "That will do, Captain," he said, "and, as I said before, that position must be held at all hazards."

As Capt. Dahlgren and I wheeled to the left, the Captain turned to me and said, "Capt. Roemer, I am sorry for your battery." Knowing full well what he meant, I replied, "Captain, if I die to-day, I won't have to die to-morrow." "Capt. Roemer," said he, "I wish I could say so." "Well, said I, "all I wish is, if I must die, to sell the Battery as dearly as possible." I sent my orderly to bring the Battery westward. I then said to Capt. Dahlgren, "I will take the opportunity, before the Battery comes up, to look over the ground I will have to occupy. The enemy have ten pieces with which to attack the position, while I have but five with which to defend it; the odds against me are very great." I did not at all like the position we were to take. There was a little farm-house on the southern slope of the hill, and I saw at once, that that place would be a splendid position for the Battery in its contest with the ten rebel guns, as it afforded more protection. Just before the Battery came up, I called Capt. Dahlgren's attention to the position, and, telling him it was the best position possible for the Battery, asked him to allow me to take it in preference to the one the general had ordered me to take. "Here," said I, "I can shield both men and horses, and even my ammunition will be half covered from the enemy's fire. I'll fix the ten rebel guns if you will let me stay here." Finally he consented. To save time in getting the Battery into position, I ordered the cannoneers to the front with axes. After cutting down chicken-coops, hog-pens, corn-cribs, etc., the Battery went through the door yard into a fine orchard, which gave the Battery a splendid position. We had fired but three or four shots, when an aide came galloping up the hill towards us. He brought orders for the Battery to take the position that had been occupied by Capt. Schirmer's Battery. I knew we must obey, so, after giving the order to "cease firing," I rode in front of the men and said : "Boys, it is no longer of any use to keep from you what may be in store for us. Before the sun sets to-night, many of you may have given up your lives ; perhaps I myself will have to, but all I have to say is—Die like men ; do not run like cowards. Stick to your guns, and, with the help of God and our own exertions, we may get through. Forward, march."

We went west about half a mile, and then came to a sunken road on the right, with a bank on its eastern side about seven feet high. The cut through the road would allow but one carriage to pass at a time. Capt. Dahlgren and I rode forward to be at the head of the column. Guns and caissons followed immediately. Soon all had entered and were passing through. The enemy had calculated upon this from the moment we left our former position and entered the road. Just as soon as we emerged from the road, they were ready for us. Shot and shell flew thick and fast. I took in the situation at a glance and knew they would have a chance to destroy us utterly. I raised my right hand to Heaven, and said to myself, "Good-bye to all the dear ones at home, for I will not see the sun set tonight." I gave the order, "Come on, trot, march. Gallop, march." To get over the plain as quickly as possible. While passing a small belt of woods, the enemy opened upon us from it, and while we were taking position, they had us at their mercy and opened fire upon our left flank.

This was too much for me. I rushed forward, raised my saber, and, after saying to Capt. Dahlgren, "The command is mine," gave the order. "Head of column to the right. Follow me. Each sergeant will command his own piece." We were right in front of the enemy as we went back to our former position, and at the mercy of their ten pieces. We had to go back to save the Battery. I gave the orders as I did, that we might get back as speedily as possible, no matter how we went. On we went, pell-mell, over fences, stone-walls—everything had to give way before us. We were back in our former position in just twenty-five minutes after we had left it. I put the right piece on the western side of the garden fence just where it had stood before, but instead of placing the guns fourteen yards apart as before, I now placed them forty yards apart, so that the enemy would have to fire directly at each piece to do any damage. On looking around, I found that three guns only had followed me. One of my lieutenants had turned left instead of right in the sunken road and gone down Manassas Valley into the bushes, thinking, no doubt, that to be a safer place. I placed the three pieces, so that it was eighty yards from the right piece to the left one.

Capt. Dahlgren came up to the center gun, where I was standing, and said, "Capt. Roemer, you cannot stand this fire thirty minutes. I will hasten to Gen. Sigel and ask him to send a battery to assist you." I said to him, "Do so, and, meanwhile, I will try my best to overcome the rebel fire, although, you know, Captain, ten to three is very great odds." The sergeant asked me, "What fuse shall we use?" I told him to wait a little, and I would ascertain what the enemy were using. They had four rifles and six twelve-pound Napoleons. I took out my watch and timed them. I soon ascertained they were using 8-second fuses, while their shells exploded half a mile in our rear. I then ordered my men to use 5-second fuses with forty yards cut-off. As soon as the three pieces had been sighted by their respective gunners, I said, "Boys, the life of the Battery hangs on the first and second shots. I want young Bell to look over these pieces before they are fired. I want them all aimed at the cherry tree you can see from here." After looking over the three guns, Bell pronounced them all right. Taking my field glass, I knelt down beside the center piece and gave the command, "Fire." As if fired from a single gun, the three shells went whizzing through the air. I was triumphant, for the execution was great. I said to the men, "That was first rate, let them know this is Battery L, 2nd N. Y." Immediately, the guns were reloaded, and again sighted by Bell. Again I knelt with my glass and commanded, "Fire." I dropped my glass, ran up on the trail of the gun, and shouted. "Hurrah! Hurrah for Battery L! Their ten pieces are retreating before our three. The day is ours, boys, give it to them now." Just then Capt. Dahlgren came up from our rear, and greeted me with, "Well, Capt. Roemer, how do you stand it?" "Well, Captain," I replied, "every man and horse of Battery L still stands on his own legs, and yet the Johnnies have put 500 yards more space between us and themselves." "You have done well," said he, "Capt. Hampton was to come to your support, but I understand he has lost two pieces in the position where he relieved your battery."

It was now near 5 P. M., and we had completely the upper hand of the enemy's ten-gun battery. Our first two battery fires had cost them 30 horses and almost the same number of men. By 5.30 P. M., Battery L had had no casualties among either men or horses, and had so far during this engagement fired 207 rounds.

Capt. Hampton now reported with two pieces and took position on my left. Just as he was moving into position, a shell struck one of his pieces, killed three horses, and wounded several of his men very severely. At this time also, my brave (?) lieutenant, who had sought shelter in the bushes, finding we had so far silenced the ten-gun battery, came up. The ten-gun battery still kept up a desultory fire, but by 7 P. M., they were using one gun only and that very feebly.

After 7 P. M., Battery L was relieved by order of Gen. Sigel, who, after complimenting it, ordered it, as soon as it was relieved, to go to the rear camp and refresh men and horses, a privilege to which the Battery was fully entitled for having held the forlorn hope so bravely on the battle-field, during the whole afternoon. This compliment from Gen. Sigel, the boys felt, fully repaid them for all the anxiety and hardship they had experienced during the day. The Battery marched to the rear camp to enjoy one good meal that should be dinner and supper together, and, if possible, to obtain one good night's rest for both men and horses. At 7:30 P. M., the only casualties that had occurred in Battery L, were two men slightly wounded, and one horse killed.

One of the strange things that sometimes occur during a battle, happened to Private Billy Green on this day. A shot of some kind passed and Billy either took his cap off, or it was knocked off, at any rate, he was standing with his cap in his hand. Looking at me, he said, "Sure, Captain, them Johnnies have shot the 'L' off me cap." "Never mind, Billy," said I, "I will give you another one." Billy was No. 1 of his gun detachment, and handled the ramrod in loading the gun. One of the enemy's shells struck the ground about eight feet in front of him, entered the earth, and passed under him, compelling him to turn a complete somersault. He scrambled up, looked around and then at me. "Billy, are you hurt?" I asked. "No, Captain," he replied. "Well, Billy," said I, "what have you done to the Johnnies, that they pick you out for a target? First, they take the 'L.' off your cap and then they try to make a circus actor of you. They don't trouble the other boys." "Sure, Captain," he replied. "I don't know what they want with me. Faith, I never meant them any harm." "Well, Billy," said I, "all I have to say is—give it to them. I don't want them to insult my best cannoneer."

By 8 P. M., we were all settled in camp. Billy Howard, the Battery cook, had made all preparations for our supper, which consisted of coffee and crackers. I told him to give the men quantity, if he could not give quality, to make the coffee hold out so they could have all they wanted to soak their crackers in. I was thankful that there was plenty of water to be had. We had a good night's rest, and, in the morning felt quite fresh and thoroughly rested.

At 5 A. M., August 30th, the Battery reported as reserve, at the crossroads under the hill in rear of where it had been in position the previous day. The Battery was mounted at 8 A. M., and was held in readiness for instant action. While it was still waiting for orders, at 10:30 A. M., a number of infantry regiments passed. Among them were the 9th N. Y. S. M. (83d N. Y. V.)* and "Duryea's Zouaves," (5th N. Y. V.)† While the former was passing, when they learned that we were the Flushing Battery, cheers for the

---

* In 3d Brig., 2d Div., Third Army Corps.

† In 3d Brig., 2d Div., Fifth Army Corps.

Battery came from the Flushing boys in the regiment. Prince, Howard, Cassady, Hicks and others whom we had entertained at Warrenton, were as glad to see us as we were to see them. Then came the Zouaves. I can yet see the smiling face of Corporal Geo. Huntsman, as he passed in red jacket and tasseled cap. When he saw the Battery he gave the regimental cheer, three times three and a tiger. This flower of Flushing marched away to the left (I watched him as long as I could) and to death. He gave his life for a noble cause, but the sacrifice was great. Before the sun sank below the western horizon, the blooming cheeks of the morning had become ashen pale; he died for his country. This was the first sacrifice Flushing was called upon to make. When I heard the news of his death my heart went out to his mother. I was thankful that I had had that opportunity of seeing familiar faces. How they inspire one, these chance meetings, in the intervals of war.

At 11:30 A. M., the ambulance arrived from the rear camp with dinner. Sergeant Heasley had the bugle dinner call sounded at once. Dinner was soon over and apparently none too soon, for, by the firing, the battle seemed to be on, and we might be called at any moment. Just then Capt. Rawolle, formerly of Battery L, rode over from Headquarters to learn how we had fared the preceding day. I invited him to the ambulance to have a cup of coffee with us. We were just drinking it when Gen. Schurz galloped up. "Capt. Roemer," said he, "I want your Battery immediately. I have a battery up on the hill that isn't worth a cent." I mounted my horse, said "Good-bye" to Capt. Rawolle, and rode off with Gen. Schurz to survey the ground. While looking over the position, I learned that the drivers of the battery Gen. Schurz had named, had turned so short that they had upset the gun, broken the limber pole, and found themselves unable either to unhitch the horses or right the gun. I saw there was no time to lose, and had Battery L come up into line the best way it could amid the debris.

Battery L then formed behind the other, piece by piece, left into action, and opened fire at once. Of course, the enemy had seen the mishap, and had redoubled their fire, but when we gave them two shots by battery, from all five pieces, that seemed to paralyze them. Then they brought more artillery to bear upon us, and pushed their infantry also against us, but, as we had no idea of allowing this, we soon caused the latter to fall back. By this time we were having shots aimed at us from several directions. We had had an infantry support but we learned later that they had deserted us. Suddenly, Gen. Schurz appeared on the scene and ordered us to limber to the rear, then to proceeed left into a hollow, because the enemy were coming in on the right.

It was then that I discovered the desertion of the infantry supports. They had left some three hundred muskets lying around on the ground. I learned from Gen. Schurz, where he wished to place the Battery, and then started to go across the valley to Benjamin's battery on the hill. We had to pass over these discarded muskets, and while passing, some of our men stopped to pick some up. I called to them, "Throw those muskets down. I don't want any of my boys to touch much less take one of those cowards' muskets. I would not have you disgrace yourselves so. Drive over them." While passing through the Manassas Valley, the heavy rattle of musketry and booming of cannon gave me to understand that the left wing was being heavily pressed by the enemy, and that most likely some of us would have holes in our jackets or trousers before the day was over.

While ascending the hill, I gave the order, "Battery, front into line," so it could take its position in line at once.

Coming up to level ground, I saw that the 6th Me. Battery held the right, and that Battery L's position was to be to the right of this battery, in close quarters to the enemy's line, and, as I thought, only from six to seven hundred yards from it. I now gave the commands, "By battery, left wheel. Halt. Action rear, horses facing to the rear. Caissons, pass your pieces. Commence firing." Bullets, shot and shell flew like hail in a heavy storm. We were getting some of them, too, for bullets were dropping all around and shells were ploughing up the ground. Men were tumbling, and horses falling, and it certainly looked as though "de kingdom was a-coming." Our ammunition was getting very low. When we first went into position, there were 56 shots in the limber chests, but in ten minutes these had all been spent. The sergeants successively reported, "out of ammunition," but in a low tone that the infantry might not hear. Just as the last sergeant reported, the order came, "Artillery to the rear, infantry to the front." I ordered Battery L, "Limber to the rear, march." I think that was the quickest limber to the rear the Battery ever made. The commands given to the Battery both on going into position and on leaving it, as given above, were never given by me at any other time during the whole war. When the guns are in such position as they were by the orders given at going into position, and the commands, "Cease firing, Limber to the rear," are given, the cannoneers simply lift the trails of their respective guns and hook them up to the limbers. If the same orders are given, when facing front, the horses have to be turned around before the trails can be hooked to the limbers, and this takes more time. Thus we were the first to get away, for it took the 6th Me. three times as long as it did us, at least, so I was informed afterwards. In consequence of this delay, they lost nineteen men taken prisoners, and had two pieces captured.

Thus it is evident what quick action during an engagement may accomplish.

The Battery fell back about seventy-five or eighty yards and went into position in battle array. Many shots from the enemy were received, but no reply could be made. Gen. McDowell with his staff rode up and inquired in an excited tone, "Captain, why don't you fire?" I went to him and whispered in his ear, "Not a shot in the ammunition chests, General." He turned quickly and asked, "Does the infantry know of this?" "No, General," I replied, "but I have picked up seven of the enemy's unexploded shells; shall I fire them?" "No," he replied, "but don't let the infantry get wind of the fact that you are out of ammunition." "Very well, General," said I, "I would like to have some. Is there any possibility of getting any?" "I will try and send you some," he answered. "But here is my aide, who has reported that you drew your saber against him, when he told you he would report you. You said he could report you to the devil." "That is all true, General," I replied, "but did your aide recount the circumstances that made me say that? My Battery was in position with the pieces quite widely separated. My men were doing their best to support the infantry. Your aide went to the sergeant commanding the left piece and ordered him to cease firing, as he was firing on our own troops. At the time I was with the right piece. Noticing that the left gun had ceased firing, I galloped over to ascertain the cause and asked the sergeant what was the matter. He said this officer had ordered him to cease firing. I then said to the sergeant: 'I command this battery. Open fire again at once.' I then returned to my place with the right piece. This same officer again went to my sergeant and ordered him to cease firing, but the sergeant then told him that he (the officer) had nothing to do with him; and that he (the sergeant) took orders from his Captain only. Your aide then asked where I was and the sergeant directed him. Your aide came up to me and said, 'Cease firing with your battery. You are firing on our own troops.' 'What do you say?' said I, 'cease firing? Who are you, anyhow?' 'I am on the staff of Gen. McDowell,' he replied. 'Well,' said I, 'if you are, that gives you no right to come here and accuse my sergeant and myself of firing on our own troops. I want you to leave.' At the same time I wheeled my horse, grasped my saber, and went up to him. He then said he would report me and I said what I did. I was in the position I was holding, by order of Gen. Schurz, and my officers and men can verify my statement as to what was said and done." "Well," said Gen. McDowell, "if that is the case, Captain, it is all right." "No, General," said I, "it is not all right." "Well, what else do you want?" the General inquired. "I can't recognize this man," said I, "as an officer on your staff, unless he apologizes for the insult put by him on my sergeant and myself on yonder battle-ground." Gen. McDowell then turned to the young man and said: "If what Captain Roemer says is true, you are in duty bound to ask his pardon. Be more careful in future, how you approach this old artillery officer." The aide shook hands with me and said, "Captain Roemer, I beg your pardon."

This incident being satisfactorily closed, I turned my attention to the matter of replenishing my ammunition. Through Gen. McDowell I obtained fifty rounds, but was ordered not to fire unless necessary. The Battery remained in this position until sundown, firing an occasional shot. Some shots were fired at the Battery from various points. One of these shells coming our way, exploded near where I was sitting on my horse. The latter immediately began plunging and rearing. Thinking this was occasioned by fright on his part I gave him the spur, but he did not go forward, on the contrary, he reared so high that he nearly overbalanced himself. I threw myself forward upon his neck and spurred him again. He then plunged forward, nearly striking Lieut. Van Nostrand. The lieutenant turned, grabbed the horse's bridle, and said, "For God's sake, Captain, don't spur your horse, his right fore-leg is cut off." I dismounted in a hurry to consider the damage, and found the hoof split and the fetlock cut. I called for a grain bag and bound up the leg as well as I could. Just then one of the men standing near said, "Captain, what is the matter? There is blood coming from your leg." I clapped my hand right on the spot where the wound was. Then it occurred to me, that, at the time my horse was struck and made his first spring, I struck the saddle, as I thought, but when I saw the blood, I realized that I had been wounded in the right thigh.

During this battle, generally known as the Second Battle of Bull Run or Manassas, August 29-30, 1862, the casualties in Battery L were fourteen enlisted men wounded (including Sergeant Adam Wirth, mortally wounded) besides myself, three horses killed, and twenty-one wounded.

While we were in our last position, I saw one of our infantry officers lying on the ground right in front of the Battery, and with my glass, I could see he was absolutely helpless. I called J. N. Mosser, the ambulance driver, and sent him out with two men who volunteered to go, and the ambulance, to bring in the officer. They went bravely out, put the officer into the ambulance, and turned around to return, but just at that moment a cannon shot came and struck it, killed one horse, smashed the front axle of the ambulance, and also turned it upside down. The two men made their way back to the Battery as fast as their legs could carry them, but Mosser, the wounded officer, the ambulance and one horse fell into the hands of the enemy.

Within these two days, the Battery expended 1217 rounds of ammunition. At 7 P. M., August 30, an aide brought an order for the Battery to guard the crossing of Manassas Brook or Young's Branch, until all the troops had passed. Here it remained until 2 A. M., of the 31st, when it marched to the Stone Bridge arriving there at 8 A. M. Here it was ordered to remain and guard the bridge. A heavy rain storm now set in and the men were very hungry. On the preceding day, all our baggage wagons had been sent on to Alexandria for safety as the enemy were close at hand. We had nothing to fall back upon and all must go hungry until "Massa Lincum" sent us something from Washington. We had plenty of time for eating but had nothing to eat. This was a sad state of affairs. Our Flushing friends would have thought so if they could have seen the eager faces of the troops watching and hoping that food would soon arrive. On the road from Manassas to Centerville, were thousands of stragglers asking everybody they met for a piece of bread. If they could buy it, they did, but if they could not, they would try to steal it.

I rode out and came to a row of log huts. Here I thought I might find something for my men, but the men here were equally as destitute as my own. I saw a man come out of one of the huts with a large piece of salt pork, (something I never cared for at home). The sight of it made my mouth water. I reined up and asked the man if he would give me a piece of it. He looked at me and said, "Capt. Roemer, you can have it all." "No, my son," I replied, "I won't take it from you. If you will give me a piece an inch wide, I will be satisfied." "Captain," said he "I have no knife to cut it." So I pulled out my own knife which he took and cut off the desired piece. I ate that piece of salt pork with enjoyment. It seemed as though I had never eaten anything sweeter. I realized the truth of the old proverb, "Hunger is the best sauce." I rode on further, found the Quartermaster and told him if he did not send me rations for my men, they would butcher him. He asked where the Battery was stationed. I told him it was at the Stone Bridge. He then and there promised he would send double rations both for my men and myself. Just at the same moment, word came that rations had arrived from Washington. The Quartermaster then told me that on that morning, he had not had a single ration in store. I now rode rapidly back to the Battery, and when I told them the good news, the smiling faces that greeted me, gave me great pleasure.

At about 11 A. M., that Sunday morning, the double rations arrived. These were soon cooked and the men of the Battery were soon making merry over their great feast. Not only Battery L, but all the other troops here suffered greatly for want of food.

CHAPTER IV.

ANTIETAM.   FREDERICKSBURG.

The Battery marched on September 1st, from the Stone Bridge six miles, to Centreville, where it replenished its supply of ammunition with 290 rounds of fixed ammunition and 321 rounds of blank cartridges. September 2nd, it left Centreville in a blinding rain-storm for Fairfax C. H., where it arrived at 12 M. on the 3d. The same day at 1 P. M., the enemy attacked our flank quite sharply and followed us on our retreat to Langley, which was reached at 2 A. M. on the 4th, after fighting all the way. The march was continued the same day to the Chain Bridge, fighting the enemy by sections, the whole distance. The Battery, however, suffered no casualties. It marched on the 5th, twelve miles to Tenallytown, where it encamped for the night. On the 6th, it marched to Rockville ten miles distant, and went into camp for two days. During this time, I went to Washington to bring back the piece that had been sent from Warrenton in a disabled condition for repairs, on August 25th, and also to draw the stores and ammunition, the Battery still needed. While I was absent from the Battery, two sections were ordered to join the command of Gen. D. N. Couch.

September 8th the Battery was transferred from the 1st Corps (Sigel's) back to the 2d Corps (Banks's), to which it was first assigned. I returned from Washington, September 10th, and on the 11th, the Battery joined the other batteries and marched twenty miles to Poolesville, then ten miles to Barnesville, and afterwards to Noland's Ferry, where it encamped. One section was with Gen. Couch, and another was engaged in guarding the Ferry in company with Col. Neal's Cavalry and the 36th N. Y. Inf.

September 15th, I received orders to bring the Battery together, one section from Point of Rocks, and one from Monocacy, by the 16th, and then, to report to the commanding officer of the Ninth Army Corps. On the 17th, the Battery was ordered to follow Gen. Hartranft's Brigade, consisting of the 51st N. Y., 51st Pa., and the 21st Mass. to take the stone bridge over Antietam Creek, since known as Burnside's Bridge. The fighting at the storming of the bridge was terrific. When the bridge was carried, the Battery followed the 21st Mass. over it, then turned sharply to the left and then to the right to ascend the steep west bank. As it was about to pass along the road, the dead bodies of thirty-seven men and a colonel were found lying in it, right in the way. They were removed so that the guns would not have to run over them. The Battery then turned to the right in rear of a house and went into position facing in the direction of the cornfield and the school house, and opened fire.

The school house stood where the Antietam and Sharpsburg roads cross, thus making the point a most important one for either side to hold, and the fighting at that place, as shown by the number of dead and wounded lying around, of both armies, that had fallen there, was truly frightful. The road passing the school house is very wide; it seemed to me, to be fully one hundred feet in width. From our position, we had a good view of both this road and the cornfield, and hence could plainly see the hand to hand contest between the blue and the gray that took place there. At times, it seemed as if our army must lose the day.

At about 5 P. M., as I understood, Gen. Burnside sent to Gen. McClellan, a request for reinforcements to the extent of two or three thousand men to push our line forward. Gen. McClellan answered in person, after crossing with his staff the bridge taken by Gen. Hartranft's Brigade. Gen. McClellan told Gen. Burnside he could not possibly give him the reinforcements desired, and that Gen. Burnside should simply hold his line and not attempt to press forward too much. From that time on, therefore, our line was not pushed forward, and, although the fighting continued until sundown, we simply maintained our position. I received orders to be ready to march at 5 A. M., on the 18th, but the order to march did not come until the 19th.

After the battle, I went around to look at the destruction wrought by it. I examined the fences on either side of that wide roadway, and found each twelve foot rail for some distance had been struck by bullets, some by two, others by five, six, eight and ten, and some even by fifteen. The school house had been so perforated through and through by cannon balls that, it seemed to me, there was scarcely a whole brick in the building. The shots must have been thick and heavy. I could see pieces of brick and mortar scattered from fifty to a hundred yards away all around from southeast to west.

The wound in my leg had been very painful during the last two hours of the battle. I had been in the saddle almost constantly for the last two days, and this, no doubt, had greatly aggravated it, and then the wetting I had received at Sandy Hook, where I had been obliged to swim across the canal, was a still greater aggravation. In fact, I suffered so much, that I wished a bullet would hit me and end it all. On the morning of the 18th, Capt. Rawolle, my old lieutenant, rode over from Headquarters, and invited me to ride over the battle field with him. I had to decline and told him my leg was so painful I could not sit in the saddle. He asked to see my leg, and I showed it to him. It was black and blue. He had no sooner seen it than he called for his horse. He soon returned with Dr. Thompson, Medical Director of the Ninth Corps (and, by the way, a former resident of Flushing Township, living on the "Thompson Farm," just outside of Flushing Village). The doctor examined my leg and then asked, "How, under heaven, could you ride a horse with a leg like that?" Then he continued, "I order you to your tent for four weeks, and if you come out before that time is up, I will have you court martialed for neglecting yourself." It was twenty-one days before I could use my leg again.

After the examination was over, Capt. Rawolle was anxious to know how I had managed to contract such a cold in my wound. I then told him the whole story as follows: "After receiving the order to bring the sections of the Battery together, I started out with my orderly, Corporal Rierson, for that purpose. We had to go to Monocacy, Point of Rocks and Frederick City. While on the road to Harper's Ferry, we learned that the enemy had burned the bridge across the Potomac. We were then on the towpath of the canal, between the canal and the river. When we reached the place opposite Harper's Ferry, we found ourselves unable to cross the canal on account of the debris of the burned bridge. It was quite dark, yet I perceived some infantry on the other side of the river. I called out to them, "Hallo, what regiment is that?" In answer, we received several shots accompanied by the remark, "If it was only daylight, we would show you, you Yankee sons of guns, what regiment we belong to." I then said to Rierson, 'Now we know how the land lies. All we can do is to go back to Sandy Hook and swim the canal.' We retraced our steps some three miles, to a place where there was a sloping descent to the canal. I went in first and the corporal followed. Wet from head to foot we lay all night in our wet clothes, waiting for the morning light, to go on. That is my story, Captain, and now I don't think you will wonder that my leg is so badly swollen. Furthermore, the strain of yesterday's fight did not improve it any." Capt. Rowelle now left me, after telling me to obey the surgeon's orders to the letter.

September 18th, orders were received to be in the saddle ready to move at 4 A. M. The Battery was held thus ready all day. On the 18th, it fell back from the battlefield of Antietam. During the day it fired 87 rounds and suffered no casualties. Three days after the battle, the stench arising from the dead bodies of men and horses, became so great that nearly every one in the surrounding country became sick. In many cases these dead bodies, both of men and horses, had swelled to double their normal size. One could easily distinguish the Union dead from the Confederate dead; the former were white while the latter were black. This was caused, it was said, by the want of salt experienced by the Confederates, who had had but very little for a long time.

From here, the Battery marched September 20th, to Darnestown to join Gen. Couch's command, and remained there three days in camp. It marched on the 26th under orders to join Gen. Banks's command, to Sharpsburg, Md., eight miles distant, camping there for the night, and the next day, went to Sandy Hook, Md., and joined Gen. Banks's command. It left Sandy Hook, October 4th, to join the Ninth Corps of Gen. Burnside and arrived at the camp of that Corps near Antietam Creek during the evening in a rain storm. The next day, it was inspected by Capt. Rawolle, and as a result of this inspection, about one-half of the ammunition was condemned. On this same date,

October 4, 1862, the Battery was formally attached to the Ninth Corps, commanded by Maj.-Gen. A. E. Burnside, and with which it remained during the rest of the war.

The Battery remained in camp until October 7th, on which date, it was aroused at 3 A. M., but did not march until 7:30 A. M., when it marched to Knoxville. Md., arriving there at 3 P. M., after marching fourteen miles. It went into camp at Pleasant Valley, Md., and remained there until October 24th.

Second Lieut. Wm. Cooper was discharged on surgeon's certificate of disability, by Special Order No. 284, dated Headquarters of the Army, Adjutant-General's Office, Washington, D. C., October 8, 1862. Also the resignation of Second Lieut. Jerome Van Nostrand was accepted by Special Order No. 56, dated Headquarters, Ninth Army Corps, Pleasant Valley, Md., October 8, 1862. On the 16th, First Sergeant Moses E. Brush was promoted Junior Second Lieutenant, and Sergeant Thomas Heasley, to First Sergeant and Acting Second Lieutenant.

October 24th, the Battery was ordered to Berlin, Md., to support the U. S. Engineers under command of Capt. Cross, who had been ordered to build a pontoon bridge across the Potomac at that point. The Ninth Corps crossed this bridge on the 25th on its way to Fredericksburg, Va. October 28th, First Lieutenant Henry J. Standish resigned and left the Battery. On the 29th, the Battery arrived at Lovettsville, Va., and was in the field near Wheatlands on the 30th and 31st. November 5th, it was near Upperville and on the 8th near Orleans, and at Jeffersonton on the 10th, from which point one section went out with Gen. Pleasanton's Cavalry on a reconnoitering expedition, and was in action, firing fourteen rounds. November 12th, at 2 A. M., the Battery left Jeffersonton and marched six miles to Sulphur Springs, where it remained until the 15th. On the 14th it had quite a lively set-to with the rebels, during which it fired twenty-two rounds.

The Battery left Sulphur Springs at 8 A. M., on the 15th, and went to Fayettesville, six miles distant, and the next day to a point near Warrenton Junction, also a distance of six miles, whence on the 18th and 19th it marched to Falmouth, just north of Fredericksburg, on the left bank of Rappahannock River, where it arrived on the 20th, after marching about thirty miles. It was assigned to a position on the left of the Fredericksburg and Washington Railroad, while Battery E, 4th U. S. Art., Capt. Geo. Dickenson, took position on the right of the same railroad, about 200 yards from the river. The river at this point is only about fifty yards wide, and each battery threw up embrasures to protect each gun, in accordance with orders from Headquarters to do so whenever such close quarters were to be held. We were only about 250 yards from the city of Fredericksburg. It took several days to construct these embrasures.

It is my opinion that Marye's Heights could and should have been occupied by our troops on their arrival at this point, for at that time there were no works of any consequence on either side, and our troops could have taken the position the rebels took as easily as they did the position they did take. As it was, every movement made on our side was made so slowly that the enemy had twenty and more days, ample time enough, to build works that proved far too strong for our troops when, at last, an assault was made upon the Heights. Many others have expressed like opinions on this point. The strong massive works built by the Confederates, extended in a curve from the Rappahannock River, north of Fredericksburg around over Marye's Heights, west of the city, southward till they reached the Rappahannock again.

Every night at 9 P. M., for twenty-seven days, a fresh regiment was sent to support our batteries in case we were attacked by the enemy in an attempt to turn our right. Every night during this period I had to go out, no matter what the weather might be, to see that the infantry were properly posted. It often happened that these infantry supports would have to march four and five miles to report for this duty, and frequently they were wet to the skin when they arrived. I had a large hospital tent, eighteen feet by fourteen, and, at such times, I gave this up to the officers, but as an infantry regiment has thirty line officers besides the field and staff, it will readily be understood they were in rather close quarters; yet they had shelter from the storms. If I had not had this tent, I could not have given my brother officers the shelter and comfort I did.

One regiment in particular, reported to me on one of the stormiest days of that winter. They had had to march five miles. They had started at 2 P. M., but they did not arrive until 9 P. M., and were, by that time, completely wet through. If I ever felt sorry for soldiers, I felt sorry for them. When welcoming the commanding officer, I remarked, "Colonel, you have had a bad day." In reply, he said, "Captain, I have been out in rough weather before, but this beats anything I have ever seen." I called the First Sergeant and told him to shelter as many as he could in my big tent. Forty of the men and officers had to go on duty at once. I slipped out, called Billy Howard, the cook for the officers' mess, and told him to make three kettles full of good hot coffee. I then made the rounds to station the pickets. Just as I was returning to my tent, I smelled the aroma of the coffee, and then went into the big tent. The colonel asked me about the weather. I replied that there was no let up, and that, as there was so much water outside, I had ordered our cook to make some coffee for the sake of a change, and, that it was at their orders if they wanted some. There was a great hurrah and they had a jolly time over their coffee.

By the 27th of November, the earthworks for the protection of the guns were completed, as well as quarters for the men and stables for the horses. The hard campaigns of the past few months had told heavily on both men and horses; seven men had died. Some seven or eight of the younger men in the battery were feeling very bad, as a result of the hardships they had undergone, and they asked for a furlough, for they wanted to go home. I consulted the Battery surgeon, Dr. Freeman, concerning them. After talking the matter over, we concluded that it would not benefit them much to go home, for the people at home might kill them with kindness, and probably some of them might never come back again. I then told the surgeon to send me a written request that they be relieved from duty and be ordered to exercise like boys—to run, play and jump—in fact, to be boys again. The rest of the Battery men and officers (including the Doctor himself) joined in their sports. They soon forgot their home sickness, and came round again all right. During the following summer these same men were the healthiest members of the Battery.

On the last day of November, orders came to strengthen the four embrasures, the better to resist the heavy fire of the enemy. To do this, required the use of 12 or 14 cords of wood, and hard work for three days and three nights. A few days after the works were completed, a young staff officer called on me and said, "Captain Roemer, I am on the staff of Gen. Sumner,* and have been ordered to inspect your works." "All right, Captain," said I, and, taking my

---

* Gen. E. V. Sumner was at this time Commander of the Right Grand Division, consisting of the Second and Ninth Corps and Gen. Pleasanton's Cavalry Division.

100-foot tape measure, went out with him along the earthworks. I was very proud of them, for I thought they were the very best we had ever made, and I expected to occupy them in our next engagement. We walked around the works, while he examined them very closely. He then said I must take out all the revetment and put in hurdles. "All right, Captain," said I, "if you will furnish them, I will put them in." "No," said he, "you must furnish them yourself." "No," said I, "we are not engineers. If you don't furnish them, my works will remain as they are." "Well, Captain Roemer," said he, "I will have to report you for disobedience of my orders," and then left me. I then went out with my tape measure and accurately measured every detail of my works, from base to top, height, thickness, etc., and put the record of the measurements together with a trace of the works, into an official envelope, mounted my horse, and rode over to the Headquarters of Gen. Sumner. His Headquarters were in one of those fine old southern mansions, with a high stoop in front. Just as I arrived, he was descending the steps with some ladies. Seeing me with the envelope in my hand, he said, "Leave of absence, Captain, I can't see you." "I beg pardon, General," said I, "it is other business of importance." "Walk right in, Captain," said he, "I will see you as soon as I have taken leave of the ladies." I walked into the office where were many officers and clerks busily engaged. Soon Gen. Sumner returned and asked me into his private office. I then handed my report to him. He glanced at it, then looked at me, and said, "Captain, this is the way I want my officers to act. Are you sure your works are built according to this statement?" "I will vouch for it," I replied. "I will send some staff officers," said he, "this afternoon to inspect your works again."

I returned to my quarters, and, about 3 P. M., three

engineer officers rode up and said they had been sent to inspect my works. "All right," said I, "I am at your service." They took my tape measure, and went over the whole of the works, to see if the actual measurements and description corresponded with those made in my report to the General. These officers measured every detail of the redoubt, and when they had finished their inspection, they told me their measurements agreed exactly with those given in my report. Later in the afternoon, I received a note from Gen. Sumner, saying that the officers' report was perfectly satisfactory, thanking me for reporting as I did, and, furthermore, saying I should follow the same rule hereafter.

Our stay in these winter quarters was of but short duration, for on the 10th of December, orders came to leave the redoubt just built in front of Fredericksburg, and take position on Falmouth Heights, on the extreme right of our lines, in company with Lieut. S. N. Benjamin's Battery E, 2d U. S. Art., Capt. Chas. D. Owen's Battery G, 1st R. I. Art., and Lieut. Rufus King, Jr.'s Battery A, 4th U. S. Art. This position assigned me by Lieut.-Col. Hays, Chief of Art., Ninth Corps, and Commandant of the Artillery Reserve, Right Grand Division, was on the farm of Mr. Bryan, Falmouth Heights. In the afternoon an order came to take the position assigned us that night. Battery L's position was on the bank of the Rappahannock River, facing due south with Owen's, King's, and Benjamin's Batteries to the right of Battery L in the order named, and at right angles with the main line. At this point, the river flows east a short distance and then makes a sharp turn to the southeast just in front of Falmouth. The position was fully fifty feet above the river, and was a very prominent position for a battery as well as a very conspicuous target for the enemy.

After viewing the position, I was convinced that Lieut.-Col. Hays was right in saying, "Captain Roemer, you have the crown of positions." I thanked him for the honor conferred on the Battery, by giving it the preference, even if the position was hazardous. The Battery was soon prepared for the enemy if they should attack us during the night. The order was to be watchful, and, if necessity demanded, to open fire at once without waiting for further orders. All was quiet during the night.

At about 9 A. M., on the 11th, the enemy opened fire upon our troops south of us, from the rear of the town. By special orders from Lieut.-Col. Hays, to Capt. Owen and myself, we were prepared to enfilade the enemy's batteries, as our other troops were not in a position to silence the fire. Accordingly, we moved our batteries nearer the river, and soon silenced the enemy's fire. Battery L then received orders to take position in the peach orchard on the left of the Bryan house, from which position, it exchanged about 25 rounds with the enemy. It then returned to its former position. Soon the firing on the right became more pronounced, and I was ordered to send one section to the peach orchard on the left of the house again, close to the river bank. This section fired seventeen rounds and remained in the orchard during the night. The other section was retained in its position and ordered to construct four embrasures which were completed by the next morning. During the day ninety-one rounds in all were fired by the Battery which suffered no casualties.

On the 12th, orders were received to withdraw the section from the river bank and place it with the other within the embrasures, to watch the enemy's fire, and to open fire upon them only when they opened fire upon our troops. At 7 A. M., the enemy opened upon our works. The Battery exchanged shots with such batteries as it could reach, whereupon they ceased firing. At 9 A. M., a dense fog settled down in our front obscuring everything. As soon as the fog lifted, the enemy opened fire again. Finding that we could not reach these guns of the enemy from our embrasures, especially with the right section, the latter was moved to the left to the bank of the river where it opened fire. This drew the enemy's fire which was, however, soon silenced. At 4 P. M., the enemy opened fire on our redoubt again, this time from the woods north of Marye's Heights, with twelve or fifteen pieces. This was answered by the four batteries of Benjamin, King, Owen, and Roemer, which soon silenced it. Battery L suffered no casualties and fired 67 rounds.

The Battery remained in the redoubt the night of the twelfth, and opened fire the next morning at 7 A. M. During the night, there had been a heavy frost, and when the sun arose, the dampness caused such a dense fog, that orders were received to be very careful in firing, especially, as our cavalry pickets were crossing the river under cover of our fire. Nothing of importance to the Battery occurred until 3 P. M., when an order came for it to report forthwith to Gen. Sumner at the Lacy House where it arrived and reported at 5 P. M. Gen. Sumner ordered the Battery, to take position behind the Lacy House, out of reach of the enemy's fire (though shot and shell were flying around on all sides), to be kept in readiness for any emergency. During the day, the Battery expended 128 rounds of ammunition and suffered no casualties. It remained at the Lacy House until 4 P. M., on the 15th, when by order of Lieut.-Col. Hays, it went to occupy the redoubt previously occupied by Benjamin's Battery E, 2nd U. S. Art. on the extreme right. From there it was ordered to its old position on the left of the Fredericksburg and Washington R. R. to resume its former occupation of looking after the four redoubts and posting the infantry regiments on picket as they arrived each evening at 9 o'clock, in our front, near the river and on the left flank of the Ninth Corps.

While sitting in my tent after the battle, it occurred to me to review it on paper, and thus preserve my impressions of it.

On the 11th of December, Lieut.-Col. Hays held a consultation with the commanders of the four batteries stationed on the extreme right of our lines, viz., Benjamin, Owen, King, and myself. Benjamin and King were officers of the regulars while Owen and I belonged to the volunteers. He questioned each of us as to our knowledge of our lines. As I am writing the history of my Battery, I will mention only what was asked of me. When it came my turn, Col. Hays asked me, "Well, Capt. Roemer, what knowledge of our lines do you possess?" "Colonel," I replied, "the other day, I made a tour of inspection for my own satisfaction, along our lines from right to left, but being interested chiefly in artillery, I gave my attention almost wholly to that arm. I located 127 pieces of artillery and made a small diagram of their positions." I then handed the diagram to Col. Hays, who, after looking it over, said, "Very good, Captain, this may be of use for future reference, and, therefore, I will keep it."

Every battle will have connected with it, incidents that are interesting whether important or not. On the night of December 10th, before the fighting of the first day, I was making the rounds to post the pickets of the infantry regiment that was to be our support that night, and giving them instructions as to what must be observed by the pickets on their several posts, and especially by those near the river. While I was at the point nearest the enemy, a voice was heard from the opposite bank, saying, "Hallo, Yanks!" "Well, Johnny," said I, "what is it?" "Say, Yanks," said the voice, "what's the meaning of your three days' rations in your haversacks? If you come over here we'll give you h—l." They were well informed. Three days' rations had been issued to our troops, and the rebels well knew that that meant a fight or a march.   I think that every rebel knew of this issue, and, furthermore, that this information came to them through female spies in the War Department in Washington, and also that this was only part of the knowledge the Confederate officials had obtained through these spies.   Our troops certainly had a smell of brimstone, in fact, it was the principal thing they did smell. When the enemy said they would give us hell, they surely meant it, for the butchery of our brave boys was terrible, especially at the sunken telegraph road and at the foot of Marye's Heights, where they fell like grass before the scythe.   This was one part of my impressions regarding the battle.

The second part relates to the arrangement of the troops, the advance, and the time of the attack.   Three pontoon bridges were successfully placed, and the several Corps Commanders had their orders as to where and when their corps should be ready for the duties assigned them.   It was not to be a simultaneous attack by all the corps.   At the time, I was informed that Gen. Franklin, away on our left, had orders to attack Lee's rear on the Richmond Railway, about one hour and a half or two hours ahead of the attacks to be made by the other Grand Divisions.   This would have been dangerous to Lee's rear, and would have compelled Lee to draw upon his reserves when our troops should attack him in front two hours later, and thus would have had to call on all his troops, including his reserves, to keep Franklin from destroying the railroad or falling on his rear, and, at the same time to meet the attack in front.   But at the time when our troops advanced to attack in front, Franklin had not arrived in Lee's rear, and, consequently, Lee could and did throw his whole force against our troops in front, and this force was too overwhelming for our men to withstand. There was, furthermore, some difficulty encountered by our troops in crossing the river that night, which had not been expected. Had the crossing of the river been carried out as contemplated, I have no doubt the troops would have succeeded in doing what had been planned.

The Battery spent the 18th in repairing damages received during the three days' engagement. During this time also, the Battery fired 414 rounds of ammunition and had two men and five horses slightly wounded. I give below a verbatim copy of my report made to Lieut.-Col. Wm. Hays, Chief of Artillery, Ninth Army Corps.

HEADQUARTERS BATTERY L, 2D N. Y. VOL. ART.,
FALMOUTH, VA., Dec. 18th, 1862.

LIEUT.-COL. HAYS, CHIEF OF ART., NINTH ARMY CORPS:

COLONEL:—I have the honor to report the part taken by my Battery during the late engagement with the enemy on Thursday, Friday and Saturday, the 11th, 12th and 13th inst. On the 10th inst, a position was assigned me by yourself on the farm of Mr. Bryan, above Falmouth, on the Rappahannock River and on the right of our line. The Battery reached this position at 11 P. M., on the 10th, went into park and so remained until daybreak, when it took position ready for action. I then received orders to be ready for any emergency, and, if I found the position the Battery then occupied was not suited to return the enemy's fire, to move to the front of Mr. Bryan's house, where I would have a better range on the enemy's guns and also on the town, that position being on the crest of a hill and on the bank of the Rappahannock River.

About 9 A. M., the enemy opened fire on our troops in front, from the rear of the town. I received from you special orders to enfilade the enemy's fire, which, in combination with Owen's Battery, was done by moving both batteries to the front. After I had expended about twenty rounds of ammunition, the enemy ceased firing. I then received orders to place the Battery in the peach orchard on the left of Bryan's house. The enemy now opened fire on the Battery on the left of the house and about twenty-five shots were exchanged. From this position, the Battery went back to its former position, as the enemy's fire had changed from left to right. This change enabled us to silence the enemy's fire against our right.

I now received orders to place one section again in the peach orchard on the left of the house, and several shots were exchanged. This section remained in the peach orchard during the night, while the other section was retained in its original position. At the same time, I was ordered to construct embrasures in our first position, which work was done during the night of the 11th. During this day, I expended seventy-four rounds of ammunition. On the 12th, I received orders to withdraw the section in the peach orchard on the river bank to the embrasures, to watch the enemy's fire, and to fire my guns only when the enemy opened on our troops.

The enemy opened fire from their works at 7 A. M. I returned it with my Battery, firing on such guns as I could reach. After several shots, the enemy ceased firing. At 9 A. M., a dense fog obscured everything. When the fog lifted, the enemy again opened fire on our troops, but I found I could not reach these batteries from our embrasures, and especially, with the guns of the right section. On this account, I moved this section to the left and to the river bank, and opened fire which soon silenced the enemy.

Nothing of importance again occurred until 4 P. M., when, the Battery being within the embrasures, the enemy opened a brisk cross fire from the woods and hills, which was soon silenced by a very brisk fire from the four batteries of Benjamin, King, Owen and my own. The enemy's guns numbered some 12 or 15 pieces. Battery L fired about sixty-seven rounds. The Battery remained in the embrasures during the night of the 12th, and opened fire again at 7 A. M., on the 13th. A dense fog having arisen between 8 and 9 A. M., I received orders to be cautious in firing, as our cavalry pickets were advancing under cover of our fire. The Battery fired at intervals during the day, changing position according to the varying changes of the enemy's fire, and expended one hundred and twenty-eight rounds of ammunition.

At 3 P. M., I received orders to report with the Battery immediately to Gen. Sumner at the Lacy House, which order was promptly obeyed. The Battery arrived at the Lacy House at 5 P. M. I then received instructions to hold the Battery in readiness for any emergency that might arise during the night. It lay ready for orders till between 3 and 4 P. M., on the 15th, when I received orders from yourself in person again to occupy the redoubts on the right. I am now in the position previously occupied by Benjamin's Battery E, 2d U. S. Art.

I have the honor to be, Colonel, your most obedient servant,

    [Signed]   JACOB ROEMER,
        Capt. Comdg. Battery L, 2d N. Y. Art.

On the 19th, the work of putting the Battery in perfect trim for action was continued, that it might be ready for instant service, whenever it might be called upon. The ammunition in limber and caisson chests was replenished, and the thousand and one things required to put the Battery in complete order, were carefully looked after. Late in the day, it took its former position on the left of the railroad. I now learned, to my infinite regret, that Lieut. Geo. Dickenson, who commanded Battery E, 4th U. S. Art., when it was stationed with us on the right of the railroad, was no more. After we had left our several positions and had arrived at the Lacy House, he was ordered to cross the pontoon bridge opposite that point. The next morning he was ordered to take position on a knoll well in advance. He had hardly reached the position assigned him, when he was killed with two of his men, while several more were wounded. He was shot squarely in the forehead. The last words he uttered before he died (which was almost instantly) were, "Bury me where I fell." His battery had not, as yet, fired a single shot. Few of our brave comrades recrossed the Rappahannock. The bones of those who fell were left on the right bank of the river they had so recently crossed.

I can distinctly recall the fine soldierly bearing of Lieut. Dickenson when he left us at the Lacy House. He came to me with outstretched hand, grasped mine, and said, "Well, Roemer, good-bye. We won't see each other again. This is our last farewell. We won't grasp hands in friendly fellowship again. We have been good friends all through our work of guarding the railroad, but now all is over, good-bye." I replied, "Don't talk like that, Lieutenant. We will meet again before many days and talk over our victory together." But he said, "That will never be." Then he was off, waving his hand, bidding us good-bye. He really had a presentiment of his fate. Afterwards many others have said similar things to me, and in many cases their words came true.

The 20th was spent in drilling both on foot and mounted, to perfect ourselves for the work we might at any moment be called upon to perform. In war, whoever can gain the advantage by his skill in maneuvering, usually wins the day.

CHAPTER V.

FREDERICKSBURG TO VICKSBURG.

Christmast 1862. The usual greetings were exchanged by all with one another during the day. All seemed happy and contented, yet, doubtless, the thoughts of both officers and men, were with the folks at home.

January 1st, 1863. New Year's Day was a gala day in the camp of Battery L. Over one hundred officers were entertained in its big hospital tent, behind the redoubts. Good wishes were exchanged, and we had as sociable a time as our means could afford. We were safe from the enemy's fire, though only about 250 yards from the city of Fredericksburg. The next day, Sergeant J. J. Johnston was promoted 1st Sergeant, vice Thos. Heasley, promoted Acting Second Lieutenant.

Orders came January 19th, to be ready to move at a moment's notice. At 4 P. M., the order came to go to Falmouth Heights, and take the old position on Bryan's farm, in company with our old associates at that point, the batteries of Benjamin, Owen and King. At midnight a tremendous rainstorm set in. Men and horses suffered terrribly from the cold and wet. Near the Battery's position there were several stacks of corn, and I ordered the men to use these as best they could to shelter themselves. The heavy rains made the ground so soft that it became almost impossible to move artillery from one position to another.

On the 22d, an order came from Brig.-Gen. Hays, Chief

of Artillery, to return to the old position in front of Fredericksburg. To reach this position it would be necessary in following the roads, to march north from Falmouth, then west, then south, and then east again, a total distance of six miles. The bank at Mr. Bryan's house was about ten or fifteen feet above the level of the road leading into Falmouth, and from this point, it was only about three hundred yards to Falmouth. I examined this bank and came to the conclusion that I could let the gun-carriages and caissons slide down it into the road, and thus save the men and horses from making the six-mile march around, during this dark and stormy night, for I discovered that this could be accomplished with a little work. I at once sent an order to 1st Sergeant Johnston in the camp before Fredericksburg to send all the spare Battery horses to report to me at the lower part of the street in Falmouth (there being only one street there) at 5 A. M. the next morning. The Battery remained in position until 4 A. M. on the 23d. The other three batteries started at 6 P. M., on the 22d, on their march to the positions assigned them, by the roads through the woods, as above indicated. They were the same roads by which we had all gone previously to reach the positions we were now leaving.

At 4 A. M., on the 23d, all preparations had been made to slide the gun-carriages and caissons down the bank, and all had been enjoined to refrain from talking loud, as the enemy were on the opposite bank of the river, and it would have been "good-bye to Battery L," if they had known anything of our movements. One thing was in our favor; the earth composing the bank was very soft and loose and hence no noise would be caused by the actual movement of gun-carriages and caissons. In sliding these down, no teams were used except the pole-teams. By means of the prolong ropes which were attached to the rear of the carriages, eight men to each carriage kept them from pressing too closely upon the teams. As soon as the carriages and caissons were safe in the road, the other teams that were in waiting were hitched on, and to each carriage one or two of the extra teams were attached, as circumstances required. Everything being ready, the Battery started off to go to its old camp before Fredericksburg. Just after it had passed through Falmouth, the other three batteries which had made the six-mile march around, came up with their horses wholly used up. Our regular teams, as well as the twelve extra teams were perfectly fresh. We had the lead on the road, and when our sixty horses and eight carriages and caissons had passed, the road was, of course, pretty well cut up, and those who followed had to get along as best they could.

By 10 A. M., the Battery was again in its old camp. An hour later, Gen. Ferrero came into camp and looked around in astonishment. Spying me, he said, "Roemer, I thought you went out with the U. S. Batteries to Falmouth Heights?" "Well, General," I replied, "we have been there." "Well," said he, "how in hell did you get back into camp again so soon?" "We have arrived, General," I replied, "but if I tell you how, I am afraid you will have me court martialed." "Nonsense, Roemer," said he, "but were you really out?" "Of course we were, General," I replied. "Well," said he, "you don't look it." I then told him about our plan of descending the bank. Just then we looked out of our redoubts, from which we had a good view of the level ground around the Lacy House, which was some three or four miles in length and over a mile in width, but all we could see was artillery carriages and ammunition wagons, to the number of eighty or one hundred, stuck fast in the mud. This was the famous "Mud Campaign", of Gen. Burnside, that was fought without artillery or muskets.

There were no casualties, and no ammunition was expended. Many of the cannon could not be pulled out of the mud for three or four days, and some were so deeply imbedded that they had to be pried out with fence rails.

The Battery spent several days in repairing harness that had been badly damaged, in examining the ammunition, and repairing the redoubt. During these days, there were rumors floating about that the Ninth Corps was to go west. On the 6th of February, orders came for the Ninth Corps to get ready to march, and at 6 A. M., the next day, an order came to march immediately to Aquia Creek. The Battery left camp at 8 A. M., but as the road was found to be in a terrible condition, our progress was extremely slow. As all teams, baggage-wagons, gun-carriages, caissons, etc., had to pass over this one road, it consequently happened, that the farther we went, the worse it became, and from time to time, some carriage would stick fast.

At one place quite a hill was encountered. To take the guns and caisons up, from eight to twenty-two horses were required for each, in addition to the six regularly belonging to it, and even with twenty-eight horses attached, a piece would sometimes stick fast. Even my own horse became mired, and I was compelled to dismount and allow him to jump to pull his forelegs out of the mud. I saw plenty of bad roads during our marches, but this one from Fredericksburg to Aquia Creek was the worst of all. It was a nine-mile march only, yet both men and horses had to work their hardest for two days to make it. It arrived at Aquia Creek at 9 P. M., February 9th, when orders were received to embark the guns, caissons, etc., on the canal-boats *Wm. T. Mooney* and *Empire City*, and the horses on the boats *Sarah Ann* and *M. T. Corbin*. Loading a battery on canal boats is somewhat of a task. Some fifteen cannon-carriages, caissons, battery wagon, forge, ammunition and baggage wagons, seventy-eight horses and ten mules, had to be transferred from the shore to the boats, but by 1 A. M., the next morning, all were embarked and ready to sail.

Our vessels then joined the rest of the Ninth Corps' fleet and steamed down the Potomac on the way to Fort Monroe. On the way down, a heavy storm was encountered and the boats had to lie at anchor in St. Mary's River for two days. Long Islanders, as is well known, are fond of sea food, and as St. Mary's River abounded in oysters, the Battery boys managed to dispose of five or six bushels on each of these two days. The Battery arrived at Fort Monroe on the 15th, disembarked on the 16th, and went into camp back of Hampton. On the 21st, it marched to Newport News, eight miles distant, and placed one section in position. Here the Battery remained until March 23d. On March 9th, I started for home on a ten days' leave of absence, and returned at 10 A. M. on the 19th. An order came at 12:15 P. M., March 22d for the Battery to return to Hampton. It started the next day at 10 A. M., and arrived at Hampton at 1:30 P. M. It left Hampton on the 26th for Fort Monroe where it embarked during the following night on the steamer *Champion*. The steamer left Fort Monroe at 10 A. M., on the 27th, for Baltimore, where it arrived at 8 P. M., a distance of 160 miles. The Battery, then numbering 82 men with 74 horses, disembarked and marched to the B. & O. R. R. station whence it departed for Pittsburg, Pa., 334 miles distant, where it arrived at 11 P. M. on the 29th, in company with rest of the Ninth Corps.

The people of Pittsburg received the Ninth Corps right royally. They brought us the best of everything, fed us, and petted us. Wherever we went, the cry was, "Hurrah for the soldiers of the Ninth Corps." But the boys could not stand such luxury, coming, as it did, right on the heels of the hardships and meager fare that had so long been their lot. It occasioned much trouble to the commanding officers, for the mixture of so many good things was altogether too much for the boys, and when the time came to board the cars, it was hard to get them on the train. I am sorry to say that I had to leave behind some eight or ten men, who had become so crazed with liquors I could do nothing with them, for the Provost Marshal to forward. He could handle them, in whatever condition they were. When men fell into his hands, they were compelled to come to terms, whether willing or unwilling.

We now left Pittsburg for Cincinnati where we arrived at 2 A. M., April 1st, after a journey of 337 miles. The men here partook of a good breakfast, and were then given leave to view the sights of the city, with orders to report at a certain hour. In the meantime, I drew what horses and stores were needed to complete the Battery's equipment for the field. At 5 P. M., all being in readiness, the Battery crossed the bridge over the Ohio river, to Covington, Ky., four miles distant. Here, it took the train at 2 P. M., April 2d, for Lexington, Ky., where it arrived the next day at 10:30 P. M., and went into camp near the city.

The next day drilling was begun, and some fine drills, both on foot and mounted, were had. As the Battery needed overhauling badly, I asked Gen. Wilcox, then commanding the Ninth Corps, for an order granting the Battery three weeks' time to make the repairs so much needed, such as painting, renewing tires, etc. Eighteen days were given and the men, at once, set to work. Everyone worked with a will, and when all was finished, the gun carriages, caissons, harnesses, etc., looked as if our old equipment had been replaced by a new one. When everything was ready, I reported the fact to Gen. Willcox. Soon an order came for the Battery to go to Winchester, but that before it went, it would be reviewed by Gen. Willcox. The review was made April 28th, and Gen. Willcox, by saying that the appearance of the Battery showed that its members possessed great mechanical skill, paid the men a compliment that fully repaid them for their labor and trouble.

The Battery started for Winchester at 6 A. M., April 29th, and arrived at 3 P. M. The day was a very fine one and I can yet recall how fresh and green everything appeared. Here Gen. Sturgis, our Brigade Commander, visited the Battery and reviewed it on the 30th of April. The Battery left camp at Winchester at 9 A. M., May 4th, and went into camp near Lexington at 5 P. M. It passed through Lexington on the 5th, and went into camp seven miles beyond the town, whence it went to Lowell during a terrible storm, arriving on the 9th. From this place, it went to Lancaster where it remained until the 23d, when it moved to Crab Orchard nine miles distant. On the 25th it was moved to a point two miles south of the village. Here the Battery was drilled mounted for two days and afterwards, until June 3d, in the manual of the piece. All this time, it was doing picket duty among the mountains. The pleasant mountain air soon freshened up every one. The camp was from two to five hundred feet above the sea level, and the air had a very beneficial effect upon the men's appetites. I noticed that there were very few crumbs left when they had finished their rations.

Crab Orchard is quite noted, or was before the war, for the medicinal qualities of its sulphur, magnesia, and iron springs, for miles around. Its situation at the foot of high mountains, is very fine. To sit in the shade of its immense oak and ash trees, with the springs close at hand, was a luxury one could greatly enjoy. During the two years of fighting in Kentucky, it suffered much. I regard Kentucky as one of the finest of southern states in two particulars: first, for its blue grass region, and second, for its good roads. In 1863 the state had the finest turnpike and macadamized roads in the United States. I could not help being impressed by this fact, as we marched over them, for there was no difficulty in marching quite rapidly at any time, day or night. As stated previously, the Battery was forty-eight hours on the march from Falmouth to Aquia Creek, a distance of only nine miles, but in Kentucky it made the march from a point three miles south of Crab Orchard to Hickman's Bridge over the Kentucky River, a distance of thirty-five miles, in eight and one quarter hours. Thus it is readily seen of what advantage good roads are to both men and horses.

On June 3d I received orders to have the Battery ready to march to Hickman's Bridge and over Kentucky River, and to report in person at the Headquarters of Col. S. G. Griffin, commanding 1st Brigade, 2d Div., Ninth Corps, for further instructions. Accordingly, I reported at 10.30 A. M., and was told that the Battery must, by all means, cross the river not later than 7:15 A. M., June 4th, and that Mosby was around and they were watching out for him. He furthermore told me the Battery would have no infantry support during the march. At 11 P. M. the Battery arrived at Crab Orchard, where I received another hint from Col. Griffin. "Roemer," said he, "if you don't want to be gobbled up by Mosby, see to it that the crossing of the bridge is made, as I said before, not later than 7:15 A. M., for I have just received news of his whereabouts and he can't possibly reach the bridge before 7 or 8 o'clock to-morrow morning. Now look out, old boy. Good-bye."

The Battery left Headquarters at 11:10 P. M. and reached the bridge at 7:15 the next morning. The bridge was guarded by infantry and artillery, so, as soon as it reached the bridge, the Battery was safe. On this march of thirty-five miles over a smooth macadamized road, where the horses could go at full step without trotting, it was a pleasure to ride at the side of the Battery and listen to the even tread of the horses, although the march was made chiefly during the night. After we had halted and partaken of a good breakfast, we felt we could defy Mosby or any one else to do us any harm. Then, when the horses had been fed, we were ready for the march to Nicholasville, on the north side of the river. To reach the bridge, the Battery had to go down a steep descent from the south, and to reach the road to Nicholasville, it had to go up an equally steep ascent on the north. The climb up that hill was awful, both on account of the heat of the direct rays of the sun and that of the rays reflected from the water. Men and horses suffered much, and, although it was a march of but three miles, they suffered more than they did during the thirty-five mile march of the preceding night.

At the end of this three-mile march, the Battery came to a beautiful clover field. I gave orders to park the battery in this field; to unhitch the horses and give them an hour in it; afterwards to water them; and then to feed them with grain. By the time all this had been done, dinner was ready for the men, and strange to say, the men were ready for the dinner. After this hearty meal, the men soon found comfortable places where they could lie down and rest till 12 midnight, for it was expected that the Battery would have to be again on the march at 2 A. M. Just at the moment when men and horses were comfortably settled, an orderly came with a telegram from Gen. Willcox, ordering the Battery to hurry on to Lexington for the train that was to carry the Battery was ready to be loaded. I really did not have the heart to disturb the men, they were resting so quietly after their fatiguing march on the previous night and the morning following. I put the telegram in my pocket and thought I was justified in doing so, since Col.

Griffin had stated in his instructions to me, that it was not expected the Battery would be shipped until the fifth of June.

At the same moment a man entered the field; it immediately occurred to me that he must be its owner. I at once went up to him and said, "Sir, I have taken possession of your field." "That is all right, Captain," said he, "I am glad I am able to furnish your Battery with something that will benefit it." He was accompanied by his young son, who was, apparently, of about the same age (thirteen years) as my own son, Louis, who was with me on this campaign, and was at the moment but a short distance away. I called Louis, and he came marching up as soldierly as an old veteran, clad in his full regalia, soldier's coat, high top-boots and slouch hat. I introduced him to the farmer, who looked at him and said in wonder, "Do you mean to tell me this young boy is making this campaign with you?" I told Louis to answer for himself, and he did so with a soldier's courtesy and then related some of his adventures. The two boys soon became friends, and when the farmer was about to leave, he asked my permission to take Louis home with him to stay with his son over night, for he wanted his wife to see a soldier only thirteen years old. Of course, I was greatly surprised at this request, and stopped to consider. I left it to Louis, knowing he had good judgment, and asked him if he cared to go with the gentlemen and spend the night under a roof and in a bed. For that part of it he said he did not care, but if I thought it would be all right, he would like to go. So it was settled.

I told the farmer, however, I should hold him responsible for my son's safety, and, as the Battery was to march at 2 in the morning, he should take care of my son's horse and start him on the road to Lexington at 4 A. M., so that Louis could reach that place by 5, as he was a good rider. The farmer made the required promise and the three set off for the farmer's home.

The Battery reached Lexington at 5 the next morning, and had but just halted at the station, when, off in the distance, I descried Louis galloping towards us on his gray mare. He was all smiles as he reined up beside me and began telling me of the good time he had had.

Everything was now in a bustle as the trains were in waiting. An officer came up and I asked him which train had been set apart for Roemer's Battery. He pointed it out and, at the same time, said it had been expected the night before. Orders were then given to load the Battery on the train at once, and the men were promised two hour's leave when the loading was done. It was astonishing how this prospect inspired the men; within thirty minutes everything was on board the train; then the men took their two hours' leave. I then started out to go to Gen. Willcox's Headquarters to report the arrival of the Battery, but met him on the way in company with the Depot Quartermaster and thirty men who had been detailed to help load the Battery on the train. I went up to Gen. Willcox, saluted, and reported that the Battery was on the train. "Who loaded the Battery?" he inquired. "My men, General," I replied, and the officer in charge of the trains corroborated my statement and added, "I have never seen a battery loaded so quickly before in all my life."

The train left Lexington at 11 A. M. and arrived at 6 P. M. at Louisville, where the Battery, after being unloaded, marched to the wharf five miles distant, and was shipped on board the steamer *Mariner* for Vicksburg, Miss. The 36th Mass. Vols. accompanied the Battery as its support. On the 6th the *Mariner* steamed down the Ohio River in fine weather and under favorable circumstances, and arrived at Cairo at 7 P. M. on the 9th, and then started on the voyage down the Mississippi River. Nothing of importance occurred until the steamer reached Lake Providence. Here they were fighting on the land, and we could hear the rattle of musketry. Our flotilla consisted of eleven transports led by two gunboats. The *Mariner* was the rear boat of the flotilla, and two of the Battery's guns were in position in the bow of the boat ready for action. The current was very strong, although the river is here from one to three miles wide, because the strong current had eaten away the banks at varying intervals. All the vessels had to follow the channel, and so had to pass down the river in single file the *Mariner* being the last boat to pass.

Just as the boat neared the bank and swung away from it to the left, several companies of Confederates rushed out of the canebrake, and let us have the contents of their muskets. When they had fired three volleys, I made up my mind that some of us might suffer. My first thought was for my son. I made him lie down and then covered him with mattresses. I then went to the guns in the bow, had them loaded with canister, and fired. That the guns were well aimed, was proved by the fact that we could see the "Johnnies" hop. The latter started to run and we sent some shrapnel after them. It was all over in a few minutes, but the "Johnnies" got the worst of it, for we suffered no casualties. When the first volley of rebel bullets struck our boat, and rattled against the pilot house, one might have thought the Chinese had come to town with their big gongs, as the pilot house was sheathed with heavy sheet iron. The gunboats were at the bend of the river, where our colored troops were having a sharp fight with the enemy near Lake Providence. As soon as the gunboats could get near enough to reach the enemy with their guns, they opened fire. The colored troops seeing they were well supported, took fresh courage, and, without waiting to reload their muskets, clubbed them and dashed forward, rending the air with their cries of "Fort Pillow!" "Fort Pillow!" Those on the boats could hear the echo, "Fort Pillow, men! No quarter!" The enemy broke and fled. During the encounter we received many stray bullets, and after it was well over, we looked around to see if they had done any damage. It was found that some eight or ten horses and two men had been slightly wounded. On further investigation it was found that the *Mariner* had somehow caught fire just over the boilers, but as the fire had as yet gained no headway, it was easily extinguished, while the boat had suffered no material injury.

At this time a heavy wind was blowing, which finally became a severe gale that tossed the boat from side to side. The 36th Mass. were on the upper deck and suffered much discomfort. The boat would probably have been swamped, if Capt. Collier had not wisely headed the boat to windward, and put in the lee of the bank, where it was safer. The waves in the river were so powerful and heavy that a small stern-wheel boat, not three hundred yards away from us, was carried by one, the high wind aiding it, right upon the land, where it remained when the water receded, about one hundred and fifty yards from the edge of the river, with its stern-wheel revolving for all it was worth.

The steamer arrived at the Yazoo River at midnight June 17th, under a clear full moon. As it turned the point, the lovely live-oak trees draped with the silver-gray hane, or Spanish moss, bathed in the moonlight and contrasting strongly with the light background of the river bank, presented a picture that cannot be described. I took my field glass and drank in the beauties of the landscape, and, as I gazed, I thought that a more beautiful view could not be found in all creation.

CHAPTER VI.

HAYNES'S BLUFF, JACKSON AND VICKSBURG.

At six o'clock in the morning of June 18th, the *Mariner* arrived at the foot of the bluff known as Haynes's Bluff. The banks were so high and steep that it seemed impossible to disembark the artillery there. I reported the matter to Gen. Parke, commanding the Ninth Corps. He told me I was in command of the *Mariner* and should find a suitable place to land the Battery. I sent word to Capt. Collier to drop down towards Vicksburg, and that I would walk along the bank and give him notice as soon as I found a suitable place. With some other officers I walked down the river some three miles, where we found a good landing place, with stout trees near, to which the block and fall could be fastened to haul cannon-carriages, etc., on shore. When all were landed, the horses were attached and the Battery marched to its destination, Haynes's Bluff.

Here was found the wreck of Pemberton's siege train, guns, and both shot and shell by the cartload. We were told that Pemberton's men rolled the siege guns down the bluff into the Yazoo. The gun-carriages were partly burned. The shot and shell were of all kinds and sizes. The enemy must have been in a terrible hurry when they left, judging from the promiscuous way things were lying around. From this position was a splendid view of the surrounding country and even Vicksburg could be distinctly seen. Up the river toward Memphis could be seen the rice plantations on the lowlands for twenty-five or thirty miles.

These rice fields are very expensive to construct. Each one is surrounded by a wall three or four feet high, and wide enough to drive a horse and cart along the top. In the wall are sluices with gates, through which water may be let into the fields or out of them, as may be required.

On this bluff the Battery went into camp, occupying some of Pemberton's old redoubts, which were now reversed. The place was so elevated that it seemed useless to build redoubts, for no ordinary gun or mortar could reach it. Pemberton was caged safely enough; the iron girdle was completely around him; and he could never get out without first handing his sword to Gen. Grant. We were placed here merely as outposts to watch Gen. Johnston.

As this was my first visit so far south, I was willing to take a few hints from Mrs. Collier, wife of the *Mariner's* captain. She had said that Northerners did not know how to take care of themselves in this fever-stricken country, so I asked for instruction. She then said that Northerners were so imprudent as to sleep out-of-doors without any covering. After midnight there was always a cool breeze, and then, if people didn't have the proper covering to protect them, the southern fever would surely seize them. I thanked her and said I would profit by her advice. After dinner Dr. Freeman, our Battery Surgeon, and I held a consultation about the matter, and it was decided to have the Surgeon issue an order that every man in the Battery must, under penalty, be covered with his blanket, especially after 12 midnight. The order was made out and read to the men at retreat roll-call for several successive nights thereafter. I also ordered the sergeant of the guard to call me at midnight just before the guards were changed, to make the rounds with the relief. The first night, three men were

Johnston, who was, at that time in the neighborhood of Jackson. Battery L was occupying its position as a picket battery.

During this time one of Gen. Grant's spies, named Kelly, made his headquarters with me in my tent. He was accustomed to come and go at all hours of the night, to pass our pickets, and enter the rebel lines, and visit Vicksburg to see what was going on there. He attended balls and parties in Vicksburg and mingled in the best society in the city, both civil and military; he courted the ladies and made himself agreeable to all he met. On such occasions he always wore a fine rebel uniform and posed as an officer from some distant part of the Confederacy. When he returned from these visits to the rebel city, he would come to my tent, change his clothes, and then go to report to Gen. Grant.

I well recollect the evening of the surrender of Vicksburg. That same day I had asked Gen. Parke, commanding the Ninth Corps, for an order to go out to examine the approaches to the position the Battery was then holding. Gen. Parke gave me the order and then asked me what escort I would have to accompany me on such a perilous expedition. I told him I should take two of my sergeants, the Captain of a Missouri Battery, and three of his men. He replied, "Captain, that will never do. I will send you twelve cavalrymen and a sergeant for your escort to-morrow morning at 9 o'clock, but you must be careful, Captain, and not venture out too far. What you want to do in front of your Battery, is, I understand, to ascertain the character of the approaches to the position you are holding." I returned to my quarters with Gen. Parke's order which read thus :

"Pickets and vedettes will pass Capt. Roemer and escort to examine the roads in front of his battery's position on the Mill Dale road July 4th." [Signed] "John G. Parke, Maj.-Gen., commanding Ninth Army Corps.

At 9 P. M., July 3d, news came that Lieut.-Gen. Pemberton had surrendered, and immediately thereafter came an order for Battery L to march at 3 P. M. July 4th. Kelly, the spy, was in my tent when the order came, and I said to him, "Kelly, this is too bad. We have helped to take Vicksburg, yet now we are hurried off without being allowed to have a chance of seeing the inside of the city." Kelly rose, came over to me, and said, "Captain Roemer, where is that order Gen. Parke gave you? Let me see it." I gave it to him, and he, after glancing at it and returning it, said, "That order is all right. I will get you into Vicksburg before Gen. Grant gets there. We must start very early, as we shall have to ride some seven or eight miles. We can not get in from the front for every road is heavily guarded, but with that order we can easily blind the pickets and vedettes. The order reads July 4th. Now send for the Missouri captain and his lieutenant. If we don't go then, you won't have another chance as your Battery moves at 3 P. M. to-morrow, to the Big Black River in the direction of Jackson."

[In order that certain events that follow may be fully understood, it will be necessary to know what are the several duties of pickets, vedettes, and the main line, or line of battle. Pickets are guards placed in front of the main lines of infantry, while vedettes are guards stationed in front of the cavalry and also of the infantry pickets. The vedettes are always the nearest to the enemy. Seated on their horses, they hold their carbines in their right hand with their fore-fingers on the triggers. At the least suspicious movement of the enemy they give an alarm or fire a shot. This will cause the pickets to be placed under arms. If there is any further trouble, the vedettes fall back to the picket line, and then, if they are pressed too hard, both vedettes and pickets will fall back on the main line, firing as they retreat. This was the usual practice of both armies in the field.]

At 5 A. M., July 4th, our party consisting of Kelly, the Missouri Battery Captain, and his lieutenant, myself and two of my men, a sergeant and a bugler, six in all, started on our perilous journey to Vicksburg. We had selected horses good at jumping ditches, for Kelly had informed me we would have to do some jumping, if we wished to see the city, as the main rebel ditch was five feet wide and as many deep. We had, however, perfect confidence in the ability of our horses. Kelly had a mule which he said he would not exchange for the best mule in Gen. Grant's army. We passed our main line of pickets and vedettes without trouble. But now the officers of the advanced guards asked to see my pass. I showed it. "Correct," they replied, "pass on."

We were now between our own and the enemy's lines. The enemy's vedettes and pickets had all been withdrawn. Their main line, furthermore, had been ordered to advance from their main ditch five paces towards our lines, stack arms, and return without them. We had now arrived at this main ditch, where our horses must show their mettle. Kelly took the lead and gave his mule the spur, but the mule shook his head, as much as to say, "I'm not going over that ditch." I then said, "Kelly, let me try it." "Why, Roemer," said he, "your old plow horse can't make it, if my mule can't." However, I determined to try. I rode up to the ditch to let my horse see what it was, then turned and rode round in a circle and then went over without any especial exertion. Kelly tried to follow, but still his mule would not jump. I went back and formed a ring of all the horses, taking the lead myself, with Kelly last. This time all went over safely. Now we were really in rebeldom. In the gullies along which we rode and into which the shot and shell had rolled down from the hills, one could have gathered these missiles by the cartload. They were of all sorts and sizes, from 3-pounders to 300-pounders.

Up hill and down dale we went, but it was terribly severe on the horses. We finally reached the city which showed many marks of the shells of the "swamp angel," the name given to a big gun throwing a 400-pound shell. This gun opened fire at 6 P. M. every day, and was fired at intervals of half an hour all night till 6 the next morning. In different sections of the city, we saw where a single shell had gone through several houses in succession, making in each a hole sufficiently large for a man to crawl through with ease.

By 10 A. M. we had made a pretty thorough survey of the city, and as the formal surrender was soon to take place in front of the City Hall, we started for that point to obtain a good view of our late opponents, who were now compelled once more to bow in obedience under the glorious stars and stripes, the emblem of the free and the brave. We arrived at 11 and, through the influence of our friend Kelly (whose cheek could never be broken by a fall) secured a splendid position. He led us straight through the crowd, to a point right in front of the City Hall, whence we could look southward for a full mile.

At 11 A. M. precisely the head of the column came in sight with Gen. Grant on the right, Gen. Sherman on the left, and Gen. Pemberton in the center. They were followed by all the members of Grant's and Sherman's staffs, all looking well, though many of the shoulder straps were faded, and well they might, for they had been through many a march beneath a southern sun and been wet by many a southern rain. Then came a heavy escort of U. S. Cavalry, followed by a large force of infantry. After these came the prisoners of war, without arms, numbering in all some 30,000. All the ammunition, guns, horses, harnesses, ambulances, in fact, everything had been surrendered except the side-arms of the officers, which they were allowed to retain. I am not certain, however, that any below the rank of captain were permitted to do so. The ceremony was very imposing, but as it was now two o'clock, I told Kelly it was high time for me to make my way back to my command, as I had quite a distance to go and my horse was not overfresh. We had so far ridden somewhere about fifty miles, and I knew it was too much to expect of my faithful "Dick" that he should go much longer without rest. "Dick is all right, Roemer," said Kelly, "but my mule is the best for traveling around Vicksburg." "Yes," said I, "but he comes after Dick, for Dick had to lead the way this morning."

Time was precious, so, after thanking Kelly for his escort so far, I bade him good-bye. But Kelly would accept no thanks. Said he, "Roemer, if you thank me, I will have you court-martialed. How about the time you were instrumental in saving my neck from a rebel gallows when they were after me. I had to lie in that ditch for sixteen hours, and you gave me a cup of delicious coffee to revive me?" "Well, Kelly," I replied, "if the rebels get after you again come to me and I will save you, and give you all the coffee you can drink." I now set out to return to the Battery. After some miles had been traversed, my splendid horse Dick began to act as if he were hurt in some way, but I could not locate the injury. As soon as I reached camp I charged my groom to examine the horse thoroughly, and find out if possible the cause of his peculiar actions. Soon after the groom reported that the saddle had worn quite a hole in Dick's back. I was much relieved and very thankful it was no worse, for Dick was such a faithful horse I did not want to be compelled to part with him. That day I was in the saddle for fifteen hours.

At 3 P. M., July 4th, the Battery left camp and advanced three miles in the direction of the Big Black River, and halted for the night. The next day it went three miles farther and halted at a point about one and one-half miles from the river, and remained the whole of the 6th as guards for the troops engaged in building a bridge over the river. The next morning orders came to cross the river. Not more than three-quarters of the troops had crossed before the bridge broke down, and some horses and ammunition wagons went down with it. The troops that had not crossed were now ordered to march the next day to Messinger's Ford and cross the river over the bridge located there. During the night of the 7th a pouring rain storm set in. The rain came down by the barrelful, and the ground soon became so saturated that it would not hold a tent-peg. Lieut. Heasley and I had to stand up all night and hold the tent up the best we could to keep it over us. I might say without exaggeration, that about forty pailfuls of water ran down my back that night.

The next morning the Battery started for Messinger's Ford, five miles distant. It arrived but it was a pretty soft march. It then crossed the bridge and joined the First Brigade, 2d Div., Ninth Corps, commanded by Col. Griffin. On the 9th it continued the march and arrived at Jackson late in the evening. On the 11th I received orders from Col. Griffin to report the Battery to Gen. Potter, commanding the 2d Division, at 3:30 P. M. Gen. Potter directed me to remain in reserve with horses harnessed and the Battery in readiness for instant action during the 12th. Late in the afternoon of the 12th the Battery was ordered to move to a point near the Asylum, and near which it remained in different positions until July 20th.

On the 15th, as we were very desirous of learning something concerning the construction and true position of the enemy's works which, we had been informed, were built of cotton bales. Lieut. Benjamin, commanding Battery E, 2d U. S. Art., and I crawled out as near as possible to their works and found a place where we had a good view of them. We could see plainly that they were built of cotton bales, and that leaves had been used in making the bales in an endeavor to disguise their true character, and, furthermore, that they made fine breastworks. The rebels fired over us, for they did not have the slightest inkling of our presence so near them. It was raining at the time, and as we had to remain there for over an hour, we, of course, had our jackets thoroughly soaked. We then made our way back to our own lines as best we could. Lieut. Benjamin was made very sick by this exposure.

On the 16th the Batteries were in position on low ground, but still near the Asylum. Both Lieut. Benjamin and I were very eager to get the range of the State House in Jackson, and we could get it only from some high point. I at once thought of the Asylum tower. If I could only reach the top of it and give Benjamin the cue, we could obtain accuracy in aiming our guns. I made my way to the top, and under shelter of the Asylum's flag managed to give the proper signals by motions of my hands previously agreed upon. After firing four shots Benjamin had established accurately his line of fire, but by this time the rebels had detected me behind the flag, and now they sent a 42-lb. shot crashing through the Asylum. It did not take me long to come down the ninety-four steps leading down to the ground. When outside I stopped to fasten my spurs. Just then I heard the clatter of a horse's hoofs and, looking around, I saw Gen. Parke come galloping up, pell-mell, around the Asylum. Calling me, he asked, "Roemer, have you been up in the tower?" "Tower?" said I, "What tower?" "The tower of the Asylum," he replied. "No, sir," I answered. (This was only a little white lie, and I don't think the goblins will get me for telling it). "I came here just at this moment." "Well," said he, "some one must have been up there or the enemy would never have aimed that shot at the Asylum." "General," said I, "I know nothing about it." Gen. Parke then rode off to make further investigation. Inasmuch as the line of fire had already been established and Benjamin had obtained accurate range on the State House, I did not mind the story I had told Gen. Parke. Benjamin peppered them well during the ensuing night, and the next morning it was found that nearly all the rebels had left the town.

As I wanted to know how many shots Benjamin had put through the State House, I went there to find out. The investigation showed that some seven or eight had gone straight through it. In the Governor's room it was clear "He took his hat an' lef bery sudden, an' I 'spec he's run away." One of his shoes lay in one corner, his vest in another and confusion reigned throughout. The bed was strewn with brick and mortar. Leaving the State House I rode over to the Pearl River. Our infantry were in possession of the approach to the bridge, and a guard was stationed there. I was just about to ride over the bridge when an infantryman sprang up and seized my horse by the bridle, at the same time calling out, "For God's sake, Captain, don't go another step or you are a dead man." He then with his bayonet picked a hand grenade out of the sand It seemed that when the rebels left Jackson they also left many grenades at various points in the road, and so covered with sand that they could not be seen. I was not aware of this fact until this soldier informed me. He also told me that our infantry had found the matter out through having some of their men blown up by these hidden grenades. While I was conversing with this soldier a rebel prisoner a little distance away was telling how the enemy had fooled our troops. In the midst of his story he accidentally stepped on one of the grenades and it exploded, tearing his legs from his body. Instantly he lay dead in a pool of blood. While sitting there looking at that dead rebel, I could not but wonder at the quantity of blood in a human body. I have seen hundreds of wounded men, but I have never witnessed another scene like that. I felt very sorry for this poor fellow, who had lost his life through the actions of his own people. It was a most sickening sight.

Now, no longer caring to look at the beautiful Pearl River, I turned and rode back to Jackson. At the entrance to the city I was met by one of the men, Sergeant Rossbach, who said, "Captain, I have found a lot of salt in that long building yonder." I told him to go to a store and get two bags. He did so, and we put about a bushel of salt in each. While engaged in this matter, one of the aides galloped up, and called out, "Roemer, get out of this building with your sergeant as quickly as possible. The rebels have just attempted to blow up the gas-house, and a big fire is raging only two doors above this around the corner." We hurried out of the building, but the salt was not left, for it was far too precious. The sergeant and another horseman who had come out with him, each took a bag and carried it to camp. I then rode around the block to where the fire was raging like a furnace. I had to cross one of the main avenues of the city to go away from it and just as I reached the middle of the avenue, a blast of hot air struck me. My horse bounded, and if I had been sitting loosely in the saddle, I would surely have been thrown off, and yet I was a hundred yards away from the burning building. I had gone but one block farther when the gas-house was blown up with a crash that shook the town.

The salt found in Jackson was a great acquisition for the

Battery, for both men and horses had needed it for some time. Salt is one of the necessities of life, and must be provided in order to maintain an army in good health. The same is true, in a measure, of pepper. I often think that Battery L would have suffered more from sickness than it did if I had not been careful to keep a proper supply of these articles constantly on hand, in accordance with the advice of the Battery's surgeon, Dr. Edwin Freeman, to whom, indeed, the men of the Battery were greatly indebted in many ways.

To Dr. Freeman great credit must be given that so few of the members of the Battery were sick during the time they were in camp around Vicksburg and Jackson, where so many died of malarial fever. Even when he was sick and confined to his cot, the Doctor measured out quinine in varying amounts, which my son Louis (who was sitting by the Doctor's bedside) put up in packages suitably marked. These packages were given to me and I would then treat the men to a dose of the requisite amount whenever they might chance to need it. I must say that the men did not always relish the dose, although to take it was compulsory under General Orders. Sometimes as much as twenty grains were given in one dose, and often when the men were very weak, a little commissary (whiskey) would be given in addition, which, strange to say, they always took without a murmur, and, in fact, seemed willing to take the quinine for the sake of getting some of the commissary. Our care in this respect was well rewarded, for only one man died of the fever; and he was my own body-servant, a colored man named Stonewall Jackson, whom I had brought with me from Virginia.

I now give my official report of the part taken by Battery L in the Mississippi Campaign made to Gen. Potter, commanding Second Division, Ninth Corps:

HEADQUARTERS, BATTERY L, 2D N. Y. ART., }
NEAR JACKSON, MISS., July 18, 1863. }

CAPT. H. R.—A. A. G. 2d DIV., 9TH ARMY CORPS:

SIR:—I have the honor to report according to General Order, No. 13, from Headquarters, 2d Div., 9th A. C., received July 18th, 1863, as follows:

At 9 P. M., July 3, while before Vicksburg, this Battery received orders to march at 3 P. M., July 4th, towards the Big Black River. At that time it marched out three miles from the Bryan House. July 5th it again marched three miles and encamped one and one-half miles from the river. On the 6th, it remained in camp all day awaiting the building of the bridge across the river. On the 7th that part of the 9th Corps began crossing the bridge and was engaged in crossing all day. Near sunset the bridge broke down and a part of Durell's Battery, my own Battery, and a regiment of infantry were unable to cross. July 8th, I received orders from Col. Griffin, commanding 1st Brig., 2d Div., 9th A. C., to take my own Battery and the remaining part of Durell's Battery to Messinger's Ford, some five miles down the river on the right bank and cross at that point at 11 A. M. I joined Col. Griffin's command at 8:30 P. M.

July 9th, by orders from Col. Griffin, I put my right section in position on the Jackson road. I started again on the march July 10th, and at 9 A. M. arrived at a point within three miles of Jackson, Miss., where I received orders from Gen. Potter, commanding 2d Div., 9th A. C., to take position on the right of the Vicksburg and Jackson R. R. On the 11th I received orders to follow the 2d Brigade and park the Battery east of the Lunatic Asylum. The Battery remained at that point part of July 11th, and all of the 12th, on which day orders were received for all batteries to fire 30 rounds per gun. I asked both Gen. Potter and Gen. Parke for permission to assist Lieut. Benjamin in ascertaining what effect his fire had upon the State House by ascending the tower of the Asylum with which Gen. Parke is acquainted. On the 13th, in accordance with orders to move the Battery to a more sheltered position, it moved one-half mile northeast to the position I am now holding.

I regret that Battery L has not been of more service to my

new commander than it has been. The Battery is now, as it always has been, ready for any emergency. During the time covered by this report, the Battery has suffered no casualties whatever and has fired 115 rounds of ammunition. I have the honor to be, Captain,

     Your most obedient servant,
      [Signed] Jacob Roemer,
    Capt. Com'd'g Battery L, 2d N. Y. Art.

On the 19th the Battery received orders to be ready to march back to Vicksburg at 4 A. M. on the 20th and to go with the last Brigade. Its time to fall in did not come till 9 A. M. It marched the whole of that day to get into position so as to be at the head of the column on the 21st. How the men suffered on that march in rear of that great mass of troops, horses, wagons, ambulances, etc., from heat and dust, of which the latter was the worst, being fairly knee-deep. At 5 P. M. it passed the first bivouac, but it was not until 12.30 A. M. on the 21st, that it reached its own place of bivouac. It had marched twenty-four miles. I need not say that everybody was thankful. As soon as it halted the horses were ordered to be unhitched and tied to the picket-rope but not to be watered until 2:30 A. M. as they were so heated. The men then dropped where they stood for a short rest, for the Battery had to start on the march again at 4 A. M.

At 4 A. M., July 21st, the Battery left camp with the 1st Brig. of the 2d Div. Ninth Corps at the head of the column, and reached the Big Black River at 5.30 P. M. having marched nineteen miles. It bivouacked on the left bank of the river in a field of fine grass on the right of the road, while the infantry supports bivouacked on the left of the road. Orders now came to be ready to march at 5 A. M., July 22, but the order to march did not come until 6, and with that came an order for each command to return to its old quarters near Vicksburg without further orders.

Immediately the bugle call, "Boots and Saddles," was sounded and the Battery was soon on the road. It crossed over Messinger's Bridge to the other side of the Big Black where stood the beautiful Messinger mansion, for the time being the headquarters of Gen. Parke of the Ninth Corps. While marching by, Gen. Parke came out on the piazza and the Battery passed in review. Then the general called me and asked, "Captain, how many horses did you lose yesterday?" "None, General," I replied. "How is your saddle-horse that was ailing yesterday?" he again inquired. "He is under me, General," I answered. "I can't understand how it is," said he. "I have received reports this morning from three batteries that they have within two days lost ninety-four horses while you have lost none. I would like to see you, Captain, this evening at my headquarters at Mil Dale. I see you are the first on the road this morning. Keep clear of the ambulances." "I will be six or eight miles ahead of everything on the other side of the bridge," said I.

The Battery went on trying to get as much headway as possible during the cool of the morning. The big hill three and one-half miles from its old camp soon came in sight. The men did not like to look at it long, for they knew they had to climb it and under a hot sun. Crawling slowly up the hill, all felt as if the sun would melt us, but knowing that gaining the top meant dinner, we persevered. The Battery soon reached the top where a grove of live oaks stood to welcome them. What a feast for weary eyes it was after that wearying climb. Here a halt was made for one hour and a half to refresh men and horses. The men ate what they had in their haversacks for lunch washing it down with good hot coffee. At 1:30 it started for the old camp ground at Mill Dale and arrived at 3. The horses were soon unharnessed and then the boys set to work to get up a good dinner.

Some ducks and chickens perambulating around annoyed them considerably and they were not long in capturing them, thus putting an end to the annoyance, and at the same time, obtaining good materials for a dinner. They looked around for the planter who owned them that they might pay him, but did not succeed in finding him. This fact did not prevent them, however, from going on with their preparations for a feast. They sent us officers, for our especial benefit, several splendidly roasted ducks. Our mouths watered as we gazed at them.

Just as we were about to begin operations on the ducks, a very heavy thunder-storm accompanied by a high wind broke over us with such force that our ducks and the boys' feast as well as everything else that was loose, were swept away and carried over to the Yazoo to feed the buffalo-fish. Some of the boys declared that they saw the fish open their mouths and swallow a whole duck at a time. I, of course, cannot vouch for the truth of this story, as I did not have my field-glass ready to investigate the matter. However, I told the boys they shouldn't mind, for on the 9th of August we would have a buffalo-fish chowder, and then they might have a chance to recover some of the ducks and chickens they had just lost.

Nothing further of importance occurred the remainder of the month outside the usual routine of camp life except that the tents were shifted to higher ground. Several mounted battery drills were held to give the men and horses a little exercise. On Sunday, August 2d, there was an inspection of tents, clothing, and horses.

The 9th of August was approaching and the chowder party had to be provided for. This was to celebrate the anniversary of the Battery's first battle, that of Cedar Mountain in 1862. The Committee of Arrangements consisted of Lieut. Heasley, First Serg't J. J. Johnston, Q. M. Serg't

Miller and three privates. They purchased three buffalo-fish, weighing respectively 87, 93 and 98 pounds, a total weight of 278 pounds which was thought to be fully sufficient for the needs of the men and their guests.

An order came the day before to have the Battery ready to embark as the steamer would arrive on the 9th. This was a most important order and had to be obeyed at once, yet the preparations for the chowder and the celebration went on. On the morning of the 9th, everything looked favorable for the celebration of our anniversary. Friends, both civil and military, were invited to partake of our feast and every one made merry at our celebration on the banks of the Yazoo, and all pronounced the chowder to be a complete success.

The steamer *Emerald* arrived at 9 A. M. We looked down upon her while still sitting at our feast and wondered when we should have another similar feast. When all had finished their repast, they were ready for work, and at 6:30 P. M. everything pertaining to the Battery was on board the boat. It then started for the Mississippi but its progress was, for some reason, rather slow. During the following day, the 10th, nothing of importance occurred. The chowder had produced a beneficial effect. All felt happy and contented, but no one cared to feed the buffalo-fish again.

CHAPTER VII.

VICKSBURG TO KNOXVILLE.

The steamer arrived at Memphis, Tenn., on the 12th and after coaling, started for Cairo, Ill., where it arrived on the morning of August 15th. I then reported at once to Gen. Buford for orders. In accordance with his orders the Battery was disembarked and placed on cars for transportation to Cincinnati, O., where it arrived at 5 A. M. August 18th. I immediately reported to Gen. Parke who ordered the Battery to cross the Ohio and encamp at Covington, Ky., on the banks of Licking River. The camp was established on the 19th.

The 10,000 infantry and four batteries of the Ninth Corps which had assisted Gen. Grant in taking Vicksburg and for which Gen. Burnside had sent after the fall of Vicksburg, were inspected on the 24th to ascertain how many of them were fit for hard service. About 1000 infantry and Battery L were the only troops found fit to form the rear guard of the troops that had been ordered to take Cumberland Gap and advance into Tennessee to effect a permanent lodgment in that state. During the six days following the review spoken of above, there was a great mortality among the troops from chronic diarrhoea. Battery L had 44 officers and men out of a total of 99 in all, sick with this dread disease.

On the day preceding the review orders came from Gen.

Willcox for the Battery to be ready to go by rail to Nicholasville, and, in the meantime, to make out requisitions for all ammunition and stores needed and to draw the same from the arsenal at Cincinnati.

The next morning I went with Serg't Werner and four men and a four-horse wagon to draw these supplies. While in Cincinnati I called on Dr. Freeman, the Battery surgeon, and my little son Louis, both of whom were on the sick list with the Yazoo fever which they had contracted at Vicksburg. Both were doing well yet they had to be left behind. Great credit is due to Dr. Freeman for his exertions in behalf of the men of Battery L while they were at Vicksburg. Many of them would never have reached Covington but for him. All that went to Vicksburg returned to Covington and this occasioned much wonder among all commanding officers, because the mortality among the other troops was so great. The U. S. Battery and Durell's Battery together did not bring as many men back to Covington as Battery L alone did. These batteries were not able to move on account of the sickness among the men, until the spring of 1864.

Having obtained the ammunition and stores required, we returned to Covington and camp at 10 P. M. I at once visited all the sick and learned that they had had nothing to eat during the entire day. I immediately ordered three camp kettles to be filled with water and hung over the fire to boil. As soon as the water was hot enough, I put into the kettles the proper quantity of farina and sugar, to make three kettles of gruel, and as I had on hand three bottles of whiskey given me by the Sanitary Commission, I added these to the gruel, thinking the whiskey would give it a better flavor. Each of the sick was served with a bowl of this gruel, and after it was disposed of, the roll was called to ascertain how many would be able to go on the march with the Battery the next day, the 25th, if ordered to march. All but seven were found able.

On the receipt of Gen. Willcox's telegraphic orders to be ready to march, I had immediately telegraphed back that I was not able to load the Battery on the train because so many of my men were sick. He had at once replied by telegraph, "Call on a regiment of infantry to load the Battery. Do not use any of your own men. I will have fifty men ready to unload it as soon as you reach Nicholasville. I have a fine camp-ground prepared for you. You must come."

Having completed all the preliminary arrangements for our departure on the morrow in anticipation of the receipt of marching orders, I went to bed at about midnight of the 24th, but before 2 o'clock A. M., I was seized with the dreaded fever. I at once sent a horseman post-haste to Covington for Dr. Z. Freeman, brother of our Battery Surgeon. He came with his wife in a carriage at 5 A. M. His first salutation was, "Hallo, Captain, what is the matter with you?" "That's what I want to know," I replied, "and that's why I sent for you." I then told him all about myself, and after this, he remarked, "I consulted my brother Edwin about you before coming. He said you had a good strong constitution and I could use extreme measures with you, and that I shall do. Now put yourself under my care and we will see what can be done." I did so and in about three hours I was in condition to move around.

On the morning of the 30th orders came from Gen. Potter to proceed to Nicholasville. I sent for First Sergeant Johnston and directed him to ascertain how many of the sick were determined to go to the Hospital. He returned shortly and reported the number. These men were immediately sent off in an ambulance in charge of a sergeant who was directed to call afterwards on Col. Gerhardt, 65th N. Y.

V., give him the compliments of Gen. Willcox and myself, and ask for a detail of one hundred men to assist in loading the Battery and the sick of my command on the cars. I assured all the sick men that if they went with the Battery the best of care would be taken of them, and that as soon as we reached the mountains a change for the better would certainly occur.

On the morning of the 31st one hundred men of the 46th N. Y. V., reported for duty. By noon the Battery was loaded on the train with the sick placed under the gun-carriages and caissons. Now, everything being in readiness, the train started for Nicholasville. It was wonderful to notice the change for the better that took place in the condition of the sick during this ride through the blue grass region of Kentucky.

The Battery arrived at Nicholasville September 1st. Gen. Willcox and the Division Quartermaster were on hand with a detail of thirty men from the 46th N. Y. V., to assist in unloading the Battery. The sick men were soon made comfortable in tents that had already been provided for them by Gen. Willcox previous to our arrival. The Battery's camp was situated in a fine grove of trees, with a spring of good water near by. This camp was called Camp Parke, in honor of Gen. Parke, the commander of that part of the Ninth Corps that went to Vicksburg. The Division Surgeon visited all the sick and began at once to administer heavy doses of quinine. Here we remained five days, or until all the troops that were expected to come, had arrived. These troops formed the reserve guard of Gen. Burnside's Army of the Ohio, and consisted of those found fit for duty after the Vicksburg Campaign, new recruits and various details from Covington. To make up for the Battery's lack of men, caused by sickness, etc., thirty men were detailed from the 46th N. Y. V. to serve temporarily with it, although more than half of the sick who came with it from Covington, had, by this time, fully recovered. The Surgeon gave me a two-ounce vial of quinine for use during the expected march over the mountains.

September 6th the order came for the Battery to start on the march over the Cumberland Mountains and follow Gen. Burnside into Tennessee. I was very sorry I was obliged to leave Sergeant Werner behind at Camp Parke, for he was a very promising young non-commissioned officer, and was likely to be promoted to a higher grade. He was with me in Cincinnati, August 24th, assisting in drawing supplies, and was taken sick at the same time I was. I tried to persuade him to go with the Battery, but he said he was too sick by far to do so. There was not much excitement during this march over the mountains, although there were one or two hair-breadth escapes from being crushed by rocks rolling down the mountain side while the Battery was climbing the high precipices over which passed the military road around the mountain, constructed by the pioneers. At some points on one side of the road the mountain's top could not be seen, while on the other side its base was not visible. The woods below, as seen from the tops of the high cliffs, had rather the appearance of a potato patch.

One most striking incident occurred in the Battery while on this mountain march. It was climbing up a steep grade with the mountain on the left, and on the right, a precipice at least two hundred feet down, while the Cumberland flowed along far below us. Just then one of the Battery officers called out, "Captain, the battery-wagon is going over the precipice. The horses won't pull; they are letting it run." I saw at once there wasn't a second to spare. I galloped back and wheeled my horse alongside the pole team. I threw myself over to the right, hanging to the saddle with my left leg, seized the end of the pole with my right hand and pulled with all my might until I felt the left wheel strike the stock (or reach, as it is commonly called). I then ordered every wheel to be blocked, the horses to be unhitched (as they could not be trusted in such a situation) and the wagon to be moved, inch by inch, by the cannoneers, until it was once more in the regular road. Had this wagon gone down that two-hundred-foot precipice, four drivers, myself and nine horses would have been dashed to pieces among the woods or on the rocks below. It was a very narrow escape, as the hind wheels of the wagon came within eighteen inches of the precipice. Even to-day, while writing about it, the thought of it causes the hair to rise on my head like the quills on the back of a fretful porcupine.

I have said on a preceding page that there was not much excitement during this march over the mountains, but the reader may, perhaps, think by the time he has finished this account of it, that there was really an abundance of it, for as the Battery went on farther, another strange occurrence took place. The Battery had come to position of the road around the mountain that was so narrow for a distance of three miles that but one wagon could pass at a time. While the Battery was coming up the road going south, a train of three hundred baggage wagons was also coming up from the other side going north. As I rode up to the guard station, the sergeant on duty there said, "Captain, you will have to wait until the train coming from the south passes you. Park your battery so that the wagons can pass it." I then rode over to the officer in command of the station and asked him how much of a train was coming north. He could not say for certain but he thought it was a very large one. After the Battery had been so parked that any number of wagons could pass easily, I rode leisurely southward to ascertain the number of wagons composing the train.

I had not gone far before I saw the head of the train coming around the mountain with an officer riding in front. I rode forward to meet him and just when I was near enough to him to speak to him, the first baggage-wagon with a snow-white canvas cover came up. The wind was blowing a gale. Suddenly, a puff of wind caught the white cover and it fluttered. At once there was a clatter of hoofs, my horse made a side-spring, and over the bank we went, my horse and I, before I knew what had happened. At the instant he rose to jump, I closed my thighs hard against the saddle. The horse jumped fully ten feet down amongst a mass of bushes and landed upright on all fours. He knew he had done wrong, and as soon as he had landed, he scrambled back to the place whence he had sprung, bringing me also back safe and sound.

The officer commanding the train was completely dumbfounded by the occurrence, our disappearance had been so sudden, and his face was as white as the wagon-cover. His salutation when I came up again, was, "Captain, there was one chance in five thousand for you and you had it." Had my horse not been so sure-footed as he was, we would both have been hurled into the Cumberland River after tumbling over huge rocks, stumps, etc.; nothing could have saved us from meeting a watery grave. The Battery, after this train had passed, went on without any other mishap, and reached Barboursville, Sunday, September 13th.

This was a day of rest for the whole reserve. I did not feel at all well; my head ached so at times that I thought I should go crazy. The surgeon came to my tent early in the morning and gave me a dose of quinine, and that turned my head completely. Gen. Ferrero called to see me and ask how I was. I ordered him to shut the tent and not speak to me. Afterwards the general always regarded it as a good joke that I had ordered him out of my tent.

In the afternoon the Battery was inspected and sick-call held. The next morning, of the forty men brought along sick from Covington, all but two reported fit for duty. I also received word from Covington that five of the seven enlisted men left there had died. Among these were Sergeant Werner and Corporal Edw. Johnston whom I was very sorry to lose, for they were most excellent non-commissioned officers, and just then the Battery was greatly in need of such.

After our Sunday's rest the march was resumed and Cumberland Gap was reached on the 20th, and that night the Battery bivouacked on Tennessee soil. Some of us inspected the earthworks the rebels had built there and learned how our advance army had taken the Gap. It had advanced over rocks and ledges and burnt the mill and storehouse before the rebels were aware of it; the latter had had no idea the "Yankees" were so close at hand. Thousands of bushels of grain were destroyed by this burning of the mill and storehouse. Three States, Virginia, Kentucky and Tennessee, meet at Cumberland Gap. On one side of the road is a large square monument of stone about three feet square, and standing four feet above the ground. If one walks around this, he will put his feet successively in each of the three States, whose boundaries it marks.

At this place most of the men who had been left sick in Covington having recovered, came up and rejoined their respective commands. Thus by the return of the convalescents, the reserve army was constantly being reinforced, and had by this time been considerably increased in numbers. It consisted mainly of the troops that had been in the Vicksburg Campaign, viz., the 36th Mass. Vols., the 46th, 51st and 79th N. Y. Vols., the 51st Pa. Vols., and the 2d, 8th, 17th and 27th Mich. Vols. All of these regiments were of the best quality and would support and defend Battery L, to the last, and at all hazards, and Battery L would do the same for them. Troops that have fought side by side as we had, become well acquainted with one another, and friendships formed under such circumstances are almost always lasting.

The Battery left Cumberland Gap on the 21st, taking the road to Knoxville, Tenn., and the next day reached Clinch Mountain, over which it had to climb three miles up and the same down, making six miles of most tiresome marching. The ascent was comparatively easy, but when the peak was reached, how to make the turn there in safety was the great problem, for the top is composed of immense flat blocks of stone, and as the road-bed over these was not sufficiently wide, the width had been increased to some extent by a wall of stone built against the rock. The wall was four feet thick and about eight feet high from its bottom to the level of the rock. All the gun-carriages and caissons passed over in safety and without difficulty, but when the battery-wagon drawn by eight horses came up, the eight horses had to take a wider swing than any of the others, and the hind wheel slipped off the rock upon the wall. The immense weight of the wagon tore the wall from the rock. The result was, the wagon, eight horses and four drivers went down the mountain side, turned over thrice in the descent, and finally, struck a stump, which stopped them and saved wagon, men and horses, from rolling a mile down the mountain side.

Imagine every one's astonishment when one of the drivers, without his cap, and with his clothing almost completely torn from his body, crawled out from under his horse, stood up, rubbed his head, and called out, "The Berliner is alive yet!" (Berliner was his nick name in the Battery; his real name was Henry Kasemeyer). Strange to say, none of the men or horses were injured to any great extent. Just as the "Berliner" called out. Gen. Ferrero, who was riding beside me, turned to me and said, "This is the most singular occurrence I ever witnessed." He then gave orders to relieve the horses and to let the wagon remain where it lay, as it was securely held, until the next day. The Battery then proceeded on its way down the mountain breaking, in the meantime, fourteen lock chains. No ordinary wagon could pass along such a road as this was; only the most strongly built artillery carriages could stand the racking. The Battery reached Morristown the same day. Just as it was entering the place, an aide on Gen. Willcox's staff rode up to me and said, "Captain, the general wishes to see you." The Battery went on into camp, while I accompanied the aide to the general's headquarters. As soon as he saw me, he helped me to dismount and said, "Your looks, Captain, tell me you saw severe service at the Siege of Vicksburg, but, my boy, I am proud of the Battery. Gen. Parke has told me all about it. Come in and sit on my cot. I have a bottle of wine for you, and we'll drink it while you are telling me all about your horses. Gen. Parke could not understand why it was that the two U. S. Batteries and Durell's Battery lost 94 horses, while yours lost none, though they marched the same distance you did and under the same orders from Gen. Parke. But let us first have a glass of wine together, for you look wearied and worn, Captain. I told you in Lexington, when I inspected your Battery previous to sending you to Vicksburg, I would hear good news from your Battery. Now, tell all about your management of your horses." "General," I began, "I told Gen. Parke at Mill Dale, Miss., that if I should tell everything relating to my management of my horses on that famous march from Jackson to Vicksburg, he would have me court-martialed, because I had gone directly contrary to U. S. Army Regulations, but as you want to know the whole story I will tell you all."

"On the first day's march the Battery was in rear of the whole column of 15,000 men. The column started at 4 A. M., but my turn to fall into the column did not come until 9. The day was exceedingly hot and the dust in the road was knee-deep. As my battery was in the rear, it had to halt every ten or fifteen minutes. This is very wearisome for horses in column. The column, furthermore, was to be reversed at the bivouac. My Battery was with the First Brigade of the 2d Division, and had to be at the head of the column the next morning. At 5 in the afternoon I arrived at the place where the first troops bivouacked, and it was not till half an hour after midnight that the Battery arrived at the place where it was to bivouac. I saw that all the horses of the batteries that had reached their appointed places had been unhitched, unharnessed, and sent to water, but I considered it wrong to water those horses at that time, for they were all too wet with sweat and too fatigued by the heat. When the Battery reached the place assigned to it on the left of the road, and had been properly parked, my First Sergeant, Johnston, asked, 'Where are the horses to be watered?' I replied, 'Not a horse of this Battery is to be watered before half past two, under heavy penalties.' I then gave orders for the horses to be unhitched, unharnessed, and tied to the picket rope, and then each one to be rubbed down while so tied, but to have no feed or water until half past two."

"I then rode over to Gen. Parke's quarters and told as pitiful a story as I could about my horses,—how fatigued, worn down and exhausted they were,—and asked as a favor to be allowed to march the next day with the First Brigade, and also to have four or five hundred yards distance at the head of the column so that the Battery need not be compelled to halt every ten or fifteen minutes, for the main column, as we had had to do the day before. Gen. Parke replied. "I cannot allow you any such distance, but will give you two hundred yards as you have always been very careful of your horses.' The next day the Battery went on until it was within two or three miles of the Big Black River when Gen. Parke rode up to me and said. 'Captain, when you reach the river, you and your brigade will bivouac close to it. Post the infantry so that they can easily support you during the night.' I immediately galloped ahead and selected a position on the right of the road in a field of splendid grass in which I could refresh the horses. I sent my orderly back with orders for the brigade and the Battery to come up at once. When the Battery arrived, I ordered it to be parked in the grass field on the right, and also ordered the horses to be unhitched, unharnessed, and to have one hour in the grass, during which time they were to be rubbed down, and, when this was done, to be watered and fed. I posted the infantry support on the left of the road, as the river on my right, made a sharp bend to the left. Messinger's Ford and Bridge were directly in front, and I, therefore, considered the position of the First Brigade and the Battery to be a very strong one. The next morning, the march towards Vicksburg was resumed at 6 o'clock and on the 26th of July the Battery reached its old camp ground at Mill Dale. This, Gen. Willcox, is all the story I have to relate regarding the care bestowed upon the horses of Battery L, while it was in Mississippi. Now, General, good-by, for I must follow the Battery." "Very well done," said he, "good-by."

The next day, the 23d, I went back up the mountain with twelve men, ten horses, tackle and tools to make a road out to the battery wagon to bring it back to the road, and even then, fifteen men more had to be sent for to finish the job of recovering the wagon. The battery wagon was so essential a part of the Battery's equipment, that it could not be left behind. This wagon always contained stores of all kinds that might be needed, except ammunition; in fact, it was the Battery's storehouse.

To give some idea of the roughness of these roads over the mountains, it is only necessary to say, that, before leaving Covington, I drew five hundred horseshoes, (as I usually had about one hundred horses with the Battery), and that when the Battery reached Morristown not one was left. The loss per day was from twenty to thirty-five. Every evening the sergeants had to report to me the number of shoes lost by the horses of his command during the day. The horses had to be shod at night by the Battery's two farriers, that all might be ready for work in the morning.

The Battery left Morristown the same day at 1 P. M. for Russellville, and shortly after its arrival there, orders came to return to Morristown the next day. It returned as ordered and on the 25th left Morristown for Knoxville where it arrived on the 26th in company with the Ninth Corps. As soon as the enemy saw the Ninth Corps advancing against Knoxville, they evacuated it and our entrance into the town was comparatively easy. Accompanying the Union troops was a man very widely known at that time, named Wm. G. Brownlow and generally called "Parson" Brownlow. He was quite a prominent man during the whole of the Tennessee campaign and did good service in conducting hundreds of women and children across the Holston River and into Kentucky. On the second day after our arrival, word passed through the Corps that the "Parson" would deliver one of his characteristic speeches in the evening at his residence. It is needless to say that when evening came, thousands of people, both soldiers and citizens, were on hand to listen to him. I can see him yet, as he appeared when we approached the house. He was standing on a porch in front of it, and welcomed us as we drew near. He began to speak, and his voice was so loud, so distinct, and so penetrating, that every word he uttered could be clearly understood by everyone in that vast assemblage. Of course I cannot repeat his remarks, but I know his speech impressed everyone who heard it, most forcibly. One sentence I remember very distinctly, it was so emphatic. Speaking in his loudest voice, he said: " Boys, I don't wish the rebels any harm. O! No! All I wish for them is, that each rebel had a millstone tied around his neck and then be let down into hell for twenty-four hours; then they wouldn't trouble us any more!"

Before the arrival of the Ninth Corps he had had very much trouble with the rebels, for while the latter held possession of Knoxville, he had not dared to show himself in the streets for fear of his life, and to save it he had been compelled to keep away from the town.

CHAPTER VIII.

THE TENNESSEE CAMPAIGN. CAMPBELL'S STATION.

Up to the first of October everything was quiet and peaceful, and the men took advantage of this state of affairs to put the Battery in perfect order. The gun-carriages, caissons and wagons were repaired ; the horses were newly shod and fed carefully to put them in perfect condition ; in fact, everything was done to prepare the Battery for efficient service. The Battery was inspected at 9 A. M. on the 4th. In the afternoon it went out for mounted battery drill from 2 to 4 o'clock, and then practised target-firing, during which, twenty-six rounds were fired. Of course, while the Battery remained quiet in camp the boys would have their fun, and to do a little foraging was quite natural. Woe to the pig or the chicken that came in their way, and it was astonishing how they managed to keep these captures out of sight of their officers. I have been told of many such doings, by my boys, since the war.

The Battery started out at 7 A. M. October 10th, on the Bull's Gap road and arrived at Blue Springs at about 11 A. M. Here the enemy were found awaiting our advance. The Battery was ordered to shell the right of the rebel line of Gen. Williams's army ; and they were driven out of some woods situated on a very high hill which might, perhaps, be called a mountain. The Twenty-third Corps had been in action against the enemy all the morning without being able to make any headway, and Gen. Burnside determined to put the Ninth Corps in at 1 o'clock, if, at that hour, the Twenty-third Corps should have been unsuccessful in routing the enemy. The guns of the artillery of the Twenty-third Corps had been hauled up the hill that morning by means of a block and fall. Orders were given to the Ninth Corps to advance and keep up the fighting. The Battery was assigned to a position on the extreme left, but to reach it was a difficult matter. Ten horses were needed to drag each piece to its position while the men by means of the prolong kept it from turning over. When the pieces were once up on the hill, it was comparatively easy to put them in position. The enemy would now be wholly at the mercy of our guns as soon as the Ninth Corps should drive them out of the woods. As soon as the guns were in position and properly sighted for distance, a few shells started the enemy running down the mountain side. Nine companies of infantry or dismounted cavalry, I don't remember which, armed with seven-shooters followed them. The enemy then tried to turn our left flank, but after receiving five rounds from the seven-shooters and several rounds of shrapnel from the Battery's right section, they changed their minds and retreated across an open field to a piece of woods beyond.

An order now came for the right section of the Battery to follow the infantry immediately. To return by the way it had come up the mountain and then march around to come up with the infantry, would have taken two hours, and as time is precious at such times, I determined to let the guns of the section slide down the mountain in front, as I saw it was sandy and devoid of trees. I had the lead and swing teams unhitched and taken down, all the hind wheels locked, and two men stationed at each wheel to add their weight to that of the carriage to force it through the sand,

Furthermore, four men with prolongs were assigned to each piece to hold back the carriage and thus relieve the pole-team from the forward pressure of it. The two gun-carriages now went down the mountain side with the pole-horses actually sliding down on their haunches. When they reached the level, the other teams were hitched on, and everything being ready, the section made a left turn, went down an embankment eight feet high, crossed a brook and halted.

Seeing some generals and staff-officers in a group on a road above and beyond where the section had halted, I rode up to them. Just as I came up, Gen. Parke asked me, "Roemer, how soon will your battery be here?" "General, it is right behind you," I answered. "Why, how did you get here so soon?" asked he again. "General," I replied, "look up and see the furrows we made coming down the mountain side." "Well," said he, "I am glad you are here and I consider it a great feat thus to come down the mountain, but you must not leave your guns exposed like this. Put them behind this hill for shelter."

Orders were now given for the whole line again to advance. We drove the enemy through the woods in front and across another clearing into another piece of woods beyond, while we kept possession of the woods where the enemy had been. The Battery was not called into action until about dark. It was assigned to a position on the south edge of the woods. In front of it was a clearing with a piece of woods beyond which was held by the enemy. The Battery fired a few shots before dark. The men threw up breast-works during the night, and, as they had but very few intrenching tools, it was very difficult work. The spades and pick-axes belonging to the Battery had been turned over to the infantry the night before to enable them to construct breast-works as a shelter from the enemy's fire. But as we of the Battery, did not wish to be exposed to this fire, we all, officers and men, worked with axes and a few shovels as well as we could, digging and heaping up the earth. By morning quite a serviceable fortification had been raised.

At two in the morning, while we were still at work on our intrenchments, Gen. Ferrero came along the line and found me at work loosening the earth with an axe. As soon as he saw me, he said, "Roemer, I don't want you to do such work." "General," I replied, "my men are all worn out and I want to show them I can help them build some shelter to be ready for whatever may happen. I do not think, however, that we shall have need of these works, judging from what I have seen and heard." The general looked at me and asked, "Well, old boy, what is it you *do* think?" "It is this," I replied, "about an hour ago I had occasion to go a little distance outside our lines, and while there I heard some unusual sounds. By listening carefully I could hear quite distinctly the tramping of horses and the movements of heavy artillery as the guns rattled along. I put my ear close to the ground and heard commands given, and then a long drawn out sound. By keeping very quiet, I heard the orders, 'Hello there, get out of the way.' Putting all these things together, I think you will find out, when morning comes, that the enemy have gone away." The general, however, was not to be convinced and soon rode off. So far all was perfectly quiet along the lines.

I was up again before daylight watching the enemy's lines through my glass till breakfast was announced. After that was dispatched, I resumed the task of watching their lines and kept at it till near 9 o'clock. At that hour, I saw some of the generals and their staff officers on my left, apparently in consultation about something. I walked over to them and saluted. Then I learned from their conversation that they desired to send out several regiments to charge the rebel lines. I stepped up to Gen. Burnside and said, "General, there is not a single rebel musket in those woods in our front, in fact, nothing but that line of vedettes we can see in front of the woods. In front of my line there is nothing but some Quaker guns, and of this I am absolutely sure." "How do you know that?" he inquired. Replying I said, "I told Gen. Ferrero last night at 2 o'clock that the rebels were moving, but he would not believe me although I told how I had obtained my information." Gen. Burnside turned to Gen. Ferrero and asked him, "Why did you not report this to me, General?" Gen. Ferrero replied, "I did not think it possible." "Now, General," said I, "I think that if you will charge on those vedettes they will turn their horses and show you their tails, and that that will be the last you will see of them." At once several regiments were ordered to charge the rebel lines, and, as I had predicted, the rebel vedettes instantly wheeled to the rear, and, with their horses' tails flying in the air, scampered off leaving our troops behind.

Gen. Burnside being now convinced that our front was clear, ordered the whole force now at Blue Springs to follow Williams's force. Preparations for this had already been made by Gen. Burnside. Gen. Foster had been sent out to make a circuit of ten miles and get in front of Willams at Rheatown, and, by putting all possible barriers in his way, felling trees, etc., to delay the march of that general's troops. Now, Burnside's whole force started from Blue Springs for Bull's Gap, which it passed and went on to Greenville, where it halted, twenty-two miles from Blue Springs.

Gen. Parke now came to me and said, "Your Battery has been selected to follow Gen. Foster, for the infantry cannot march any farther and Gen. Foster has no artillery. Try and get there as soon as possible, for one shot to-day is better than two to-morrow." I then asked Gen. Parke, "Is the road mine?" "What do you mean by that?" he asked in turn. "I mean this," I replied, "is everything in my front to give way for me to pass?" "Certainly, Roemer," he answered. The Battery moved off as rapidly as possible. I inquired of every person, black or white, I met on the road, how far ahead of me the rebels were. Some would express their opinion in true southern style by saying "a right smart bit." After much close questioning I concluded they must be about five miles ahead of the Battery. We kept on, and after marching two hours, I found we had gone about eleven miles and were approaching Rheatown. After passing this place, I saw what havoc Gen. Foster had wrought among Williams's troops. The school house was filled with the wounded and dying, and even the fields we crossed were strewn with the dead and wounded. I saw some hanging over the fences, having been shot, apparently, while climbing over them. Arriving at a point about a mile beyond Rheatown, I saw how effectually Gen. Foster had blocked the road with felled trees, which were lying criss-cross, one over the other, in such a way as to make it impossible for a wagon or a gun-carriage to pass. For a long distance the road was strewn with broken wagons, wheels, cracker boxes, and damaged harness, which showed how thoroughly Gen. Foster had carried out his orders, and in what a hurry the rebel troops had been to get away.

The Battery went four miles farther, and then an order from Gen. Parke was brought by an orderly, to rest for the night. There was a fine field of clover near by, and this was selected for our bivouac. Just as the Battery turned into this field three battery horses fell dead in consequence of the fatigue experienced during this forced march. In the time between 9 A. M., October 11th and 6 P. M., October 12th, thirty-three hours, the Battery had marched forty-five miles. All were glad we had a chance to rest after this long and dusty march. The next day, in the afternoon, the Battery started on its return to Knoxville, where it arrived on the 16th, and remained in camp until the 20th. That day it was ordered to go to Campbell's Station and thence to Lenoir Station, and then again to Loudon, where it remained from the 23d to the 28th. During these last six days the Battery's farriers were required to make thirty pounds of nails of various sizes for use in building a pontoon bridge over the Holston River. These nails were made of iron bars taken from a brick building near by.

All the men skilled in various trades were called upon to assist in this work of bridge building, as there were nails to be made, timber to be hewn and many kinds of iron work to be forged. The farriers and blacksmiths belonging to the various batteries were kept busy by the demands made upon them for their services. When my men had finished the quantity of nails required of them and carried them to headquarters, the men were complimented by the general for their promptness and were informed that they were the first to finish the task assigned them. The bridge was soon completed, for as many as two thousand men were, at times, employed upon it at the same time. It was never used to any extent, however, because, for some reason I never knew, it was destroyed almost as soon as it was finished.*

The troops returned to Lenoir Station October 29th, where orders came to erect log houses and go into winter quarters. Although there were very few carpenters among the men, yet each command sought to have some features about the houses they built that would be different from those built by

---

* Col. O. M. Poe, on p. 732, Vol. 3, "Battles and Leaders of the Civil War," states that "the pontoon bridge was transferred from Loudon to Knoxville, where Gen. Sanders's cavalry command crossed it to the south side of the river on the 1st of November."—EDITOR.

the others, but as the various tools usually employed in house building were wanting, many difficulties were encountered in accomplishing their object. All the old buildings found for miles around were confiscated to obtain material for building chimneys; and all the old iron found was quickly converted into nails and other necessary articles. The forges of the various batteries were kept busy night and day with this work of providing the iron work needed in constructing these houses.

Within a week after our arrival all were thoroughly at home in their new houses and ready to receive and entertain their friends. This camp at Lenoir Station had more the appearance of a permanent village than of a temporary camp. Battery L's houses were as fine as any, and my house was especially comfortable. I would have been very glad to entertain some of my Flushing friends in that house. It was ten feet long, eight feet wide and four and three-fourths feet high at the sides; the roof was a wall-tent fly, supported as such flies usually are. Thus I had ample room for all purposes. Just outside the house, on the right of the front entrance, was a hole three feet deep, called the fire-hole; from the upper part of this a horizontal flue constructed of brick, extended through the house from front to rear, six inches below the ground, and terminated in a brick chimney ten or twelve feet high. The ground within the house was thoroughly warmed by this flue, and, of course, the whole interior was very comfortable. I had used the same plan at Falmouth in December, 1862, and found it superior to any other method of heating log houses. On the 11th of November, as a number of fresh horses had been received, orders were issued calling for mounted drills and target practice to accustom them to the various battery maneuvers.

I am sorry to say that we did not have the pleasure of occupying the comfortable quarters in which we had expected to live through the winter, longer than two days and one and one-half nights, for at 1:30 A. M., November 12th, just when I had fallen into a good sleep, an order came to move immediately. At that moment it was raining, as they say, cats and dogs, and it appeared to be impossible to move. It was the worst storm the Ninth Corps ever encountered in all its marches. However, I was soon up, and then gave orders to harness, hitch up, and stand to horse. My orders also read, "Capt. Roemer will report at Headquarters in person for further orders." It was pitch dark when I went to Headquarters. I there learned that the army was to march to Loudon, but, in consequence of the severity of the storm, it would await its cessation before marching, and that, at that time, the order to move would be given. It was 10 o'clock before the storm finally ceased. At 11, Gen. Ferrero rode up and gave the order, "Captain, move your Battery out on the road yonder," and then gave me the required direction. "General," I replied, "that is impossible." "Why?" he inquired. "Simply because I shall require ten horses for each carriage and can, therefore, move out with no more than four gun-carriages and caissons," I replied. "No more?" he inquired. "No more," I replied again. "I know what my horses can do, and what they can't do. In their present condition I doubt if ten horses will be sufficient for a single gun." "Well, Captain," said he "I will report the matter to Gen. Burnside." He immediately despatched an orderly to Gen. Burnside with a message explaining the condition of affairs. The orderly soon returned with an order from Gen. Burnside to move with four carriages if more could not be taken along. I then went with four pieces to Loudon where the following order of Gen. Grant to Gen. Burnside was received: "Gen. Burnside, do not allow Gen. Longstreet to cross the Holston River, even if it costs you all the cavalry present with your command." Orders were also received to burn the bridge over the Holston built by the enemy, and over which, as we were informed, Longstreet intended to cross.

The Battery arrived at a point outside the town. Here the infantry and batteries of artillery were placed in position in the woods, there to remain until midnight, at which hour the bridge was to be burned. Just as this was about to be done a heavy rain storm set in, and so nothing could be done. The troops lay all night under arms, and all became wet to the skin, as there was no shelter for them.

November 15th all the troops returned to Lenoir Station in a terrible condition. Battery L had the rear of the column and was supported by the Thirty-Sixth Massachusetts Volunteers, which had been ordered not only to support the Battery in antion, but also to assist in pulling the gun carriages and caissons up a very steep hill outside of Loudon. For this purpose thirty men of the Thirty-Sixth were assigned to each carriage, three to each horse. They were to march beside the horses, and, in case the latter could not go forward up the steep grade, were to take hold of the traces and add their strength to that of the horses. The ascent of the hill was finally accomplished and the Battery went on and arrived at Lenoir Station in the evening. We were all a very sorry-looking lot, covered, as we were, with mud from head to heels. It was now perfectly evident that the situation was materially changed. All the troops were so placed that they could protect themselves from an attack by Longstreet's army, which was close at their heels.

Battery L was put into position on a high bank facing a pass and a high rocky cliff, from which the enemy could easily attack the Battery's position with artillery. The position also was so encumbered with stumps from three to four feet high that it was impossible to use the horses in putting the pieces into position. Every piece had to be put into position by hand. Night was fast approaching and the men had to work hard and rapidly to make all the preparations needed to be made for our defense. At 9 P. M. Gen. Willcox visited the Battery's position and was well pleased with the arrangements made to defend it. He then said, "Captain, everything, so far as I can see, is in order, and, as you have not had any sleep for two nights, you should put Lieut. Heasley in command and take a few hours' sleep." Gen. Willcox went away and I proceeded to give a few orders preliminary to my retiring for the needed sleep, but before I had completed giving them there came the whiz and bang of a thousand bullets, which, luckily, flew over us. It can readily be inferred that I did not go to sleep. The Battery replied to this fusillade with a few rounds of canister, which silenced the enemy for the night, during which, however, the whole army was kept under arms. Immediately after the firing, orders were issued for all baggage and ammunition wagons to proceed at once to Campbell's Station, to be out of the way of the troops marching in that direction.

At 4 A. M. on the 16th orders came to be ready to march, and at 6 o'clock the march began. The first section of the Battery, under my personal command, marched with the advanced guard of the column, which consisted of three regiments of infantry; the second section under Lieut. Heasley followed with the rear brigade.

The column had not been in motion more than half an hour when word came to me that three of my caissons were stuck in the mud (this was a *sticker* for me), and could not be extricated without fresh horses. I immediately sought Col. Morrison and asked permission to let the first section go on under its sergeant, while I returned to see if the caissons could not be pulled out of the mud before the main column came up. I obtained the desired permission and at once rode back and soon reached the scene of distress. First Sergeant Johnston was in command and was engaged in throwing the ammunition out of the chests. I asked him, "Who commanded you to do this?" "Gen. Burnside," he answered. "I command this battery, Gen. Burnside does not," said I. "Pick up every shot you have thrown out and put it back in its proper place. How long is it since you received Gen. Burnside's order?" "About fifteen minutes ago," he replied. Accompanied by my orderly I rode off at full speed after Gen. Burnside and soon came up with him. I saluted him and said, "Good morning, General; I have countermanded your order." "What order?" he asked. "Your order to my sergeant," I replied, "to throw the ammunition out of the caisson chests." Continuing, I said, "General, we cannot afford to lose this ammunition, for the Chief of Artillery told me a few minutes ago the army was very short of artillery ammunition." "Well, Captain," he asked in reply, "what will you do, for your horses are all used up?" "Do you see," I asked in turn, "that column of harnessed mules coming up from Lenoir Station? Can I not have some of them?" The General's face brightened up just as one sees the glorious sun rise after a stormy night, and, turning to me, he said, "Captain Roemer, you shall have unlimited power—unlimited power—to take as many as you wish." Bidding him good-by, I galloped off with my orderly to the mule train.

This train was composed of some four hundred mules that had been with a wagon train which had been burned at Lenoir Station. As soon as I reached it, I asked, "Who commands this train?" "A lieutenant in the quartermaster's department," was the answer. I soon found the lieutenant and said, "By Gen. Burnside's order I have come to you for sixteen four mule teams, and I will select them. You will please see to it that the drivers obey my orders.

Orderly, line them up as I pick them out." The drivers were colored men, not soldiers, and were somewhat frightened, not knowing what they would have to do, and, therefore, were a little shaky in their boots (although I don't remember that they had boots on). However, time was precious, and orders had to be obeyed; they were obeyed, for I sat on my horse with drawn sabre to enforce them.

As soon as the mule teams had been formed in column, I gave the order, "Column, forward, march," and off we went to relieve the caissons. The first four teams I turned over to Benjamin's Battery, as it was sorely in need of them. (Lieut. Benjamin, U. S. Artillery, was Chief of Artillery of the Ninth Corps in this campaign.) The remaining twelve teams were used in pulling my own caissons out of the mud. This was soon accomplished and the caissons went on.

The First Brigade, together with Battery L's first section (each gun-carriage and caisson being drawn by six horses and four mules) arrived on the field of battle at Campbell's Station, nine miles northeast of Lenoir Station and seventeen miles southwest from Knoxville, at 10 A. M. The artillery section under my personal command, was assigned to a position on the extreme left between two mountains. There were two roads entering this valley, the Loudon and Lenoir road and the Kingston road more to our right; our troops came up by the former and the enemy's by the latter. The orders given to the First Brigade and to myself were, to use all speed possible and reach the valley before the enemy, as they were trying to get between our army and Knoxville and thus cut us off from that place. However, our troops arrived first and most of them were placed in battle array a full half hour before the enemy showed themselves, or, as the men put it, before the head of the column of graybacks came in sight. As we came into position we faced about so as to confront the enemy who were not far away in our rear.

Lieut. Heasley, with the other section of the Battery, accompanied the last brigade commanded by Col. Humphrey, and this brigade had not yet come up. I learned later that this brigade had had to fight their way the whole distance from Lenoir Station to the battle field. At times the artillerymen could not use the horses, and then the pieces were dragged along by the infantry, who also shielded the artillerymen and horses from the enemy's fire. Every little while, the infantry would open and then the cannon would fire double charges of canister at the enemy. The infantry would then close up around the guns and resume the onward march. This maneuver was repeated many times during the march.

We had the advantage in position, but not in number of troops, for Longstreet's army outnumbered ours by about two to one. From my position I could see the enemy as they emerged from the Kingston road. The first graybacks came in sight just before 11 A. M. Then the battle line of the First Division moved forward to cover our left. Now I saw my chance. The battle had not yet opened, but I did not want to let such a chance as I now saw, escape me. Full of excitement, I galloped over to the Chief of Artillery, and before I quite reached him, shouted out, "Chief, I see my chance. May I open fire?" "Yes," he answered. No grass grew under my horse's hoofs while returning to my section. I sighted my two pieces directly on the enemy's advancing line, upon which I had a direct flank fire. The first two shots made quite a gap in the line. Turning to the gunners I said, "Boys, that was well done." Two shots were again fired, then two more and so on, till twelve shots had been fired, and then the whole rebel division broke and ran. Each shrapnel fired contained forty-two bullets, and the fuse was cut in such a way that the shrapnel exploded at just the right point. Therefore the eyes of the gunners must have been very good to judge the distance so accurately. It was this very exactness in cutting the fuses that made our shots so effective. I directed the gunners to aim their pieces at the feet of the advancing troops as they came down the mountain's side, and at their waists, when they turned and retreated. When the enemy started to run the whole of our line saw it, and also knew by that what execution had been done, and now they all shouted, "Hurrah for Roemer's Battery."

Gen. Ferrero now rode up and said, "That was well done. You gave them a good welcome, but, Roemer. I am afraid your second section, in charge of Lieut. Heasley, with the last brigade is gone up" (meaning captured). "What are the supports?" I asked. "Col. Humphrey's whole brigade, comprising the Fifty-First New York and the three Michigan regiments," he replied. "Then, General," said I, "if the second section is gone, you won't see any of the men who supported it come up." "Why," he asked. "Because," said I, "I know that no men of that brigade will see my section captured or any of my men taken prisoners." "What confidence you do have!" said he. "General," I replied, "you will see that my statement is true." After fifteen long minutes the brigade arrived and Lieut. Heasley joined me, his section going into position on the left of the first. As they came up, a cheer burst out all along the lines from right to left and back to the right again, for it had been supposed by almost everyone that they had been captured.

Now the battle opened in earnest. Shot and shell flew like hailstones in a heavy storm. The fighting was constant and fierce until night brought it to an end. Our casualties were not half the number of those sustained by the enemy, although they greatly outnumbered us. We punished them more than they did us. We had to hold on as long as we possibly could on this battle field, so that our baggage and ammunition trains might reach Knoxville in safety.

During the afternoon the enemy tried three times to turn our left flank by marching around the mountain, but our eyes were too sharp, although I must admit they came pretty near accomplishing their purpose. Each time the guns of Battery L were quickly turned from front to left and welcomed them with a shower of grape and canister. The ever true Fifty-First Pennsylvania infantry, our support, worked nobly, and the rebels thought so too, for they went up the mountain much more quickly than they came down ; they were entirely routed. This incident occurred between 3 and 4 o'clock in the afternoon. The Battery's casualties in this engagement at Campbell's Station were two men slightly wounded, one colored mule driver killed, three horses and two mules killed, and six horses wounded. Several wheels were splintered and the axle of a gun-carriage was broken. The Battery fired 441 shots in all.

CHAPTER IX.

THE TENNESSEE CAMPAIGN. SIEGE OF KNOXVILLE.

As soon as it was dark the troops began leaving the battle field of Campbell's Station, but it was 9 o'clock before the last of our army departed; the killed and wounded had to be left behind. Knoxville was reached at 5 o'clock in the morning of November 17th, with men and horses entirely worn out. The troops were halted in the valley between Fort Sanders and College Hill. When the command "Halt," was given every man dropped just where he stood, and it did not take them long to fall asleep, for they had been in constant motion for four days and four nights. Every regiment and battery received, on its arrival, written information of the position to which it had been assigned by Col. O. M. Poe, who had reached the city previously with instructions to make these arrangements.

Gens. Sanders and Foster had been holding Knoxville pending the arrival of our army, but as soon as the army came up they left the city to go out and guard those approaches by which the enemy would probably come. Gen. Foster went to the south side of Holston River to the point where a pontoon bridge had been placed, while Gen. Sanders went just outside of the city north of the river on the Loudon road to guard our rear and delay the advance of the enemy. He did this successfully the whole of the 17th and till half past two in the afternoon of the 18th. At that hour he fell mortally wounded. His command then fell back to Knoxville. Fort Sanders was named in his honor. After about three hours sleep the various organizations proceeded to occupy the positions to which they had been assigned.

From the 17th of November to the 28th, the officers and men of Battery L were busily engaged in building a fort on College Hill, which was afterward named Fort Byington, in honor of Major Byington of the Second Michigan Volunteers, who was mortally wounded during the siege. The fort was completed at 3 P. M., Saturday, November 28th, and was strong enough to withstand any assault made upon it. The parapet was seven feet high and twelve feet thick at the base. The work was lined with green bullock hides to prevent splinters from flying, as the revetment was made of boards and shutters taken from the College, and of similar materials obtained in the neighborhood. Logs could not be obtained because the enemy had possession of all the woods around Knoxville.

That the reader may more thoroughly realize what our troops endured in this campaign, it is only necessary to say that, in pursuance of an order from Gen. Burnside issued October 18th, 1863, to the effect that "not more than one-half, nor less than one-quarter rations per day shall be issued to the officers and men until further orders from these Headquarters," all had been living, marching, fighting, and working on a very scanty allowance of food since that date. This order was not revoked till long after the siege of Knoxville was over. Men and horses suffered greatly from hunger, to say nothing of cold and sickness. Every man in Gen. Burnside's command, from the general commanding to the private soldier, was thoroughly aware of what was in store for him, if we did not succeed in defeating Longstreet's army, and that was, to be taken prisoner, if he were not killed in the inevitable battle impending over us. All preferred death to capture.

To replenish the magazine, five hundred shell besides a considerable amount of other ammunition were received during the afternoon of the 28th. The men of the Battery now began to prepare for the coming assault by laying out the friction primers, making spikes, and putting all other necessary implements in their proper places. Never before had it been deemed necessary to prepare for spiking our guns. The spikes were made from small rat-tail files ; they were barbed and as hard as fire and water could make them, yet extremely brittle. When the artificer brought one to me for inspection, I took it between the first and second fingers of my right hand and snapped it in two as easily as if it were a pipe-stem. "Artificer," said I, "that's the stuff the Johnnies willl have to tackle in boring out the vents of our spiked cannon, if they get any that are spiked."

I now inspected the ammunition and found it to be in good order so far as I could see. Then I inspected the fort on College Hill and the rifle-pits in front of the fort. The fort on the Hill just completed was provided with seven as good and well-protected embrasures as could be built under the circumstances. Below the fort were two rifle-pits running from the north or right bank of Holston river around to the west, then south towards Fort Sanders—most formidable works. These were to be held by our most trustworthy troops.

The elevation of College Hill is about the same as that of Fort Sanders, each being about forty or fifty feet above the level of the surrounding country. College Hill has a very steep incline southerly extending back to the river some 400 yards, and it is fully one hundred feet from the bottom of the hill to the water's edge. Fort Sanders stands on a knoll, with a descent on all sides, the steepest inclines being on the west and north. Battery Zoellner was a small fort to the right and rear of Fort Sanders. Fort Byington on College Hill was somewhat to the left and rear of Fort Sanders and distant from it about 550 yards in an air line. Between Forts Sanders and Byington was a short but deep valley that would have been a spot very dangerous for the enemy, had they succeeded in entering it in an attempt to charge either fort. In such a case, the loss of life would have been appalling, for those in the valley would have been exposed to an enfilading fire from both forts of grape and canister, as well as shrapnel. The last missile is a terror to troops in a charge, for a single one can and may destroy forty men when it explodes.

Nov. 27th two of my pieces, those under the charge of Sergeants A. Townsend and Val. Rossbach, and commanded by Lieut. Heasley, were ordered to Fort Sanders. Sergeant Townsend's piece was put in position at the northwest embrasure, and Sergeant Rossbach's at the northeast one. Between these two, and occupying the northern embrasures, were two of Lieut. Benjamin's 20-pound Parrotts. The artillery in position in Fort Sanders consisted of Lieut. Benjamin's 4 20-pound Parrotts (Battery E, 2d U. S. Art.), Capt. Buckley's 4 12-pound Parrott rifles (Battery D, 1st R. I. Art.) and Capt. Roemer's 2 3-inch 10-pound rifles (34th N. Y., Ind. Battery). The infantry in the fort comprised the 79th N. Y. (Highlanders), the 2d, 8th and 17th Mich. Vols., and some detachments from other infantry regiments.

At 9 P. M. on the 28th, a feigned attack was made on Fort Byington with musketry and artillery. Several hundred bullets and dozens of cannon-shots were exchanged and then suddenly, everything became still. I now called together all the members of the Battery remaining in Fort Byington and thus addressed them :—" Officers and men, that which has just occurred was merely a feint; the real attack will be made before daylight in the morning. Guards will now be changed every half hour instead of every two hours. Fuses must be dried, and a stick having notches cut in it, showing the number of seconds the fuse will burn, two to seven, as the case may be, attached to each, so that No. 7 (the man having charge of the fuses) can find them in the dark, as I may call those numbers."

It was now 9:15 P. M., and just as I finished speaking to the men, an aide on Gen. Ferrero's staff rode up and said, "Captain, I wish to see you privately." We two went aside out of hearing of the men, and then the aide said, "I have a verbal message for your ear only. The general desires that if things go against us in the coming attack, you shall destroy the horses and so disable your guns that they cannot be used against us." This was a thunderbolt to me. After a moment's hesitation I said "I cannot obey such an order as that. Tell Gen. Ferrero that, when it comes to such a pass as that, I want to use my own discretion." "Captain," returned the aide, "you know you will be held responsible for what you say." "Yes," I replied, "I know full well what I am saying. I fully understand what Gen. Ferrero wants me to do, but pray tell him that I cannot obey this order, and also say to him that I fully understand the matter and will give the enemy a shot for every spoke he wants me to cut and a shot for every horse he wants me to kill, but will not cut a spoke or shoot a horse, and, when I can shoot no longer, then I will spike my guns and let them go. That is my answer to the general. I have the spikes in my pocket. See," said I, taking them from my pocket, "here they are."

The night was cold and dreary. Every man was forbidden not only to undress, but also to take off his accoutrements, so that he would be ready to take his post at his gun or elsewhere at any moment. The guns were loaded and shotted, ready to be fired at the very first notice of the attack. The men passed a long and wakeful night, for their bellies were empty and their bodies only half-clad, yet not a murmur escaped them. All on duty were watching and peering out into the darkness to catch the first inkling of the dreadful things they felt sure were in store for them. Midnight came, but there was no change. Two o'clock A. M. November 29th came, and still no change was noted. Five o'clock, and still all was silent. Soon after five the gleam of fuses and signal rockets became suddenly visible through the western embrasures. Instantly Fort Byington and Fort Sanders were alive, but remained silent though watchful. In a few minutes thereafter, all the guns of the rebel artillery along the Union front opened fire with the evident intention of smashing all the guns of the Union artillery.

Immediately the 34th N. Y. in Byington opened fire upon the eight-gun rebel battery in its front, near the Armstrong house. But four shots had been fired when I discovered that none of the shells exploded. "Cease firing," I ordered. "Hand me one of those shells." I pulled out the fuse plug and found that the powder would not run. "These shells are corroded," I said; "every one must be bored out before it can be fired. I want two brave men to bore them out. I want volunteers and at once." But no volunteers stepped forward. At last, I offered myself as the first brave man, whereupon Sergeant Volkmar offered himself as the second, saying, "Captain, if you are willing to risk your life, I am ready to risk mine with you." The boring of the shells was at once begun just behind the parapet between the two guns. Soon we began firing again. The gunners aimed their pieces exactly at the flash of some one of the rebel pieces, since it was quite dark. They made many excellent shots, for the shells exploded right in the rebel ranks and created great havoc among them.

At last the enemy managed to send a shell right over Fort Byington. It passed over the parapet just over the heads of Sergeant Volkmar and myself and struck an ammunition chest, bursting as it did so, and sending eight 10-pound shot spinning around the fort like marbles. They would not, however, have been as harmless as marbles if they had struck any on the ankle as they whirled around. Sergeant Kaufman became greatly excited, jumped up and cried out, "For God's sake, stop your work; you will have us all blown up if you bore those shells here in the fort." I instantly thought that, if I had anything to say, now was the time to say it. I rose from my kneeling posture and called out, "Sergeant, mind your own business and I will mind mine." Then stepping out into the center of the fort, I said, "Boys, I want to know if you will stand by me in this fort or not. I mean to die here rather than surrender. What have you all to say?" With one voice all cried out, "Captain, we will die by your side." "That is all I want to know," said I. "Now, not another word from any one of you. Obey my orders implicitly, and everything will be in our favor."

At 5:30, while still quite dark, a horseman came galloping into Fort Byington. It was an orderly from Fort Sanders with an order from Lieutenant Benjamin, Chief of Artillery. He halted and gave me the order. It read thus, "Capt. Roemer, send to Fort Sanders fifty rounds 10-pound shrapnel, fifty 20-second fuses, and all available canister, without delay, by your own teams, under escort." The order was at once obeyed and the ammunition sent.

By 6 o'clock, everything was at at a boiling heat. In Fort Sanders it was even hotter, with a tendency upward, on account of the canister and the wire entanglement in its front. Looking through my glass, I could see the teams sent with the ammunition in accordance with the order mentioned above. How they plunged and tore along! On they went at a dead gallop, almost flying! Sergeants Townsend and Rossbach could be plainly seen working their guns to their utmost capacity, sending 156 bullets at every discharge of their guns into the ranks of the enemy.

Although Longstreet thought on the day before, it would be an easy thing to take Fort Sanders, he did not think so on the 29th, when he saw his brave men march up in solid columns to face the embrasures of Fort Sanders only to be struck down and broken by the grape and canister hurled at them by the well-served guns of the fort.

By this time it was broad daylight, as the sun rose at half-past six. The ditch surrounding Fort Sanders, and especially that part around the northwest bastion, was half full of dead and wounded. The living scrambled over them and over the parapet in their endeavors to take the fort, only to meet a broad-ax, a bullet, or a bayonet, which hurled them back, dead or wounded, into the ditch below. There stood brave Benjamin with his fifty rounds of shrapnel, each fitted with a twenty-second fuse. Lighting the fuses with his cigar, he hurled them one after the other, over the parapet into the ditch below, to intensify the terror already prevailing there and on the ground in front. Every one of the steady solid columns of the enemy that came marching up within reach of the grape and canister hurled at them by the guns of the fort, broke and fled despite all the efforts of their officers to re-form them.

Everything on Longstreet's side was hopelessly lost, for, as it was reported of the 5,000 brave men who, in light marching order had charged on Fort Sanders after 5 o'clock, three-fourths had, by 7 o'clock, been killed, wounded or taken prisoner. The garrison occupying Fort Sanders during the fight, did not exceed 450 men, infantry and artillery together, not counting those belonging to the Eighth Michigan, who were stationed in the trenches on the northeast side to support the gun of the Thirty-Fourth New York Battery in position there, and who, from their peculiar position, could do but little in repulsing the attack on the northwest bastion.

A flag of truce was now raised,* and firing ceased all along the lines. The officers now gathered together to congratulate one another on the success of their efforts to repulse the assault made on our works. Gen. Ferrero came to me and said, "Say, Roemer, you sent me a hell of an answer last night." "General," I replied, "I couldn't help it." "Captain," said Ferrero, "when I received that message I knew old Roemer was all right."

Just as Gen. Ferrero left me Gen. Burnside rode up from behind. After saluting, he asked, "Captain Roemer, why did your shells all explode with such precision this morning, while those fired by the other batteries did not?" "I can not say, General," I replied. "I do not know." "Yes, you do know," said Burnside, "What did you tell your sergeant in the fort last night?" "I hope, General," I replied, "you will not hold me responsible for what I said to my officers and men at that time to encourage them for the impending contest of the night and the following morning." "Yes, Captain," Burnside exclaimed, "I *do* hold you responsible for every word you said to your officers and men last night, and I am proud to know what you said to your sergeant,—'Every one of these shells must be bored before it is fired.'—Who bored them?" "Sergeant Volkmar and I did," answered I. "How many?" he asked. "We bored

---

*Neither Col. Poe, U. S. A., nor Gen. Alexander, C. S. A., make mention of this in their accounts of this assault on Fort Sanders.—[EDITOR.]

sixty that were fired at the eight-gun rebel battery in our front," I replied. "How many did that battery fire at you?" he inquired. "Some three hundred and twenty," I replied. "How great are your losses?" the general then asked. "I have had two men slightly wounded, two horses killed, and two wounded," I replied. "Captain," he now asked, "do you know how much damage your shells created in the rebel battery in your front?" "I have no idea," said I. "Well, Captain," he continued, "their losses were twenty-four killed and upwards of sixty wounded. Now, Captain Roemer, tender to your officers and men my most sincere congratulations for the efficient manner in which they performed their duty last night and this morning, and also tell them I greatly admire their bravery. It is such men as you and some others that I must thank that we are free this morning." With an affectionate adieu and a smile on his face that I had not seen there in three long weeks. Gen. Burnside left me. I felt happy and grateful to him for his very kind and flattering words to the Battery.

CHAPTER X.

CLOSE OF THE TENNESSEE CAMPAIGN. RE-ENLISTMENT. VETERAN FURLOUGH.

From this time on until the seventh of December, the Battery remained in position in Fort Byington, engaged in doing everything necessary to put the Battery into perfect condition for active service.

Orders came at 7 A. M., December 7th, to move the Battery by sections out on the Morristown road to support weak points in our lines. It went out seven miles, occasionally halting to fire a shot. The next day it reached Roseberry Creek, twelve miles distant, and on the day following went to Blain's Cross Roads, seven miles farther, and on the 10th advanced to Rutledge, thirteen miles farther still, halting from time to time to go into position and fire a few rounds. It remained near Rutledge until the 14th, when it fell back two miles, and at 11 P. M. fell back seven miles, arriving at the Mills at 3 A. M. on the 15th. Six hours later it returned to Blain's Cross Roads, going into position at 4 P. M. Here it put up some huts for shelter, as there were no tents in the command. Even the officers had only one tent fly, which was used as a roof for a hut, while the gable ends were closed with blankets. These huts were our abode for several weeks, or until January 15, 1864. Most of the battery equipments had been lost November 16th, during the retreat from Lenoir's Station to Campbell's Station.

The Battery was posted on a table land or low mountain, overlooking our infantry, so that it could protect them with its fire. At this time there was a great dearth both of hard coal and of charcoal among all commands, and, therefore, it had become impossible to shoe a horse. As a result, the horses were, with a few exceptions, shoeless. How to have them shod became the question of the hour. As there was plenty of wood about, it occurred to me that it might be possible to make some charcoal, if any one could be found who knew how to make it. At retreat roll call I inquired if there was any one who knew anything about charcoal burning, and ordered those that did to step two paces to the front, whereupon three men stepped out. I told First Sergeant Johnston to bring them to my tent. He did so, and after talking with them, I came to the conclusion that it would be safe to try to make some.

The next morning bright and early we started out. I had already selected some trees, as I knew what kind of wood was necessary, although I knew nothing more. A sergeant was sent out with six ax-men and three teams to cut and haul the logs to a suitable place for our kiln, where they would be cut up and split, ready for burning. The kiln was then built and well covered with sod. By night everything was ready to start the fire. It was lighted and and the burning went on properly for four days and nights, but on the fifth day, towards morning, the guard not being very watchful, the fire broke through the sod covering, and in ten minutes eight cords of wood became a heap of ashes instead of a pile of charcoal. I looked at the ashes a moment and said, "Boys, I can burn charcoal now. Sergeant, take your ax-men and teams at once, go out, cut, and bring in ten cords of wood. We will start a new kiln to-night." I had water brought so as to have it at hand in case of need. When the wood was piled up, I caused the sods to be packed over it very firmly to prevent another outbreak. Fire was started in the new kiln that same night and five days after, we had a pile of as good charcoal as was ever burned. This charcoal I considered to be the property of Battery L, and when the general's orderly was sent to get a bushel to shoe the general's horses, I told him that the charcoal belonged to Battery L. When the orderly returned and told the general what I had said, the general replied, "I know it, but if you ask Capt. Roemer for it in a pleasant way and tell him I appreciate his efforts fully, and also know he need not give it unless he is willing, but that my horses need shoeing, I think he will give you the charcoal." The orderly came back to me and this time obtained the charcoal. When it became known that the Battery had plenty of charcoal, there was a great demand for it on all sides ; some even tried to get an order for it from the general, but he told them, one and all, that the charcoal was the property of Battery L, and they could not have any unless the Battery people were willing to give it. About this time, orders came for the men to prepare to go home on their veteran furlough, and as that was of more importance to them than the charcoal, it was given out with a free hand, in fact, it could be had without asking for it.

Between November 15th, 1863, and January 2d, 1864, sixty-nine of the seventy-one enlisted men belonging to the Battery had re-enlisted ; the majority did so on the former date. The Battery and many other organizations that had re-enlisted had expected to go home on their veteran furloughs as soon as the re-enlistment was accomplished, but the needs of the service had compelled them to wait until other troops could come to take their places. By Special Order, No. 514, from the Adjutant-General's Office at Washington, D. C., issued November 19th, 1863, Battery L was detached from the 2d N. Y. Art., to form an independent Battery, to bear a number to be designated by the Governor of New York, and the 2d N. Y. Art. was authorized to recruit a new company of Heavy Artillery to take the letter vacated by the Battery. January 16th, 1864, Special Order No. 15, from Headquarters, Ninth Army Corps, was received. This ordered me to turn over to Capt. Buckley, Battery D, 1st R. I. Art., all the ordnance and ordnance stores in my possession, retaining only one baggage-wagon and six mules for the transportation of rations and the men's knapsacks to the point where the command would take the cars on their way home to Long Island, for a veteran furlough of thirty days in accordance with orders from the War Department, Washington, D. C.

I was also directed to go to the Headquarters of the Ninth Corps at once. I went there immediately, and Gen. Burnside said to me, "Gen. Sturgis has made a formal application to me, to assign your Battery on its return from its veteran furlough to his corps in Tennessee. Now, Captain, what do you say about it?" "Well, General," I replied, "have I a right to say anything?" "Captain," said he, "you have all to say." "Then, General," said I, "it is very easily settled. If I have all to say, I will stay where I am, with the Ninth Corps." Then congratulations came thick and fast from all the generals and other officers of the Ninth Corps who happened at the time to be at Headquarters. Capt. Hicks, of Burnside's staff, then approached him and said, "General, we ought to give Capt. Roemer something as a momento from the Ninth Corps, in recognition of the meritorious services rendered to us by him while he has been with us so far." Gen. Burnside almost instantly replied to the suggestion, "Capt. Hicks, present Capt. Roemer with the flag he so bravely defended at the siege of Knoxville." Then came hurrahs for Battery

L. and, after bidding all adieu, I returned to our camp. Just as I was leaving Headquarters, Gen. Ferrero came to me and said, "I am going to your camp with you; I want to give your boys a little speech." He did so and made a very fine speech, in the course of which he referred to nearly every battle in which the Battery had taken part since it had been attached to the Ninth Corps, in September, 1862, just before the battle of Antietam. He commented on the superior marksmanship of its gunners, the accuracy of their aim, and its superiority in maneuvers on the battlefield. Referring again to Antietam, he said, "Boys, when you crossed that three-arched bridge over Antietam Creek on the 17th of September, 1862, you made a name for Battery L. I wish you much pleasure on your furlough as veterans, and that I know you will have, for you have well earned it." After bidding officers and men "good-bye," Gen. Ferrero returned to Headquarters.

At 10 A. M. that day, the 16th, the Battery left Blain's Cross Roads for Strawberry Plains, where it arrived at 3 P. M. The Battery started out the next morning to cross the Clinch Mountains on their way to Cumberland Gap. Lieut. Heasley and I remained behind to complete the transfer of ordnance, and ordnance and quartermaster's stores, four guns, battery-wagon, forge, baggage-wagons, and seventy horses, to Capt. Buckley, Battery D, 1st R. I. Art., as directed by Special Order, No. 15.

The rations served to the men before starting consisted of three bushels of corn, which was to last them until they reached Cumberland Gap. Before starting, however, I received an order from our Quartermaster on the Depot Quartermaster at the Gap, for an issue to the Battery of four rations per man, as there were none at Strawberry Plains. I also obtained five green bullock hides, for there were fifteen men without shoes. These hides were cut into strips about eighteen inches wide. A strip was wound around the foot and ankle in such a way that it would protect the feet on the march over the mountain.

Lieut. Heasley and I now followed the men, reaching the bivouac at Flat Creek at 9 P. M. on the 17th. The Battery had halted at the mill. The miller's residence was a short distance away up the side of the mountain. Some of the boys went up to pay him a visit, for they had learned somehow that the miller had two daughters, and they had thought it no more than right that they should pay them some little attention. They were soon on a friendly footing with the family, and what with singing and dancing, they made no little noise. This noise was what they wanted (they had planned it before hand), and when it had become sufficiently great, those left at the mill started the wheel and proceeded to grind the three bushels of corn issued to them in the morning, the noise of the mill being drowned by the noise at the house. Not being satisfied with the corn they had brought they did a little foraging, and found in the upper loft of the mill about four bushels of corn, which they also ground and added to what they already had. Michael Nau, a miller by trade, and another of the Battery boys, took charge of the grinding. The seven bushels of meal thus obtained were rapidly and securely packed and placed in the wagon as a resource for emergencies.

The boys also took possession of the miller's barn on the opposite side of the road from the mill. All this had occurred before we reached the bivouac. While Lieut. Heasley and I were yet some half a mile distant we could hear the singing and merry-making and smell a savory order. When we, finally, reached the place, we found the men engaged in baking corn dodgers. They invited Lieut. Heasley and myself to join them in their sumptuous meal, which we very willingly accepted, for, since morning we had tasted nothing. It was as good as a feast, though the meal consisted of nothing but corn dodgers washed down with good, cool, spring water. Such food, furthermore, was all we could expect to get for some time to come, as the order of October 18, 1863, was still in force,—"Not more than one-half, nor less than one-fourth, rations to be issued to officers and men."

The party at the miller's house did not return until after 10 P. M. During the repast, the story of the strategy used to start the mill was related. Therefore, taking all things into consideration, I thought it best, to avoid all controversy with the miller, to order a resumption of the march at 4 A. M.

At the designated hour on the 18th, the Battery marched away. Snow and rain were falling, and we marched but nine miles, halting near Flat Creek, in front of a farm house. I inquired for its owner and was told, "The mistress is boss." The mistress appeared. "Madam," said I, "what I want to know is simply this,—can I use your barn to shelter my men to-night and have some straw for them to sleep on?" She answered, "Yes." The men took possession of the barn at once. Then I asked the woman, "Have you anything to eat in the house?" She replied, "No, not a morsel." "My good lady," said I, "if you have anything in the house for my men to eat, I will pay you for it. Now, if you have and won't let me have it, my men will be welcome to what they can find, and any complaining on your part after they have taken it will be wholly useless." "Well, Captain," said she, "all I have in the house is one ham." "Bring it," I said, "and put it on the table." It was brought and it proved to be a good-sized one. "I have sixty-nine men," I now said, "now cut the ham and show me how much you will give me as one ration for each man. I will give you twenty-five cents a ration of one corn dodger and ham." The amount cut was satisfactory. I ordered First

Sergeant Johnston to see that each man received the same quantity as was shown by the sample. The distribution was made and First Sergeant Johnston reported that it was all right. I then paid the bill.

I then asked the woman if she would give my men a light breakfast in the morning. She answered, "No, I have not another morsel in the house." "Well, my good woman," said I, "I should like to give my men another good meal, for they have not had one in three months, and as we are going among the mountains I would like to have them have one good meal before we start." "I am sorry to say, Captain," she replied, "I have nothing at all in the house." "All right," said I, "but if you have lied to me, and you complain in the morning, just recollect that I shall give you no satisfaction." After their supper of corn dodgers and ham the men slept very well.

In the morning, as soon as I was up, the mistress came to me and said that during the night three of her largest hams had been stolen. "Madam," said I, "it is nothing to me how many of your hams have been stolen. You either lied to me last night or you are lying now. I cannot believe anything you say. If you had laid those hams on the table last night I would have guaranteed their safety. We are 'Yanks;' anything that is laid on the table the 'Yank' will vouch for." Nevertheless, I ordered a search to be made in the wagon and in the men's knapsacks, but not a trace of the hams was to be found, and I was then fully convinced that my men had stolen no hams.

We marched on, and at 9 A. M. reached the Clinch River, which was crossed by a rope ferry. The ferryman became quite impatient because the men were so long in embarking, for some of them had gone to visit the houses near by in search of corn dodgers or whatever other eatables they could find. Finally, we started, but had gone but a little way only, when I saw on the top of the hill one of my men with both hands full and heard him shouting, "I want to go along too." We backed to the landing and he came aboard. Soon we reached the other bank and resumed the march, which continued all day. The Battery reached Cumberland Gap January 20th, after a march of seventeen miles. Here the men were easily provided for as regards shelter, as there were regular barracks which they could use. Here, too, we expected to draw sixteen days' rations, four in arrears and twelve in advance, a total of 1,104 rations for sixty-nine men, which would last them while crossing the mountains, but, to our bitter disappointment, I found I could draw one-half a ration only per man and that for only one day at a time. I also learned that we would have to wait one week before we could draw any rations for future use, because we must wait until the provision trains should arrive from the north. I drew the one-half ration and returned to camp, and when I acquainted the boys with the facts I had learned concerning the rations, they became wild. They wanted to start off at once over the mountains without rations and trust to luck for food, they were so eager to reach home. But such a thing as that was not to be thought of, for it might result in a court martial of the Battery's commander.

I must here say that the march from Strawberry Plains to Cumberland Gap had to be conducted with the greatest caution, as the whole country around was infested with guerillas and bushwhackers who did not hesitate to shoot any Union soldiers they saw. I used my two horses, ridden by good men, as cavalry flankers, two hundred yards off on each flank when going through the woods or along roads, as circumstances demanded, to protect the men and the baggage wagon. The men of the Battery were directed to march in a body concentrated around the wagon, as that was our only fort and fire-arms were scarce. There was in the whole command but eight sabers and eight revolvers.

After distributing the rations already drawn, I made searching inquiries concerning rations and learned, much to my dismay, that nothing could be done to help us. We could draw half rations only and those day by day only, as stated before. We finally concluded to go ahead. I told the men I had no authority to go on without a proper supply of rations, and if we did start without them, every man must sign a statement exonerating me, as their commander, if any mishap should occur during the journey, from want of food, over the mountains from Cumberland Gap to Camp Nelson, Ky. Every man signed the statement and then crowded around me to induce me to give them a dollar or two each that they might buy what could be bought from those at the Gap who had food to sell. By the time I had finished giving out money, I found I had given out the sum of eighty-five dollars. They soon made their purchases and then were eager to start on their journey through the wilds of the Cumberland mountains. I was very much afraid our supply of provisions would not be sufficient to carry us through alive.

The start was made at about noon January 20th, and, at first, we did very well, but it was not long before we came to snow, and, of course, had to sleep in it wrapped up as best we could be, in our blankets, with no shelter over us. The wheels of our wagon had to be wound with ropes to keep them from slipping and sliding over the precipices covered with ice and snow. This had to be repaired every morning as the wear and tear to which it was subjected every day tore the wrapping completely off.

For two or three days during our tramp over the mountains, our cook, Billy Howard, brought me for breakfast several slices of fine ham. I questioned him closely as to where they came from, as I knew our mess chest contained nothing of the sort. All he would say was, that they had bought it at some place on the road. I knew that in that part of the country the houses were some thirty or forty miles apart, and the country itself so poor that a sparrow would starve to death in harvest time, consequently I did not believe he was telling the truth. However, I said nothing, but ate the ham and was glad enough to have it.*

The march over the mountains was a rough one, for most of the men had no shoes and all had no shelter whatever at night. Besides these discomforts rations were extremely short, for, during this march of eleven days our sixty-nine men and two officers had but the seven bushels of meal, and (what was unknown to me at the time) the three hams stolen from the widow's house at Flat Creek, together the small quantity of provisions purchased by the men individually at Cumberland Gap. Nevertheless, and in spite of these discomforts, the men were happy, for they were going home.

The Battery arrived at Camp Dick Robinson January 28th, and here the first rations were drawn. It then crossed the Kentucky river to Camp Nelson, arriving there on the 29th.

---

* Six years afterward, a reunion of the Battery was held at College Point, near Flushing, L. I., in commemoration of the battle of Blue Springs. After the banquet, when speeches and toasts were in order, one of the boys arose, and, addressing me, asked, "Captain, did you ever find out who stole the three hams from the widow at Flat Creek in January, 1864?" "No," I replied. "Well," he continued, "you ate many slices of those hams during the march over the Cumberland mountains; and this is the way we kept you from finding out anything about them. Whenever we halted, we removed them from the wagon and buried them in the snow, where they remained until we started forward again, when they were replaced in the wagon. It pleased us greatly that we succeeded in keeping the matter secret. Now, however, the secret is out." "Well, boys," said I in reply to this unexpected disclosure, which solved the puzzle which had so long mystified me, "all I have to say is they were certainly the very best hams I ever tasted in my life."

Here each man was fitted out with a suit of new uniform clothing, shoes, and the necessary amount of underclothing, including shirts, drawers, and stockings. When this was accomplished, the men were truly presentable. Had our Flushing people seen them before they were thus transformed into respectable looking soldiers, I doubt if they would have given them a night's shelter, for some of them, I must say, had scarcely clothing enough to cover their nakedness. I had had no opportunity to draw clothing for them since the beginning of the Tennessee campaign. Our greatest privation was the want of coffee, of which we had had none for six weeks. A train in which there were three wagon loads of it, came within three miles of us at Knoxville, but was captured by the enemy, and it was this same capture that prevented us from obtaining clothing. We were then completely surrounded by the enemy and no supplies of any kind could reach us.

The Battery finally reached Nicholasville, where it took the cars at 3 P. M., January 30th, for Covington, where it arrived at 4 A. M. on the 31st, and went into barracks assigned it, where the men could once more stretch themselves on a cot. Here it remained nine days, which were spent by the officers in making out muster and pay rolls, and also the bounty rolls for the enlisted men. Each man that had re-enlisted (all that were with me had done so) was paid to November 15, 1863 (the date of the re-enlistment rolls), and also received $100 bounty for services rendered. Furthermore, each re-enlisted man received for re-enlisting $400 from the United States, $300 from Queens County, N. Y., and $75 from the State of New York. No commissioned officers were entitled to these bounties.

After the men had passed three nights in the barracks, I noticed on the morning of the fourth day, that there was a great deal of coughing among them while on their way to breakfast. I halted them and said, "I thought last night that I had a lot of dogs with me instead of men, judging from the amount of barking I heard during the night. All through our march over the mountains when you slept every night amid snow and ice, I did not hear any coughing at all." At once, one of the men spoke up, "Well, Captain, we aren't used to civilization yet."

On the ninth of February, the men having received their pay and everything being ready, we started for Albany, N. Y., to report to the Governor of the State in accordance with the orders of the Secretary of War. We arrived at Albany on the 11th. Gov. E. D. Morgan received us with all the honors that could be bestowed upon veterans. In his address of welcome the Governor dwelt at length upon the Battery's work on the battlefield and upon the hardships encountered during our long marches. Among other things he said, "Boys, I am proud of you, and, Captain, the fact that this little band has re-enlisted under your command shows that they like you and are willing to follow you through all dangers. Captain Roemer, I now give you the official order changing the designation of your Battery, which will hereafter be styled the Thirty-Fourth New York Independent Veteran Volunteer Light Battery. The War Department notified me of your coming, and has also informed me of your valor in the field. Now, Captain, my friends and friends of this Battery desire to have the honor of entertaining your brave boys for one night." "Your Excellency," I replied, "I have already telegraphed to our townspeople of Flushing that we will be there to-morrow." "Captain," said he, "I beg of you to allow me and the Sanitary Commission to entertain you and your command for one night." "Well, your Excellency," I replied, "I accept your very pressing invitation to us and thank you in behalf of my command."

We were most sumptuously entertained with a fine dinner by the ladies of Albany, and, I need not say, we did full justice to it. The next day, the 12th, we left Albany for New York city, where we arrived the next morning at 5 o'clock. The Sanitary Commission at Albany had telegraphed the New York body to have a good breakfast ready for us. Then, after a hearty meal, we marched across the city to James Slip, where we took the ferry to Hunter's Point (now Long Island City) where we took the cars for Flushing. While crossing the meadows before reaching the village, I caused my two buglars to sound their instruments a few times to herald our coming. These were heard in the village, and the church bells began to ring and the people to assemble at the station on Main street. As soon as we arrived at the station, I ordered the men to fall in, and then we marched out to the street.

When I beheld the crowd of people assembled there, I was bewildered and knew not what to do. Just as we emerged from the station, Charles R. Lincoln * saw that I was overcome. He came to me and said, "I know what the matter with you is. You had not expected to meet with such a reception as this. Take my arm." The next familiar face I saw was that of G. R. Garretson, who smilingly approached, grasped my hand and said, "Words at such a time as this are useless, but I must say, 'Welcome to you and your brave boys.' Captain, you are the same true Roemer you have always been." All the while the bells continued ringing. Fire engines, hose carts and firemen were hurrying around and forming line. Citizens were crowding around me to shake my hand. Even the ladies crowded around me congratulating my men and myself. My head was in a

---

* Mr. Lincoln was at that time editor of the Flushing Journal, and to him I had telegraphed the evening of the 11th regarding our arrival.

whirl, and I knew not how to command myself. To witness the patriotism and receive the welcome of the citizens of my adopted town, unnerved me more than being on the battlefield. The line was quickly formed and we marched down Main street to the Liberty Pole, where we once more saluted "Old Glory," and thence to the Flushing Hotel. All along Main street, there were crowds of men, women, and children assembled to greet us, while ever and anon, one or another ran out to meet and grasp the hand of some one in the Battery in hearty welcome. When we had reached the hotel, the Rev. Dr. Smith was the first to meet me in welcome, while a host of ladies and gentlemen pressed around us, speaking words of hearty welcome. We were then invited into the dining room where a bountiful repast awaited us, and of which we partook while the ladies waited on us and did the honors of the occasion. The dinner was a grand success, that did great honor to its projectors. The band of veterans who enjoyed it, had good reason to feel very grateful for the dinner and the welcome that accompanied it. When the banquet was over, we separated with orders to report at Fort Schuyler, New York Harbor, March 13th, 1864, after the thirty days' furlough. We all were very anxious to visit our own homes to meet those who were impatiently awaiting us.

While we remained in Flushing, we gave, at the request of a large number of citizens, an exhibition drill with two pieces on the old camp ground, then known as Camp Todd. Of course, now all is changed, but at that time Congress avenue was all of twenty feet higher than it is now. This camp ground was then the finest piece of land that could be selected on which to organize and drill the Battery. As we lay here nearly three months before leaving for the front, old Camp Todd will never be forgotton by the Battery boys who were here initiated into the United States service, so long as they shall live. The maneuvers performed by the boys were greatly appreciated by the spectators, but I must say I did not have such complete control over the men during this drill as I was accustomed to have in the field, for, as they were on their veteran furlough, I could not put any one in the guard house.

According to all reports, the boys had a right royal time during their furlough, and were very willing to return to the field and again face the dangers and hardships of war.

One day while at home, I received as a present from Mrs. Abraham Bloodgood, a fine gold and enameled pen and pencil case. The present was accompanied with a note, which read as follows: "I send you this memento in recognition of your valor, and also for use in keeping your accounts with the Government of the United States."

A meeting of the officers of the Ninth Corps was held on the 11th of March, at the Fifth Avenue Hotel, New York City. I was notified to be present also, for the meeting had been called for the purpose of a consultation regarding the reorganization of the Corps, and the arms to be used by the different regiments and batteries, especially the latter, in the coming campaigns. At this meeting I learned that Gen. Burnside desired to have the 34th N. Y. Battery armed with six Napoleon bronze guns, for flanking purposes. I remonstrated against this, for we were wholly unused to such guns, and I did not want to have to give up my practice with rifle-guns, to learn something so different. Capt. Benjamin, Chief of Artillery, now came to my assistance and asked Gen. Burnside's permission to say a few words in my behalf. The desired permission was given, and Capt. Benjamin went on to say, "Then, General, I shall recommend that you give Capt. Roemer what he wants. He has always been extremely proud of his rifle battery, and, in every position in which he has been placed, he has always proved himself master of the situation." Gen. Burnside then said, "Capt. Roemer, you shall have your rifle battery again. I had selected you for Napoleons, to be one of my flanking batteries, but I give way. Are you satisfied, Captain?" "Most assuredly I am." I answered. Both Capt. Benjamin and I thanked him for this decision.

Gen. Burnside then asked, "How are you getting along with your recruiting—have you nearly made up your quota? I wish you to report when it is full." I had already reported in writing that same day that eighty-five men had been obtained. After reporting the number I then said, "General, I have not had a day to myself since we came home, and I would very much like to have a few days with my family." "Well, Captain," he replied, "you deserve them and shall have them." Thereupon, he wrote out and gave me an order granting me ten days' leave of absence in addition for myself.

I did not return to Flushing till the next day, March 12th, but when I did, I found awaiting me an order from the War Department directing me to report at Fort Schuyler on March 15th, and have my command shipped on the steamer *Moses Taylor* for Staten Island, where it would be transferred to the steamer *Fanny* for transportation to Annapolis, Md. The latter steamer had already on board 1,000 infantry, and these, as well as the Battery, were placed under my command. Thus it will be seen my ten days' leave was cut very short.

CHAPTER XI.

RETURN FROM THE VETERAN FURLOUGH. THE WILDERNESS. SPOTTSYLVANIA COURT HOUSE.

The men began reporting for duty at Fort Schuyler on March 13th, but not all had reported by the 25th. On that date, however, all present were embarked at 4:30 P. M. on the steamer *Moses Taylor* and were transferred to New York city, where they went on board the steamer *Fanny*. The *Fanny* set sail at 10 A. M. on the 26th for Annapolis, Md. The first day of our voyage was very pleasant, but on the morning of the second there were indications of a coming storm. At 11 P. M. it came, and with a vengeance. It blew a hurricane, and by the time we sighted Cape Henry light, it really seemed that we would be unable to weather it, indeed, the *Fanny's* captain said if we had been ten minutes later in coming around, we would have been dashed upon the rocks, a result that would probably have been fatal to the 1,150 men under my command. One mast was broken off flush with the deck and went overboard. On looking down into the hold the next morning we beheld the sorriest looking crowd one can ever expect to see anywhere.

However, we arrived safely at Annapolis at 5 A. M., and disembarked at 7 A. M., March 28th. I immediately reported to Col. Hartranft, commanding the Ninth Corps, and received orders to take the Battery to Camp Parole and draw the necessary camp and garrison equipage. For the next two days, 29th and 30th, a severe storm kept us confined to our quarters.

On the third of April there was presented to the Battery by Miss Celia L. Roe, afterward the wife of Samuel W. Bowne, and daughter of Capt. George B. Roe, of Flushing, a magnificent silk artillery guidon. It bore the names of the most important engagements in which the Battery had taken part.—"Cedar Mountain, Sulphur Springs, Second Manassas, Fredericksburg, Vicksburg and Knoxville,"—while on the staff was a silver plate inscribed, "Hamilton Light Artillery of Flushing, N. Y." For the purpose of receiving this guidon with proper honors, the Battery had been drawn up in line, and when the beautiful emblem of our contests had been presented and unfurled, I told the men they had the best reason to be proud of it, for it was presented to the Battery by one of the young ladies of Flushing as a memento of our past services. I then asked them, "What will be the duty of every man in the Thirty-Fourth New York Battery should this beautiful guidon be in danger of capture?" In reply they shouted, "To defend it at all hazards." I then passed the guidon to First Sergeant Johnston, and he in turn passed it down the line, and each man as he grasped the staff vowed he would never allow the guidon to be disgraced or captured. In order to impress upon my brave men the importance of defending their flag, even at the cost of their lives, I read to them the order of Lieut.-Gen. Grant, our new General-in-Chief, as follows:

"Any regiment, battery, troop, or separate command in the field, that loses its flag by capture or otherwise, will not be allowed to carry one thereafter until it has captured a standard from the enemy."

April 14th the Battery received orders from Gen. Burnside to go to Washington and then to Camp Marshall, and there to draw guns, caissons, battery wagon, forge, baggage wagons, and horses. All these were received April 22d. There were six three-inch rifled ordnance guns, weighing as follows: —723, 729, 747, 749, 752 and 753 pounds, six caissons, one battery wagon and one forge, and the full number of horses. I received orders on April 24th to draw all stores and ammunition needed for the full equipment of the Battery, and to be ready to cross the Potomac with the Ninth Corps on Sunday, April 25th. The Battery received at once all the supplies called for with the exception of saddle-blankets, which could not be had. I, therefore, instructed the drivers to use their own blankets as such until the proper ones could be obtained from the arsenal. At 9 P. M. the Battery being complete in every detail, a report was sent to Gen. Burnside's headquarters that the Thirty-Fourth New York Independent Veteran Volunteers Light Battery was ready to receive marching orders. Fifteen minutes later an order came assigning the Thirty-Fourth Battery to the post of honor at the head of the Ninth Corps, over 20,000 strong, to lead it across the Potomac over Long Bridge into Virginia on the morning of the 25th of April.

The next morning all were up bright and early, and made all the necessary arrangements for an early start on the march. The boys were highly elated over the honor bestowed upon them by Gen. Burnside, and performed their duties with great alacrity. The Battery left Camp Marshall at 10 A. M., April 25th, on its way to Long Bridge, and passed down Pennsylvania avenue in review before President Lincoln, Lieut.-Gen. Grant, Gen. Burnside and many other officers, both military and civil, who had assembled together on the balcony of Willard's Hotel and saluted as the Battery and the other troops passed by. We, of the Thirty-Fourth Battery, at the head of the column, with a cavalry escort in front, felt that we were being subjected to a very close scrutiny by the military officers, and were, therefore, bound to appear at our best. The cannoneers sat on the ammunition chests as rigid and erect as English cockney coachmen, with folded arms, and acted as if they thoroughly appreciated their dignity and the importance of the occasion.

The Battery crossed Long Bridge and halted near Alexandria. The next day it marched to Fairfax C. H., and on the following day to Bristoe Station, then went forward and arrived at Warrenton Junction April 28th, where it went into camp and put four pieces in position, and on the 30th was mustered for pay.

On the 4th of May, the day appointed by Lieut. Gen. Grant for a grand combined advance against the enemy by all the armies of the United States, east and west, the Battery started for Rappahannock Station. It reached Rapidan River on the 5th, crossed it over a pontoon bridge, and went into camp about one mile beyond it. At 6 A. M. the next morning (May 6th), it marched to the Wilderness. Here the Battery was ordered into a position through an aide. Looking around, I immediately saw the position was one not at all fit for artillery to take, as it was wholly surrounded by large trees. The enemy's infantry could easily advance and destroy my cannoneers, while I could not give our infantry the proper support. I then asked the aide from whom he received orders to have the Battery take that position. "From Headquarters," he replied. I then halted the Battery and rode forward to the battle line to see Gen. Willcox. There learning he had just gone to the right of the line, I followed him. Coming up with him and saluting, I asked, "General, did you assign me to that position in the woods?" "Yes," he replied, "don't it suit you?" "No, General," I said, "it don't suit me at all." "Well, Captain," he returned, "go back and take any position that will suit you, provided you can protect the infantry and your own Battery, and hereafter, if you think you can do better in some other position than in that to which you may be assigned, exercise your own judgment."

I returned and at once changed position to the rear of our line of battle, on a commanding knoll, where I found a large force under the command of Major W. A. Treadwell, 14th N. Y. H. Art., which had been ordered to support the Battery. Major Treadwell had just formed his line of battle, and his men were engaged in throwing up breastworks to protect us and his own men. After reaching a place in his rear which just suited me, the Major came over to my position and said, "You have selected an elegant position, and I am here to support you." The fighting contact was coming nearer and nearer every minute, and I told him we had no time to lose. He set his men to work, and, in the course of an hour, six fairly good shelters were raised.

By noon, the Battery was ready to give the rebels a warm reception. During a lull in the fighting that occurred just at this time, I sent word to my cook to bring up a little lunch, of which I invited Major Treadwell to partake. He accepted the invitation readily, as he had eaten nothing but one "hard tack" for nearly forty-eight hours. Our table was the limber chest of gun No. 2, and we quickly finished a can of quail, which I thought was chicken, as there was none of the toast which usually goes with quail. The Major declared it tasted better than any other meal he had eaten so far during the war. After we had finished our repast, we lighted our pipes. While we were enjoying a good smoke, the roll of musketry and the booming of cannon increased greatly in volume, but as no bullets, shot, or shell came uncomfortably near us, we paid but little attention to them.

While still sitting on the limber chest, I thought a little nap would not be out of order; I lay across the chest and closed my eyes. Hardly had I done so, when a rebel bat-

tery opened fire upon our lines, and especially upon the 34th
N. Y. Battery, but their shots went a little too high. A
moment later a line of gray emerged from the woods directly
in our front. Instantly I opened the limber chest, seized a
cartridge and a shell and had a gun loaded. In less time
than it takes to tell the story, our six guns were busy hurl-
ing grape, canister, and sharpnel into the enemy's ranks.
These and Major Treadwell's bullets were more than rebel
flesh and blood could stand, and, after a brave attempt to
stem the tide, they broke and made for cover, while we
continued pouring shot and shell into their ranks until they
were out of sight and beyond our reach. This result was
hailed with cheers by our supports. Major Treadwell was
highly delighted with the conduct of his own men and pro-
fuse in his praises of the 34th N. Y. Battery. In fact, he had
a better opportunity for observing the effect of the Battery's
fire than any of the Battery had, for his position was in
front of us. He reported to us that the Battery's fire was
terrible in its effect, and that not a single shot failed in doing
execution. The coolness of all the troops at this point was
remarkable, for a portion of Major Treadwell's command,
consisting of the 24th N. Y. Vols. and the 2d Wis. Sharpshooters, were raw troops. The sturdy old veterans of the
14th N. Y. H. A. were, however, at their backs, and, therefore, they fought well.

At dark, the advance of the army to the left, to flank the right
of Lee's army, necessitated a change in the position of the
Battery. It quietly limbered up and moved out on the Wilderness road, and was followed a little later by its supports under
Major Treadwell, who had also charge of several wagons
laden with intrenching tools. It was, furthermore, his duty
to guard our rear, and he did his work well, for all the wagons,
tools, and stores were brought off without the slightest loss.
At midnight the Battery again changed position.

Orders came at 2 A. M., May 7th, to keep a most vigilant watch upon our front, and if the enemy were found pressing our pickets back to open fire at discretion. This soon occurred, and the Battery gave them five rounds. At 5 P. M. we fired fourteen rounds more, and at 7 P. M. orders came to be ready to march at a moment's notice. The order to march came at 11 P. M. The Battery moved a few miles and then halted, remaining in column all night and until 7 A. M. on the 8th, at which hour it continued the march to Chancellorsville, where it arrived at 5 P. M. and encamped. At 9 A. M. the next day, the 9th, it marched to Gage's Hill. Here one section was put into position while the other two sections were kept ready to act when and where an emergency might require.

At 10 A. M. the whole Battery moved forward and soon a general engagement with the enemy ensued, lasting until 7 P. M. In this engagement the Battery fired 380 rounds and, fortunately, suffered no casualties. The next day, the 10th, all was quiet until 4 P. M., when the ball again opened. Here the Battery was supported by Major Treadwell's battalion on the right. The enemy charged fiercely on our front looking towards Spottsylvania, C. H., and on our left flank. The position was near the Beverly House. The battle was a severely contested one, but we maintained our ground in spite of the foe's repeated charges, and remained masters of the field. At 5 P. M. the Battery fell back across the Ny River. At 5 A. M. on the 11th orders came to take the former position at the Beverly House. Everything was quiet during the day and the succeeding night, but at 6 A. M. on the 12th the enemy opened fire on us. The morning was very foggy and, consequently, all firing was wild, producing no very serious results.

Gen. Willcox and his aide, Capt. L. Curtis Brackett, came up to the Beverly House to see how the troops were posted.

Gen. Willcox gave orders to hold the left, but said at the same time, "Captain, I must take Lieut. Heasley and your first section with me to the right and center." I remonstrated against this, saying, "There are now ten pieces opposed to my six, and if you take Lieut. Heasley and one section away, it leaves the odds against me too great—ten rebel pieces against my four." Gen. Willcox replied, "I must have one of your sections with me to-day, and if you find during the day you cannot maintain your position with the two sections left, any artillery in the rear is at your command by my order." He then rode off with the first section while Capt. Brackett remained with me.

Capt. Brackett and I ascended to the top of the Beverly House, gaining access to the roof through a skylight by the side of a big chimney. This latter shielded us for a time from the enemy's view, but when the fog lifted they discovered us observing their movements, and announced their discovery by a number of shots at us from their batteries in position near Spottsylvania, C. H. Capt. Brackett soon disappeared through the skylight, after begging me to go with him, but I had told him I was not satisfied with the appearance of things on the left and must have one more good long look through my glass. Presently, the captain looked out through the skylight and remarked, "Captain, they are getting the range on you." And so it appeared, for he had hardly uttered these words, when a number of shots rattled around the chimney, and I thereupon followed Capt Brackett's example, and went through the skylight, closing it after me. Almost instantly afterwards the whole chimney came down with a startling crash Brackett called out, "What the devil is up, Roemer? Are you hurt?" "No," I responded, "we have the best of them this time. The scuttle above us is closed." The weather was now quite clear, and we could see from our position that the rebels had everything ready to give us a heavy dose of iron pills from their batteries on the hill and on our left in front of a farmhouse where four pieces were stationed We opened with two pieces on these four, and with the other two on the six-gun battery on the hill. It was now 9 o'clock A. M., on the 12th,

At ten o'clock the battle opened all along the line and it was growing quite hot around the Beverly House. Ten rebel guns against four Union guns was rather to great odds. At 10:30 the firing was constant, but so far the Battery had suffered no losses excepting two horses badly wounded. At this juncture Gen. Willcox and staff, attended by about twenty-five orderlies rode up. The General inquired how I was making out. I replied that it was becoming pretty hot. "But can you hold your own?" he asked. "That," I responded, "is what I always try very hard to do" At that moment his attention was attracted by some object among the trees and he asked me what animal we had tied up there. I told him it was one of my men who had been playing truant for a week, and had been seen only when he came to draw his rations. On the last occasion I had ordered the sergeant to detain him, and, having provided two lariats for the purpose, had ordered him to be tied up to two trees in a position which would place him directly under the enemy's fire, as that seemed to be the only way I could keep him in action. Gen. Willcox was much amused by the incident and said, "That's right, Roemer, keep him there till sundown."

That same day, Major Treadwell's regiment with a number of other regiments were on the Battery's right. The Major, after hearing the above story, said in his quick, bluff way, "I'll bet he is a big bounty man. Keep the G-d d—d son of a —— there and get him killed, if possible, for the good of the service." But he was not to be killed. Although tons of iron and lead flew his way, nothing touched him. Upon being untied at night, he disappeared and was never seen again. At all events, if he is still living, he can truly say he went through *one* battle.

By eleven o'clock the battle on our front and left had become very hot and heavy. Seeing that my four pieces could not stand long against the rebel ten, I instructed my lieutenant, Chas. R. Lincoln, to pay all due respect to the six guns on our left and then rode off at a gallop to obtain assistance. I found and brought up two pieces of Capt. J. W. B. Wright's 14th Mass. Battery and placed them some two hundred yards apart, so that I could bring all six pieces to bear on any one of the enemy's guns I chose. While I was placing this section in position on the left, Lieut. Lincoln who commanded the right section of the 34th N. Y. Battery, came up and said he could not hold his position as the enemy had cross-fire on it. I inquired what losses he had suffered, and he replied that several horses had been shot, and that nearly all the trees in the woods had been shot down. I ordered him to go back to his section and stay there so long as he had one cannoneer for each piece, and, furthermore, told him I would soon be there. When I finished putting Capt. Wright's section into position, I galloped back to the right section of the 34th to find out what the trouble was. As soon as I arrived, Capt. Brackett met me and halted. Just then a couple of shells burst right under our horses. Each thought the other was killed, but both were uninjured. He then said, "Well, Roemer, how do you make it?" "Captain," I replied, "I can't tell you now, but this fight will have to be settled within twenty minutes." As we rode up to the right section, I said to the 34th, "Boys, Battery L has been in twenty-six battles and has never given an inch to the rebels. I want to know who of you wants to get out?" With one wild yell, they shouted,

"Captain, so long as you are with us, we will die by your side before we will flinch."

Looking over the situation I saw with my glass that the six-gun battery south of us and near a house, had some men in the house giving signals to the others to guide them in directing their fire upon us. I then told my men I would give them ten minutes to destroy that six-gun battery, and that, if they didn't, we were gone. I ordered Sergeant Rossbach to bring his right gun in front of the Beverly House into a garden, and see if he could put a few percussion shell into that farm house just over the front door, taking the panels under the windows just above the door for his target. At that moment I could see some artillerymen sitting on a bed and watching us. Sergeant Rossbach took in the situation at once and became very much excited, so much so that I tried to calm him down somewhat, but he replied, "I know I am excited, but I well know what you expect me to do. You have given me the cue and I'll be d——d if I don't open that door."

He opened fire on the house with percussion shell, and after the second shot the rebels could be seen going out of the house through the front door as fast as human legs could carry them. The fourth shot set the bed on fire, for the shell entered the room right below the window sill. Smoke now began to issue from the house, and then we knew it was doomed. I now mounted my horse and told Sergeant Rossbach that, just as soon as he saw me down at the left section, he should change to shrapnel and knock that six-gun battery into a cocked hat. The cannoneers of Sergeant Rossbach's piece were obliged to lie under the muzzle of the gun on their backs while loading it, and when the gun was fired it recoiled from six to ten feet, because the position was on rising ground.

I then galloped down to the left section and ordered the cannoneers to change from shrapnel to percussion shell and direct their fire upon the farm house so that no one on the rebel side would venture to attempt to put out the fire. I also found that my other section had been doing great damage to the four-gun battery stationed nearer Spottsylvania Court House. Sergeant Rossbach's piece made terrible work of the six-gun battery, for it was wholly knocked to pieces; so many of its horses were killed and badly wounded that two pieces only could be dragged off the field, the other four being left behind.

By this time the farm house was entirely destroyed, and I ordered Sergeant Rossbach to turn his piece and the other gun belonging to that section upon the four-gun battery near Spottsylvania Court House. Firing by battery they soon silenced the four guns, and then the enemy's artillery spoke no more. We now believed that the combat was ended, but, in this, we were mistaken and disappointed, for a cavalry charge which startled me came directly toward us. I ordered shrapnel and percussion shell to be fired, with the guns aimed at the horses' hoofs. Twelve shots caused the cavalry to halt and turn back, and as they turned I ordered four shots fired at the horses' tails. That was the last we saw of any cavalry that day.

I now took out my watch and said to the men, "Boys, I will give you ten minutes to destroy the remnant of the six-gun battery." They did it splendidly in seven and one-half minutes. I then despatched an orderly post haste to headquarters to report that all the artillery and cavalry in my front had been subdued. I then explained to the men why our position had to be held at all hazards, saying, "If we had been driven out of it we would have had to fall back five or six hundred yards directly under the enemy's fire, and many of us would, doubtless, have been shot in the back. I don't fancy having any of my men thus wounded."

Many of the officers of the infantry regiments in our front and on our flanks, who had observed the Battery's fine work, and especially Major Treadwell, commander of our immediate support, now came up and congratulated us in the warmest manner. They all thought that the Thirty-Fourth New York Battery had had a narrow escape from annihilation during the hot contest.

My orderly now returned from headquarters with orders from Gen. Willcox for me to put another battery in my position and then proceed with the Thirty-Fourth to the right, and to report in person at headquarters as soon as possible. I immediately sent for another battery, and, as soon as it was in position, sent the Thirty-Fourth to the rear of the line of battle of the First Division, and then with my orderly went by the shortest route to Gen. Willcox's headquarters to obtain further orders. I told Gen. Willcox the Battery was coming and asked for the Chief of Artillery to assign me my position. Capt. Benjamin, Chief of Artillery, was not there then. Gen. Burnside now rode up and asked, "What does Capt. Roemer want?" Gen. Willcox replied, "To find Benjamin to have a position assigned him." Burnside then turned to me and said, "Captain Roemer will not wait for the Chief of Artillery, but will look out for a place to suit himself." I thanked the General for his confidence, but he replied, "No thanks, Captain, you know best where your Battery is wanted."

I then galloped off with my orderly toward the right. The battle line of the Ninth Corps ran west from the extreme left of the Union lines toward the right, where it joined the left of the line of the Second Corps, commanded by Gen. W. S. Hancock. His line ran north, nearly at right angles with the Ninth Corps line. To reach this point we had to ford Spottsylvania Creek. In this angle was a fine knoll that was the position for a battery, as it afforded a good defense against attacks made by the enemy on either Hancock's or Burnside's lines. Two pieces only of Hancock's artillery were at all near, about six hundred yards distant to the north. Eleven pieces of the Ninth Corps artillery were about eight hundred yards west. I looked on this position as one that had been entirely neglected, and yet it was a most important one for artillery.

We then rode back to the creek, as I wanted to find out where the Battery could cross it in the easiest way and as quickly as possible. The western bank was very steep and from six to eight feet back from the water. I wished the Battery to cross as nearly south of the knoll as possible to the eastern bank, so that the gun carriages might have shelter as soon as they had crawled up the bank. I then sent my orderly to bring the Battery up to the place I had selected. The crossing was exposed to the enemy's fire. The first gun carriage crossed safely in spite of three shots aimed at it by the enemy, and all, finally, crossed in safety, though some twenty shots came from the enemy. The only casualties were splashes of black creek mud and water spattered over the men. Captain Hogan, our medical officer, who witnessed the crossing, has often said since then, "I can yet see your Battery, men, horses, and guns, getting up that bank at Spottsylvania Creek, but how they got up is a mystery to me."

The position selected had a clear field to the south and rear of it, extending some five hundred yards from the creek. The Battery was placed in position on the knoll without attracting the enemy's notice. Everything being in order and the Battery being entirely shielded and invisible to the enemy, I ordered the men to lie flat on the ground. They had lain so for about fifteen minutes, when, suddenly, the rebel yell was heard, "yi-yi-yi." The four guns were at once shoved forward and loaded with shrapnel. The enemy were charging on Burnside's line to our left, thus presenting their left flank to the Battery, and gave us a chance to send our shots directly lengthwise of their line from left to right. Taking my glass to observe the effect of our fire, I ordered the men to fire all four pieces by battery fire. The effect was terrible; we could see plainly the great gaps made in their line. This fire was repeated once, twice, and five times; and great was the consternation among the Confederates. With the fifth battery fire the charge was broken, and I gave the order "Cease firing." At this order, No. 7 of the cannoneers of each piece, whose station is at the limber chest, must put all shot, shell, or shrapnel into the chest. While they were doing this, Major Hutchins, one of Gen. Burnside's aides, came up from the rear of the right piece, and asked, "What battery is this?" "The Thirty-Fourth New York," responded No. 7 of that gun detachment. "It can't be," said the Major, "That battery is on the left." "Major, I tell you this is the Thirty-Fourth New York, sir," insisted No. 7 in a louder tone. "Well," asked the Major, "where is Capt. Roemer?" "There he is," replied No. 7, "by the left piece with his glass in his hand." No. 7's loud tones attracted my attention and I looked around to see what officer he was addressing. I recognized the Major and asked him, "Major, what's up?" "What's up?" he repeated, "Why, another feather in your cap, old fellow. Do you see Gen. Burnside up on the hill there overlooking your position? He said to me when the enemy's charge was broken, 'Go down there and see what battery that is that has just done such excellent service; it must be noticed; it was a God-send. Never have I seen such a deadly fire in so short a time.'" He then rode back to Gen. Burnside to report.

Soon after, Capt. Benjamin, Chief of Artillery, came galloping up the hill. Dismounting, he put his arm around my neck and kissed me heartily. He then said, "Roemer, it was a God-send that you were here. You want more artillery here." "This is the place, Chief," I replied. He went off and sent me three pieces more. From this time on our drivers down at the creek did not have so pleasant a time as they had been having earlier. The rebel artillery now directed their fire mainly at us, and all stray shots that went over us the drivers got. As all the baggage-wagons, ambulances, etc., were stationed there, for a time, great consternation prevailed there among the drivers. Some even cut the traces and ran off with their horses. When Dr. Hogan next saw me, he said, "Whenever your Battery takes position before my operating table again, I will get out."

Capt. Benjamin came back soon after the three pieces he had sent me, had arrived, and asked me to go with him. I told him he had better leave me with the Battery, but he said, "No, I want you to go with me. Put your First Lieutenant in command. I want your opinion regarding the line on the left on the Spottsylvania, C. H. road, as there are some very bad places in our front." We rode along the whole line towards the left. As we reached one very bad place, I said, "I would advise the placing of a regiment of infantry in the rear of this particular place." Benjamin immediately replied, "That's just my opinion, too, Roemer. I wanted you opinion because you have been around here more than I have and are better acquainted with the country. Now, I want to say, Roemer, that you did great execution with your guns this afternoon. I was also told by Gen. Burnside that you had also wiped out the six-gun battery at the farmhouse, and burnt the house, which alone was a great feat, and, furthermore, had silenced the four guns posted near the Court House." "Captain," said I, "I have some very good gunners and they are the ones I must thank for the work done to-day. You will find very few gunners that are the equals of my sergeants, Rossbach and Starkins, for accuracy of fire, and all my chiefs of pieces can hold their own with any others of that grade in the Ninth, or any other corps." "Roemer," he continued, "I want to ask you, how many shots did you fire at the rebel line that attempted to charge the right of our Ninth Corps' line this afternoon?" "Five battery fires from four guns." I replied. "The execution was terrible," he went on, "Gen. Burnside was amazed, and he was right behind you on the rear prolongation of your line of fire."

While on our way down toward the left, we called on Lieut Heasley, commanding the first section of the Thirty-Fourth New York, temporarily detached from the Battery, and found he had been right in front of the charge made on the hill.

When I returned to my command I learned that nearly all our ammunition had been expended. I reported the fact to Gen. Willcox, and asked him to have another battery put in my place. Gen. Willcox immediately came to our position and told me not to withdraw the Battery, but to send out and obtain from other batteries all the ammunition that was to be had that would fit our guns, till further orders. At midnight, May 12th, the Battery withdrew from the field. It had, during the day, fired 950 rounds. Our casualties were, two men wounded, three horses killed, and thirteen wounded. I was, myself, struck three times by spent balls, one of which might have proved fatal, as it struck my field-glass and nearly threw me out of the saddle.

The next morning, May 13th, a general order from Gen. Grant was received at the Ninth Corps Headquarters. It referred to all the troops in the field, that had taken part in the battle of the previous day, the battle of Spottsylvania Court House, and praised the soldierly spirit and bravery displayed which, he said, "deserved especial mention." The Thirty-Fourth New York Battery was not forgotten in this order. In reference to that organization, the order read thus: "The Thirty-Fourth New York Independent Volunteer Veteran Light Battery, has again signalized itself, as it has done in many former battles, but its performance of yesterday requires especial mention." Gen. Burnside, in commending the Battery, expressed the hope that the influence of its example would be felt by all. The members of the Battery received particular commendation for their soldierly conduct.

CHAPTER XII.

NORTH ANNA RIVER. COLD HARBOR. FORT FLETCHER. BEGINNING OF THE SIEGE OF PETERSBURG.

Everything was quiet along the lines during the two days following the battle of Spottsylvania Court House. The caissons of the Battery returned from the ammunition train on the 15th with 600 "Schenck" percussion shells and 70 fuse shells. The Battery had gone into position again on the 14th, but had no occasion to fire until the 16th, when eighteen rounds were fired. The next day everything was again quiet, and both men and horses enjoyed a much needed rest. At 5:30 A. M. on the 18th the enemy made an attack on our lines, which was quickly repulsed, for the Battery fired but twenty-five rounds. A second and severer attack made by the enemy in the afternoon was repulsed after 287 rounds had been fired. The next day the Battery marched three miles farther to the left by sections, and I was ordered to give men and horses a good rest, if they should not, in the meantime, be called into action. During the evening of the 22d, the Battery marched in the direction of North Anna River, and continued the march the next day and reached the river, where it encamped and threw up breastworks.

Here on the 24th the Battery was called into an action that lasted all day, and fired 473 rounds principally at the rebel works on the other side of North Anna River. At 6.30 P. M. the enemy's artillery opened fire on the Battery, but the latter silenced them after firing some thirty rounds. The next day an engagement opened at 5 A. M. and lasted until 8 P. M., but the Battery had occasion to fire but thirty-seven rounds. The only casualties to the Battery were two horses wounded. The next day the Battery received 889 rounds of ammunition from various sources, and fired forty-nine while protecting Gen. Warren's Fifth Corps during the crossing of North Anna River, after having first crossed the river itself for that purpose.

Orders came at 11:15 A. M. on the 27th to march at once to the Pamunkey River, ten miles distant. The Battery went forward and went into camp near that river at 12 P.M. At 4 A. M. the next day it moved nearer to the river which it crossed at 11:30 A. M., and went into camp one mile south of it. Men and horses were thoroughly worn out, and besides the Battery was short of both rations and forage. Orders came on the 29th to march to Hanover Town, three miles distant, where during the following night it threw up breastworks, but soon after, it withdrew and went into a cornfield one mile south of the last position. The next day it marched three miles farther south and went into position with its six guns and one section of the 7th Me. Battery, consisting of 12-pounder Napoleons. Here it fired two rounds and then remained quiet the rest of the day; five of the wounded horses died.

On the first of June, two pieces were, by order of Gen. Burnside, turned over to the ordnance officer, thus making the Battery, one of four guns. It was now in position at Salem Church. Here twelve recruits joined from Hart's Island, New York Harbor. The Battery left Salem Church at 12, midnight, June 1st, and after marching five miles, went into position with two other batteries, the Seventh Maine, Capt. Twitchell, and the Fourteenth Massachusetts, Capt. Wright, at 2 A. M., June 2d. Our infantry were being very heavily pressed by the enemy, who were trying their best to push it back or break its line, and I gave my gunners orders to give our infantry all the support they could possibly give. We were near Cold Harbor.

From the Battery's position it was not possible for me to observe the rebel line as I wished, but I found a place about fifteen yards in rear of it, on a slight elevation, whence I had a clear view of the whole field of operations. I was soon discovered in this place by the rebel sharpshooters, who evidently thought I was a good target, judging by the way their shots were directed against me. One of my men noticing the danger to which I was exposed, as also did the officers of the other batteries, called my attention to the danger, and told me to leave the hill, as I would otherwise become a fit subject for the undertaker, but, because I could find no other place that would afford me the same opportunity for directing the fire of the three batteries, I stood my ground and said, "If I have to die here, I am willing to do so, but all you have to do is to obey my commands and try your best to save our infantry." Just then one of my men, James Cavanagh, jumped up and stood in front of me, trembling violently, and swaying from side to side to cover my person. His actions sent a thrill through me, as I thought of the sacrifices my men would make to preserve my life. I tapped him on the shoulder and asked him, "Jimmy, what does all this you are doing, mean?" "And sure, Captain," he replied, "if you are kilt we are all lost, but if I am kilt you can save the boys." "Well, Jimmy," said I, "you are a brave boy and I will never forget you." All this took place in just about ten seconds.

I could now see that the enemy were being forced back; that the fire of our batteries was very effective; and that we still held our lines. The casualties this day were few. I was wounded by a bullet striking me over the right eye and slightly injuring the skull, yet it was not serious enough to compel me to leave my men. Three horses were killed and four wounded. During the day the Battery fired 237 rounds.

On the 3d of June, at 1 A. M., our three batteries opened fire from our former position, and at 1 P. M. went to a position about half a mile to the left from which we could do more effective work in silencing the enemy's batteries. The fighting was general along the whole of our lines. The casualties in the Thirty-Fourth New York were, one man killed and five wounded, three horses killed and six wounded. The number of rounds fired was 67, leaving 726 on hand. In this position the batteries remained until June 6th, when the enemy began shelling our camp, and we were ordered into position on the road to Cold Harbor. During the night following, the men of the three batteries threw up breastworks under orders from headquarters, for the Fourteenth Massachusetts on the right, the Thirty-Fourth New York in the center, and the Seventh Maine on the left. The men worked hard all night, for, according to our instructions, they had to make them unusually strong.

A very strong fort, named Fort Fletcher, was also to be built at a point one-half mile to our left. After laying out the *tracé* of the fortifications to be occupied by the three batteries, I was ordered to Fort Fletcher to superintend the construction of that work until 1 A. M. of the 7th, at which time I was to be relieved, for I had had no sleep during the three preceding nights. I was not relieved, however, until 4 A. M. During the night, it was very dangerous for the men to go on top of the works, because one man had been killed there and three wounded. Finally, I ordered the men who were at work to come in, and told the colonel commanding the infantry that I thought the work was strong enough for the infantry to hold easily during the following day. It had a frontage of between three and four hundred feet, and was four and one-half feet high, besides the ditch.

I then returned to our own camp to see how the work was progressing there, and found that all the sergeants, but one, Melsom, had each fully completed his part of the work. The men were at breakfast when I arrived. When they had finished I called out all the men of the Thirty-Fourth New York, to go ahead and help finish that part of the work. I then reported to Gen. Willcox that the three batteries were all ready for action. Early in the morning they opened fire, firing at intervals until past noon. At about 2 P. M. the enemy made their first charge. It was made without a preceding artillery fire. The charging column had scarcely reached the middle of the field before it was broken by the fire of the three batteries. Just as the retreating column reached the woods from which it had emerged, we saw that thirteen pieces of artillery were being put in position, on a bluff, in rear of the retreating troops. They immediately opened a deadly fire on our three batteries; each piece was fired at will, and as rapidly as possible without waiting for commands. Their artillery officers were evidently bound to silence our three batteries if they could. We were not long in answering this terrific fire, and deliberately shelled the woods in which their infantry were concealed from our view.

Finally, becoming convinced that their artillery were trying to destroy ours, I thought it best to let them think they were doing so, and then called Capts. Wright and Twitchell and Lieut. Heasley together for a consultation. I told them what I thought the rebels were trying to do, and that it was best for us to encourage them a little. So far, we had suffered but little from their fire. I ordered Capt. Wright on the right and Capt. Twitchell on the left, to slacken fire, and after a few minutes to cease altogether. Five minutes later, I ordered Lieut. Heasley, commanding the center battery (the Thirty-Fourth New York) to cease firing, and the gunners of the three batteries to lie low. At this stage of the game the infantry began to grow angry at our seemingly queer behavior, and were not slow in making sarcastic remarks about the three batteries in their rear, snugly esconced in their strong works, and even went so far as to say, "Roemer's three batteries are going to hell this time, sure. I guess he's met his match this time," and made other similar remarks; but, "All's well that ends well." We, behind our works were not idle a moment. The three battery commanders were taking in the whole situation and preparing for what they believed was coming, that a fierce charge was to be made on our lines. I gave orders that all three batteries should fire at the signal, which was to be one shot from the Thirty-Fourth New York, and all should aim at the feet of the charging column. Every gun was ready, loaded with shell. Soon the rebel yell was heard in the woods in our front, and this notified us that the expected charge had begun. The battery commanders gave the orders. "Attention," "Ready." When the rebel column had advanced about two hundred yards from the woods, I gave the command, "Fire." The fourteen guns were fired as one gun, and the fire was like a thunderbolt to the enemy. It stunned the entire column. This combined fire by the three batteries in unison was repeated five times. The charging column then broke and turned their faces in the direction of the woods whence they had started. Then I gave the order "One more by battery fire at their backs," which fire drove them back faster than at a double quick.

By this time our infantry supports had changed their minds regarding the three batteries, and now they shouted, "Three times three for old Roemer and the three batteries." I can not enumerate the many congratulations that were sent to us in the fort. Gen. Willcox came galloping into the fort, and said, "Roemer, you old rat, this is the best trick you have played yet." The infantry suffered the most from the rebel artillery fire directly in front of us during this great charge upon us at Cold Harbor. Directly in front of our three batteries, was Col. J. F. Hartranft's brigade, composed of the Fifty-first Pennsylvania, One Hundred and Ninth New York, and the Second, Eighth, Seventeenth and Twenty-Seventh Michigan regiments. All these shared in the glory of the occasion, for they all had had to endure the terrific rebel fire for a long half hour. No one who has not had the opportunity of being with an infantry regiment under such circumstances, can form any idea of the mental suffering endured by infantry when compelled to remain quiet while such an artillery fire is playing upon them, and they have no chance to do anything to defend themselves. Many times have I heard infantry officers say they would prefer to engage in the most desperate charge, than lie inert under such circumstances. It is the suspense that makes lying still so dreadful. The casualties in the Battery were this day (June 7th), five men wounded, two horses killed, and seven wounded. Among the latter was my black charger, which was hit in the shoulder. During the day the Battery fired 257 rounds.*

---

*On the 19th of October, 1881, I was in Yorktown, Va., attending the centennial celebration of the surrender of Lord Cornwallis to Gen. Washington. There I met a number of officers of the Ninth Corps with whom I had a talk about the days gone by. Some one of them spoke of the second charge made by the rebels on our lines at Cold Harbor, and began to guy me by saying, "You let us lie in front of you and receive the fire of the rebel artillery while you lay behind your strong works and laughed at us." During the conversation, I had noticed three men who were standing by and evidently listening to our conversation regarding that terrible charge. At last, one of them stepped up to us and said, "Gentlemen, excuse me, but we three"—pointing to the other two, —"were in the Confederate army at the time and took part in that charge on the Union lines at Cold Harbor, and you," he continued, ad-

On the eighth of June the Battery was ordered to Fort Fletcher, which work it immediately proceeded to strengthen on its left flank, while firing at intervals during the day. The next day some sixty rounds were fired. It was found that some of the enemy occupied the rear of an abrupt hill, a position which could be reached by mortars only, and these we did not have. As necessity is the mother of invention, on the 12th of June, I tried the plan of burying the trail of one of my pieces in the ground, so as to give the gun an elevation of about forty-five degrees, in order to throw some percussion shell over the hill. Although we used but six ounces of powder for a charge, it was too much, for our shells passed over them. I sent a man to a point where he could watch the effect of the shell, and then fired again; still the shell went beyond them. The look-out man could see the tents and the men there encamped. The powder charge

---

dressing me," were the Captain commanding the Union artillery at that point. Gen. Lee had himself assured us that your artillery had been silenced, and that a charge would easily break the 'Yankee' infantry line and capture their artillery. He, himself, led the charging line out of the woods, and told us we would certainly succeed. We had gone but two or three hundred yards when we heard the heaviest thunder-clap I ever heard in my life, while my comrades fell right and left. We went on until the fifth fire was poured into us, and then we could stand it no longer. Our line was completely broken, and we were ordered to retreat to the woods. While going back we picked up many of our wounded and carried them back with us. During our retreat another thunderbolt struck us before we could reach the woods. When we did, finally, reach the woods, Gen. Lee received us and said, 'Boys, this was a sad charge, and he who commanded the Yankee artillery most certainly understood his business, and all I wish is, that we had such artillery.' Now, Capt. Roemer, I wish you would grant my two comrades and myself the favor of taking a brotherly drink with us, so that we can tell our comrades at home, in South Carolina, we had the honor of taking a drink with the commander of the Yankee artillery who broke that charge at Cold Harbor." As it was over a mile to the hotel, besides being very hot and dusty, I had to decline, but gave them my hand in good-fellowship, and told them that if we met again before leaving Yorktown, I would be glad to do them the favor they had asked me. J. ROEMER.

was now reduced to five ounces, which proved to be just the right amount, for each shell dropped where it would be the most effective; the enemy were soon shelled out of their comfortable quarters by this use of a rifle gun as a mortar.

During the afternoon some prisoners were taken, and one of them said their officers were exceedingly surprised when the percussion shells began to fall into their camp, bursting and creating havoc generally, and wondered what kind of guns the d—d Yankees had that could fire percussion shells in that fashion. That day the Battery fired fifty-three shells in that way, and about twenty in the ordinary way.

While the Battery remained in position in Fort Fletcher, Lieut. Garretson, who had joined the Battery at North Anna River, proved to us that he possessed all the qualities of a true soldier. He was, at the time, in command of the caisson camp in the rear. I sent him a message to bring up 150 rounds of ammunition to the fort, but to be very cautious how he acted when he should arrive at the entrance of the covered ditch where it intersected the line of rifle pits. We had learned that some of the enemy's sharpshooters had been placed at points that would command that intersection, with orders to fire on any men or ammunition wagons, especially the latter, they might see passing through. Lieut. Garretson and his train came safely through into the fort, for the enemy's shots failed to score. The enemy knew, however, that the caissons would have to return from the fort, and, therefore, kept up a close watch for them. We had an inkling of their intentions, and I cautioned Lieut. G. to be very particularly careful, and ordered the men who accompanied him to obey his orders, strictly, when they reached the danger point. Just as the train was about to leave the covered way, Garretson gave the order, "Run," and the train went on at a dead gallop. We could hear the bullets strike the ammunition chests, but the train went through otherwise unharmed. There were all of five hundred officers and men of the infantry collected outside of the fort in its rear, who were watching the train, and thus saw the whole affair, and I could hear them praising Lieut. Garretson's courage. When the Lieutenant returned to the fort, I said to him, "Now, Garretson, you have made a name for yourself. Take good care of it." This he modestly promised to do.

At 8 P. M., June 12th, the Battery left Fort Fletcher and went to Tunstall's Station, arriving at 8 A. M. on the 14th. The march was resumed at 11 A. M. to the Chickahominy River, which was crossed at 11 P. M., and camp made just beyond. On the 15th they marched all day toward the James River till sundown, when it went into camp about one mile from the river. At noon on the 16th it crossed the James over a pontoon bridge, 2,200 feet long, from Wilcox's Wharf to Windmill Point. The Thirty-Fourth New York Battery was at the head of the crossing column, and carried unfurled, the beautiful silk guidon bearing the names of the various battles in which the Battery had taken part, which had been presented to it by Miss C. S. Roe, of Flushing. As the guidon fluttered in the breeze, the sailors manning the yards of the gunboats stationed on either side of the bridge to protect it and the men crossing it, after reading aloud the names of the battles—Cedar Mountain, Sulphur Springs, Manassas, Antietam, Fredericksburg, Vicksburg, Jackson and Knoxville—gave three cheers, "Hurrah for that Battery!" To my men and myself it was an inspiration to do and to dare. The Battery crossed in safety and encamped at McConnell's Point. At midnight the march was resumed and continued until 7 A. M. of the 17th, and it greatly fatigued both men and horses. After resting, the Battery went on and reached the battlefield at 4 P. M., where it went into position before Petersburg and fired 160 rounds.

During the afternoon it advanced three times, moving from five to seven hundred yards each time, and building new works at each point attained, although it was under fire the whole time. Just as the enemy were about to open fire on our line, when the Battery had reached its last position, Corporal James Cornell fired two shots, one after the other, which blew up two of their caissons. It was a terrible time for them, as the two caissons contained about 300 rounds of ammunition. Our troops captured the enemy's works later in the evening, and the next day we had an opportunity of seeing what destruction the explosion of these two caissons had wrought.

During the evening of the 17th of June, orders came to move at 7 A. M. on the 18th, with ten pieces, comprising the six rifles of the Thirty-Fourth New York and four of Capt. Twitchell's bronze Napoleons of the Seventh Maine, through a piece of woods in our front, south of Cemetery Hill. Thirty men of the Twenty-Fourth New York Cavalry (dismounted) were detailed to assist in moving the guns by hand through the woods. At 12:30 P. M. on the 18th, Gen. Willcox rode over from headquarters to see if everything was ready, and to have me set my watch by his, as the Thirty-Fourth New York had been selected to have the honor of opening the battle at precisely 1 P. M. At this hour, the Thirty-Fourth New York fired the signal gun, and instantly, two hundred guns opened fire upon the rebel lines. As soon as the signal gun had been fired by the Thirty-Fourth New York, its pieces, one after the other, were moved by hand into the woods in front, and the battle, which proved to be one of the fiercest fought in front of Petersburg, was fairly opened.

The enemy's lines were most heavily attacked, right, left and center. Shot and shell flew about like hailstones, and men and horses fell on all sides by the score. Right in front of our ten guns was the City Point and Petersburg Railroad, which had been taken by our troops in the first charge made that afternoon. Several attempts were made to retake it, but they all failed. Our ten guns behind the line of the First Division of the Ninth Corps, held their own bravely. One gun was taken down to the railroad cut, directly behind our line, and proved to be of great service in keeping the cut clear of the enemy, and thus facilitating the advance of Gen. Hancock's Corps, the Second. This cut was in front of Hancock's line, and was from ten to fifteen feet deep. The enemy had previously used it both as a breastwork and as a cover in moving troops. The battle raged hot and heavy until night ended it. The casualties in my command during the afternoon were, three of the 24th N. Y. Cavalry killed and four wounded, and five of the 34th N. Y. Battery wounded, besides two horses killed and six wounded.

Early the next morning, 19th, the Battery opened fire, and the first shell thrown into Petersburg was fired by the 34th that day. Seventy-two rounds were fired. On the night of the 21st, the Battery withdrew from this position to go into position at the Hare House on the extreme right, and just south of which Fort Stedman was afterward built. The house was named after the proprietor of the race course. Here the men built breastworks that were only about four hundred yards from the rebel line, and hence we were in uncomfortably close quarters to the enemy. One-second fuses only could be used. Lieut. Heasley was severely wounded in the shoulder on the 22d in these works.

It was here that, on the night of the 22d, Lieut. Garretson gave another exhibition of his indomitable courage. About midway between our line and the enemy's stood a barn. It had nearly all been taken down to the main floor, and on this floor lay about eighty bushels of corn. Garretson was still in command of the caisson and baggage camp.

He came up to the breastworks at about 9 A. M. He saw this corn and said to me, "Captain, I see a fine lot of corn over there, and I would like to get it for our horses." "Well, all right," said I, "but I think any attempt to get it will be exceedingly dangerous. It is only two hundred yards from the rebel lines, and should you be seen there, a thousand bullets will be sent after you." He said he would go back to the caisson camp and have a talk with the drivers. In the afternoon he paid me another visit and said all he wanted was my consent, as the drivers were willing to follow him, and everything was ready for the work. I gave my consent, but particularly counseled him to be exceedingly cautious, for, as Lieut. Heasley was badly wounded, I could not afford to lose Lieut. Garretson also.

At 9 P. M. he came up with three wagons and twelve men, with which he started out, at midnight, to obtain the corn. In less than half an hour he returned from his perilous expedition, having secured all the corn in the barn. During his absence, the infantry, who had been informed of the matter, as well as we of the Battery, listened breathlessly for the least sound, expecting every moment to hear the enemy open fire upon the daring men, but everything remained quiet, and the party returned in safety to the great relief of all. It was a most venturesome undertaking, and the infantry congratulated the Lieutenant most heartily for his bravery. Garretson said afterward that, from the moment they crossed the breastworks going out, until they returned, not a word was spoken by either himself or the men, so intent were they all upon succeeding in their work. On the following day, the 23d, the Battery opened fire upon some baggage trains coming from Richmond into Petersburg, and effectually stirred up the mules and their drivers. This operation was repeated the next day with marked effect. One of our men was wounded during this day.

CHAPTER XIII.

THE SIEGE OF PETERSBURG, CONTINUED. THE HARE HOUSE. FORT WILLCOX OR BATTERY XVI.

The Battery remained in position near the Hare House until June 30th, when it returned to near its former position nearly south of Cemetery Hill, and occupied works thrown up by Capt. Durell's Battery D, Penn. Artillery. Gen. Willcox inspected the works and asked me how I liked them. I replied that I did not like them at all; they were too low and we could not fire over the infantry with safety to them; furthermore, the place was too hot and my men had no shelter. "I would like," I continued, "to build a fort on the hill just on our left." "Well, Captain," he responded, "what have you again in your head? However, if you will build a fort there, I will say, go ahead." "I will," I said, "if I can get the materials." "What materials do you want?" he asked. "General," I replied, "before I begin this work, I want to have 6,000 feet of timber cut and brought up." "Ah!" said he, "I see you have already calculated upon building this work." "My plans are ready," I returned, "and I only want the materials to begin the work forthwith." Gen. Willcox turned to Capt. Brackett, his aide, and said, "Give Capt. Roemer an order to obtain whatever he wants and let him start at once." They then rode away. I then made out a requisition for twenty wagons, twenty axmen, and thirty men to handle the timber, load it on the wagons, and carry it to the south side of the hill.

By the 2d of July all the timber desired was ready at the place selected, near the site of the proposed fort to which it was to be carried by hand as needed, and, at eight o'clock the same evening the work was begun and continued all night. Fifteen hundred men worked in reliefs of five hundred men each two hours at a time and by daylight, we had a ditch five hundred feet long, six feet wide, and six deep. The enemy had not as yet had any suspicion of our intentions, and during the day, the men had shelter enough to continue the work regardless of rebel bullets. During the night of July 3d, 2,500 men were engaged in making the log revetment and building the traverses, and by morning the breastwork was four and one-half feet high, and was pronounced safe for infantry. That same night, four of the Battery's guns were safely brought in and put in position, though I did not think we would have any occasion to use them at that time.

The next day was the Fourth of July—the glorious Fourth. It was quiet all through the forenoon, but in the afternoon, presto! change! it became lively enough. The enemy had somehow learned of the existence of our fort, and they seemed to think it would be a good target for their artillery practice, for they brought up several mortars and opened fire with them on our new earthworks. They threw plenty of shells but all were absolutely ineffective except one. This one shell, a ten-inch one, landed in the loose dirt within the fort and exploded. The earth being fine and dry, an immense cloud of dust completely filled the fort. The enemy seeing this dust, were convinced they had destroyed the fort, and their works were instantly covered with men eager to behold the destruction caused by the shell's explosion. They appeared very jubilant over our supposed misfortune,

I took this all in and taking advantage of the dust cloud which partly concealed our movements, had the four pieces put in position and aimed at the largest groups of men in view and then fired. The smoke and dust so obscured our works that the enemy could not tell whence the shells had come. After the third round, we saw that the enemy's ramparts were clear of men; they had disappeared as if by magic; and, furthermore, they ceased annoying us for the rest of the day.

A few days after the foregoing incident occurred, they again brought up six mortars, to shell us out of the fort. This action on their part rather vexed me, for I did not care to leave just then. Looking over the front line with my field-glass, I chanced to notice that the hands of the clock in the tower of the Court House in Petersburg, indicated the hour of 2:10. I told Corporal Rierson to aim his gun at the dial and put a hole through it to show the rebels we could shoot when necessary. The gun was aimed and fired. I followed the course of the shell with my glass and saw it strike the larger hand and bore a hole through the tower. A second shot, a good line one, struck just under the center of the dial, while a third struck the edge of it. These shells were fired directly over the mortar battery and went a distance of two and one-fourth miles. After our third shot the mortar battery ceased firing, and as they then left us alone, we treated them in the same friendly way, at least for the time.

We had occupied this fort, which was called Fort Willcox for about ten days, when Gen. Willcox and staff came to inspect. He told me that the Battery had a right to go to the rear and rest for ten days, but I replied to this that it would as soon stay in the fort. "Well," he replied in turn, "that is at your option." I decided to stay in the fort. He then said he himself preferred to have us stay in the fort, and, furthermore, that the Pennsylvania engineers, who were about to mine the rebel works in front of Cemetery Hill would rather have the 34th N. Y. in the fort than any other battery, while they were at work.

Our fort soon became a famous resort for sightseers All who came from City Point and wished to get the best view of both Union and rebel lines were directed to go to Roemer's Battery in Fort Willcox, because it was the best place, on account of its elevation, from which to view the lines. The Battery boys soon learned to know when any people connected with the Sanitary Commission visited the fort, and were always prepared to present them with relics of our engagements and thus gain their good will. One day, a Mrs. Kimball, the head of the Ladies' Sanitary Commission, accompanied by a host of ladies, visited the fort, and the boys presented souvenirs to them all, and this action on the part of the Battery boys, had a very good effect, for, after that, none of them ever came to the fort without bringing something for the boys, which the government did not furnish, such as onions, potatoes, cabbages, sauerkraut, canned chicken, and all kinds of canned fruit. All of these articles were of great benefit by preventing the appearance of scurvy. The officers, too, were, at times, the recipients of these favors.

While the Battery was occupying this work, I was wounded by a bullet in the left leg just below the knee, and, in consequence of my not taking proper care of it, the wound became so irritated that Dr. McDonald, Medical Director of the Ninth Corps, forbade me to put on a boot, or to use my leg in any way until the inflammation had been reduced. A day or two after, some of the Battery boys brought me an antique chair, which I found to be very comfortable. I asked no questions as to where they had obtained it, for I had good reason to believe I would not have found out if I had. A few days after, we had another visit from Mrs. Kimball, who expressed great sympathy for me in my misfortune, yet took a great fancy to my antique chair. I then thought that something might be gained through it. She soon left the fort by the covered way, and then I sent it to her by one of my men, who was told to ask her to accept it with my compliments. The ladies were about to get into their ambulance when the chair was presented. Mrs. Kimball stoutly refused, at first, to accept it, saying the captain needed it, but when my messenger told her he dared not take it back, she accepted it. After that, nothing that the Sanitary Commission had to give, was too good for the boys in Fort Willcox.

Fort Willcox was named after our beloved Commander of the Third Division of the Ninth Corps, Brig.-Gen. Orlando B. Willcox. Soon after it had been so named, an order was received which directed that no fort should be named after a living commander, but Fort Willcox it had been named, and Fort Willcox it continued to be called, despite that order so far as the members of the 34th N. Y. Battery were concerned. Officially it was known as Battery XVI.

The Battery had now been in the fort for three weeks, and the enemy had been very persistent and still continued to be so, in their efforts to drive us out or to make it a mighty uncomfortable place for us to stay in. They sent their mortar shells and bullets into it night and day. On one occasion the boys undertook to count the number of bullets received in the fort in a single half hour, and their count was nearly fifty.

Thus far, we had suffered but few casualties, but it was felt by all that something had to be done to counteract their deadly fire. Unfortunately, the fort was too low to look over Cemetery Hill behind the rebel lines. We could see the roofs of some of the houses in Petersburg, besides the spires of the churches and the tower of the Court House, but they were all we could see. On looking around to learn how we could obtain a better view of the city's interior, I took note of a pine tree standing to the rear and left of the fort, that seemed to be about thirty-five feet high. I called Lieut. Garretson to consult with him concerning the rebels' terrific fire. "Captain," said he, "I don't see how we can possibly stop those d—d rebels." Pointing to the tree, I asked him, "Lieutenant, will you climb that tree and give me, by signals, the proper direction and elevation for sending our shells into the most thickly populated and most important residential portion of Petersburg?" He consented to do so. I must here note that Col. J. F. Hartranft, commanding the First Brigade of the Third Division, Ninth Corps, had his headquarters just under this tree in a large Sibley tent covered with a fly. Lieut. Garretson climbed up in rear of this tent till he reached the body of the tree, and then quickly climbed to the top of the tree, whence he communicated with me by certain prearranged signals, which enabled me to establish an effective line of fire for each gun.

Each of the gun sergeants had a book in which he recorded every shot sent from his piece, giving the distance and elevation of every one, and also the effect produced by the explosion of the shells in the streets of the city, which record would be of great service in the future. We had successfully laid down the lines of three guns, and had nearly completed those of the fourth, when the rebels, whose attention had been attracted to us because of our fire upon the city, discovered the Lieutenant in the tree. They then set to work to drive him out. First, they used globe rifle bullets, which Lieut. Garretson did not seem to mind in the least. Then they tried a Whitworth rifle, which was, at the time, for accuracy of fire, the best made. They fired four shots before they obtained the right range and elevation, but the fifth crashed through the crown of the tree. Then Lieut. G. thought it was time to go, and "not stand on the order of his going," for the next shot might come nearer than would be consistent with safety. In his haste and excitement, he missed his hold—not being a cat or a squirrel—and came down more quickly than Davy Crockett's coon.

The Lieutenant fell right on top of Col. Hartranft's tent, tore a hole through, and after landing on a pile of picks and spades, rolled over on the floor, upsetting, in the operation, the Colonel's table and scattering books, papers, pens, and inkstands promiscuously around. The Colonel was naturally startled, thinking a shell had struck the tent, but he instantly recovered himself when he saw Garretson sprawling on the floor, and then called out, "For God's sake, Lieutenant, where the d—l did you come from?" and assisted him to his feet. "Are you much hurt?" he immediately asked. "I ain't killed, General," Garretson responded in his humorous way, "but I feel mighty stiff and sore." "But where in thunder have you been?" the Colonel inquired. "Why," Garretson replied, "I have been up in the crown of this tree giving signals to Captain Roemer, so as to get good and accurate lines of fire for our guns on Petersburg, and thus rout the rebels out." "Well! Well!" said Hartranft, "That accounts for the shells I have heard passing over my tent for the last half hour. Your Battery is everlastingly up to some trick on the Johnnies."

During its occupation of Fort Willcox, the Battery had, up to the 16th of July, fired 470 rounds, most of which had been sent into Petersburg.

The buildings, seven in number, on the Griffith estate (soon destined to become famous as the ground on which the battle of the Petersburg Crater was fought), were in our immediate front, and just in front, and a little to the left, of a rebel fort on Cemetery Hill, known to the Confederates as

Elliott's Salient, or Pegram's Salient. These buildings ranged from southeast to northwest, and were somewhat lower than the rebel line, the southeast one being at the lowest point. The rebels had a habit of sending their sharpshooters into these buildings every day. These sharpshooters would raise the shingles slightly, thus making small loop-holes through which they watched our lines, and, as opportunity offered, fired at our men as they passed along, ignorant of the danger to which they were exposed. Many Union soldiers had been thus killed or wounded. We, of the 34th, in Fort Willcox, could do nothing to stop this murderous fire, in fact, not a man in the fort could raise his fingers above the parapet without having a sharpshooter's bullet strike him. These sharpshooters trained their rifles on their targets by placing them on two forked sticks, and so accurately that their bullets would sweep the top of the fort's parapet even at night, thus making it as impossible to do any work by night as it was by day. Every day from ten to twenty casualties would occur among the infantry. Gen. Willcox told me it amounted to a severe battle every day. I told him, in reply, that I had fired shot and shell into those houses, but had found that as fast as I drove them out of one they would go into another. "Well, Captain," said he, "I wish you could do something to stop this terrible fire." This set me to thinking, and I studied the matter over for a day or two, and, finally, after examining a percussion shell and finding, upon removing the plunger, it contained a space large enough to hold a fire-ball, I concluded to try these, if I could find material for making the fire-balls.

I called Lieut. Garretson and said to him, "Lieutenant, this Battery has got to burn those buildings." In his emphatic way he replied, "By God, Captain, we can't do it." However, I was determined to accomplish this feat, if it were possible. I sent the Lieutenant to Gen. Willcox's headquarters to obtain, if possible, five articles—meal powder, rosin, turpentine, sulphur, and tow—but all he could obtain was turpentine. The peculiarity of my requisition brought Gen. Willcox to the fort to inquire for what purpose the articles were wanted. I very respectfully declined to answer, saying, that if I succeeded in my plans it would be all right, but if I did not, I did not want to be laughed at. At this Gen. Willcox laughed and said, "I knew you had something in your head again. I will see if those articles can be obtained; if so, you shall have them." In the evening word came from headquarters that they could not be obtained; all departments had been searched in vain.

Then, as "necessity is the mother of invention," we were compelled to do the best we could under the circumstances. I found a cartridge bag filled with fuse clippings, which, when pealed, made very good meal powder. On searching the battery wagon some sulphur was found. I sent Lieut. Garretson with two men into the pine woods, near by, to gather all the pine knots they could find. These articles and some tar taken from a limber chest, provided all the ingredients needed for our fire-balls. For two days there was "no admission" to our tents. It was emphatically a "secret service" in which we were engaged.

After two days' experimenting we concluded to test the result of our experiments by the effect that would be produced by the compound on hard wood. Our composition proved to be excellent, for it burned a hole through the wood, while water had no perceptible effect when we tried to extinguish the fire. The mixture seemed to be just the thing we wanted. Taking the proper quantity for each we found we had enough of the composition to load thirteen percussion shells, which were ready for use by the evening of the second day of our experiments. Now, we had to wait only for a southeasterly wind to try our experimental shell on the lower buildings first, as the ground sloped very much to the southeast. Three days later the southeast wind came, July 21st. Lieuts. Garretson and Johnston had their four guns loaded with the fire shells, while the extra guns were kept ready for use in keeping the enemy from putting out the fire when it was once started. At 8 A. M., July 21st, the first fire shell was fired. The aim was good and the shell exploded within the building. The second and third exploded in the same manner. Turning to Lieut. Garretson, I remarked, "The shells have gone, but have not produced the effect I desired, for they have reached no material that will ignite." The fourth shell was fired. It struck the roof and burst; soon after flames leaped up. I now directed Garretson and Johnston to open fire with all four guns, firing one after the other with ordinary percussion shell. I did not want to have the fire put out, and this was my mild way of keeping the enemy from attempting to do so. Soon the fire was blazing briskly, and was clearly visible to every one on our entire line. When the infantry in our front understood fully what we were about, and saw now what damage had been done, burst into loud cheers along the whole line from the Appomattox River to Fort "Hell."

This terminated the existence of the Griffith buildings, for every one was burned to the ground. Only a few fence posts could be seen sticking out of the ground near where they had stood. As the buildings succumbed to the flames, one after the other, there was great rejoicing among the infantry who had been the principal sufferers from the fire of the sharpshooters who had found in the buildings a safe cover.

Nine of the thirteen fire shells were left, and as I did not want to waste them, I determined to try them on some other buildings within reach of the guns. In Petersburg and to our left, there stood a large mansion about two miles distant, and I concluded to try to burn this also. In the afternoon of the same day, July 21st, after a few trials with ordinary percussion shells, the gunners succeeded to their satisfaction in obtaining the exact distance and proper elevation. A fire shell was now thrown at the building, which had a row of large Grecian columns in its front. Several of the ordinary percussion shells fired previously, had gone entirely through the building, but the fire shell, for some unexplained reason, failed to take the grooves of the gun, and, consequently, fell about one hundred yards short of the house, and there exploded. We saw some of the enemy run out to where the burning fire-ball lay and poke at it with their ramrods, but a percussion shell was dropped among them and they scattered in a very lively manner.

It was now night and I thought it best to wait until morning, and then complete the job of burning the house. Imagine our surprise in the morning, when, on looking for it, we found it had disappeared, and that not even the foundation of it was visible. It was reported that it had been torn down by the order of Gen. Lee, and that the timbers had been used in some fortifications the enemy were building near by. The next morning some of the Battery boys met some of the rebels at the brook, and the latter said that Gen. Lee had said if they didn't tear it down themselves it would share the fate of the Griffith buildings at the hands of that New York Battery. All news of this kind spread rapidly among our men. The remaining eight fire shells were thrown that same day to the left into Petersburg, among the factories, and did a great deal of damage there.*

---

*In July, 1886, just twenty-two years afterward, George C. Strong Post, No. 534, Department New York, G. A. R., of Brooklyn, visited Richmond, Va., as the guests of Phil Kearny Post, No. 10, Department Va., G. A. R., and Robert E. Lee Camp of Confederate Veterans. Lieut. Garretson, his brother, Charles H. Garretson, and myself, accompanied Strong Post as guests of that organization. The whole party numbered about one hundred. The two Richmond organizations met our party at Dutch Gap on

During the forenoon of July 22d, the day after we had destroyed the Griffith buildings, I received an order to report at once, in person, at the headquarters of the Third Division, Ninth Corps. Gen. Willcox met me just outside of his tent and said, "Captain, I have sent for you to introduce you to some gentlemen." Taking me by the arm he escorted me into his tent, and said to those assembled there, "Gentlemen, here is my Chief of Artillery, Captain Roemer, who, yesterday, performed such valuable services for the Ninth Corps by burning the Griffith buildings." Among those present were Generals Hancock, Parke, Potter, Ferrero, Col. Hartranft, and others whose names I can not now recall. Gen. Willcox made some very flattering remarks about the Battery and its past services, whereupon General Hancock said, "I remember Capt Roemer's services at Spottsylvania Court House on the 12th of May. He did a splendid piece of work there. I was told by Gen. Burnside that he selected his own position that afternoon on the left of my Corps."

---

the James River, and Lee Camp honored us by pinning bouquets to the lapels of our coats. On arriving at the dock in Richmond, both organizations escorted our party to our hotel, and there entertained us most handsomely. Afterward they took us in carriages to all points of interest in and around Richmond. One of these points was the Confederate Soldiers' Home, an institution supported by voluntary contributions. Here we had a joyous time, and our friends of both the Blue and the Gray, worked together in harmony and good fellowship to bring about this happy result.

While conversing with one of the Confederate veterans, he referred to the fire shells thrown by the 34th New York Battery, and said they did more to alarm the people of Petersburg than all the other shells that entered the city, and he remarked, furthermore, that if the Battery had continued firing such shells, they would have destroyed the entire city of Petersburg. During our return journey from Richmond our party made up a purse of $100, which, after our arrival in New York, was sent to the Confederate Soldiers' Home in Richmond, as a remembrance of our gratitude for the kindness shown us during our visit. JAC. ROEMER.

A general conversation followed, during which Gen. Willcox asked me, "Roemer, at what military school were you educated?" I replied, "I was two days at West Point in 1840, General. In fact, I have scarcely had what is generally termed a common school education." "Never say that again, Captain," said Gen. Willcox, "You have a regular United States Battery, both on your right and on your left, and they have never done what yours has, and yet both are commanded by graduates of West Point." I thanked the general for his very flattering remarks, whereupon he said, "It is no flattery, Captain, the praise belongs to you and your Battery."

By July 23d, the enemy had established a battery of 32-pounders on Cemetery Hill, on our right, thinking, no doubt, they would certainly drive the 34th out of its fort. This day they commenced to bombard us with shells from this battery, and kept up their fire on our position the whole day. One shell entered the port hole on the left and struck the top of the magazine containing all our ammunition, but, fortunately, did not explode or do any damage to the fort, or anything within it. The magazine's damage was soon repaired, and the magazine was strengthened by placing some two hundred sandbags about it.

The next day, the 24th, they opened fire again upon the fort, and instantly we began firing on Petersburg with percussion shell from all four guns, along the lines of fire recently established. Their fire continued for about half an hour and then ceased, and then we stopped. We learned afterward that they had received word from Petersburg that our fire was greatly damaging the city. We now felt convinced that we could "hold the fort." Before this it had looked as if they had made up their minds to charge and take the fort by storm.

During these days the men were busily engaged, when

not working the guns, in building a new magazine in the fort and strengthening the parapets and bomb-proofs, that the latter might afford better protection to both officers and men, when not engaged with the guns. The bomb-proofs were underneath the traverses. For the benefit of those who may not clearly understand the matter, I will say, that traverses are works or embankments erected between the guns at right angles to the parapets or ramparts, to protect the cannoneers from any cross or flank fire of the enemy. In Fort Willcox, they were from ten to fifteen feet long, eight to ten feet thick, and about seven feet high. The bomb-proofs were under these and below the level of the ground of the fort, and, were, in fact, small rooms with very stout walls and roofs supported by logs. I always considered substantial traverses to be most important parts of a fort, and, therefore, had them constructed in every fort we ever held for any length of time.

Furthermore, a very strong parapet or rampart was constructed directly in rear of the fort. This was seven feet high and six feet thick, and behind it were constructed sleeping apartments for the men not on guard at night, who were thus well protected from the enemy's solid shot or shell.

On the 25th, I was ordered to take Capt. Twitchell's Seventh Maine Battery of four guns, and place the two sections, one on my right flank and the other on my left, to protect the flanks in case of necessity. Early the same day it was reported that the enemy were constructing a new earthwork on our left, about where the mansion previously mentioned, had stood, and was of considerable size and strength. On looking in that direction we saw several hundred men at work on it. Gen. Willcox and staff came into the fort at 10 A. M. The general immediately dismounted and went to the parapet to look over it at the enemy's lines. I at once warned him, not for his life, to raise his head above the parapet, and then said, if he wished to obtain a clear view of the enemy's lines, he should go with me through the covered way in the rear of the fort and across to the woods in front, and to the left of Durell's Pennsylvania Battery, where he could obtain the best view to be had. Accompanied by an orderly we went to that place, which was about three-quarters of a mile distant. Here we obtained a fine view of the enemy's works, and especially of the nearly completed work mentioned above.

Gen. Willcox then asked me to go over to Durell's Battery and have it open fire directly upon this new work. Durell fired ten rounds, but not a shot entered the enemy's new earthwork. After the tenth round, some of the rebels came boldly out of their works, and, turning their backs to the battery, slapped their ——— in derisive and insulting salute. Then the General gave the order, "Cease firing," and then asked me to send my orderly to our fort and have a few shots fired from the guns of the 34th. In reply, I said if he wanted guns fired from our fort, I would prefer to go myself instead of sending the orderly, as I deemed it most important for both my command and myself, that I should be with the Battery under such circumstances, and also said that if he would consent to this, I would leave my orderly with him and return myself as soon as the shots had been fired. He assented to this, and I immediately returned to the fort.

Arriving there, I told the officers and men about the firing done by Durell's battery, and, at the same time, expressed my sorrow for the mistake that battery had made. I then said to them, "I want you to fire two shells that shall explode in the enemy's new work, and thus show Gen. Willcox that you have not forgotten how to aim a piece of artillery at the right point." When everything was ready, the elevation having been determined with exactness, and the fuses properly cut, I gave the commands, "No. 1, fire," "No. 2, fire." No commotion arose in the enemy's works after the first shot, but after the second had exploded at almost the same spot the first had, it seemed as if an earthquake had occurred within the rebel fort, for at least two hundred men jumped up on top of their works and ran as for their lives.

The work was well done, and I complimented the cannoneers highly. I then returned to where I had left Gen. Willcox. He greeted me with, "Well done, Captain. Tell Durell not to fire another shot without permission from yourself, for I call such shooting as his battery did, an absolute waste of ammunition. Your two shots were worth fifty of his."

This same day some of our friends of the Sanitary Commission, both ladies and gentlemen, came to the fort in the afternoon to pay us a visit, and to obtain a good view of the opposing lines. One of them, Mrs. Kimball, whom I have mentioned before, greatly desired to fire one of the guns. Just at that moment I saw a wagon train coming out of Petersburg and heading for a fort the Union soldiers had christened "Fort Damnation."* I directed a sergeant to sight a gun on this train, then, handing the lanyard to Mrs. Kimball, told her to keep it slack and pull steadily without a jerk, when I gave the order to fire. I then gave the order, "Fire," whereupon she pulled like a veteran gunner. As the shell sped on its way she ran to the breastwork to witness its effect. The shell did its work. We saw two of the drivers running away and leaving their mules to take care of themselves. Then one of the gentlemen wished to fire a gun. The piece was prepared, the lanyard was placed in

*This fort was officially known as Fort Mahone, while the Union fort opposite it and generally called "Fort Hell," was officially known as Fort Sedgwick, and was so named in honor of Gen. John Sedgwick, who was killed at Spottsylvania Court House, May 8, 1864, while in command of the Sixth Corps.   EDITOR.

his hand, and the order to fire was given. He shut his eyes and pulled, but the gun did not respond. I think he only shut his eyes and was afraid to pull with sufficient strength.

We, of the 34th New York, had now brought the enemy in our immediate front into subjection, and they were beginning to behave themselves better. Still, every now and then, they would open fire upon us, just to let us know, apparently, that they were still there and alive. They would do this whenever a party of officers came to the fort, or any particular demonstration was made in or about the fort.

An instance of this occurred a few days after the visit of the Sanitary people, when Gen Willcox and his staff also paid us a visit. They came into the fort by the covered way, and the rebels chanced to see them just as they were entering the fort, and immediately opened fire on the fort in right good earnest. I saw at once Gen. Willcox was greatly vexed. I then saluted him. He returned my salute and said, "Why don't you stop that firing?" "Do you want me to stop it?" I asked. "Yes," he replied, "stop it." I then called to the cannoneers of guns Nos. 1 and 3, whose lines of fire were directed on Petersburg. "No. 1, ready, fire;" "No. 3, ready, fire;" "No. 1, again, ready, fire." Then Gen. Willcox remarked, "Captain, you have not hit the enemy's works." "I know I didn't," I responded, "and I don't intend to do so." Again I ordered Nos. 1 and 3 to fire. By this time the enemy had become silent, and we ceased firing also. I then saluted Gen. Willcox and said, "This is the way we silence the enemy's batteries in our front." "But, Captain," he repeated, "with all your shots you have not struck the enemy's works even once." Greatly enjoying his mystification, I replied, "No, but all of them went directly over the enemy's lines into Petersburg; three of them exploded in buildings, and two in the streets. This can be verified by my officers and men. Since you entered the fort the enemy have fired twenty-five shots. They would keep that up all day long, but they well know we have the upper hand of them and can stop them at any time." "How is that, Captain?" the General asked. I then related to him the story of Lieut. Garretson's mishap, and how it came about, and also the reason why I said we had obtained an advantage of the rebel batteries. At this he laughed heartily, and said, "Now, I recall the story Col. Hartranft told me the other day about Garretson tumbling through his tent so very unceremoniously. That action on the part of both you and your lieutenant is most praiseworthy." Soon after he and his staff left the fort.

On the morning of the 26th, the day following the disaster to the new rebel fort and the wagon, when the "Yanks" and the "Johnnies" met at the creek and talked the matter over, the rebels used very forcible language in expressing their opinions, as is shown in an article published in the New York Herald, at the time, headed:

"ROEMER'S BATTERY, NINTH CORPS."

"At last accounts all was well with the Flushing Battery in front of Petersburg. Among the most distinguished artillerists in the army is Captain Roemer, commanding the veteran 34th New York Battery, of the Ninth Corps. We have rather a good thing about him in camp just now. The Captain, as all his friends know—and their name is legion—is possessed of a set of heavy flowing whiskers, rather ruddy in color. His battery is farthest to the front, where, from its commanding position, as well as from the excellent skill and marksmanship of his gunners, it proves most annoying to the enemy. In vain they endeavor to drive him out. He returns shot for shot, and with such accuracy that the rebels are compelled to desist. His reputation is as well established in the rebel lines as in our own, and the rebel pickets are very curious about him and his battery. The other day one of them called out, 'Where the devil did that red-whiskered battery come from?'"

CHAPTER XIV.

SIEGE OF PETERSBURG CONTINUED.   BATTLE OF THE PETERSBURG
CRATER.

The position of Fort Willcox, or Battery XVI, was one of the most important ones on the whole line fronting Petersburg. "Fort Hell," the fort nearest the rebel lines, was about two miles distant to our left. Within the fort everything was lively, night and day. The enemy had a habit of sainting the fort at all times with bullets, and shell from both cannon and mortars, and there was not a day during the month of July, from the fourth, the day the Battery's four guns were first placed in position in it, until the thirtieth, that the enemy did not fire into it from the front, and both right and left flanks. It really seemed as if they all wanted to have a hack at the 34th New York. It was our good fortune to stand all this fire without suffering any serious casualties. Whenever they sent us their compliments in cold iron, we tried to be as polite as possible, and returned them as promptly and forcibly as we could. Then they thought it right to reply to our answer, and to this we responded in turn, and thus the salutations continued to be exchanged. Whenever they acknowledged our replies by ceasing to fire, we laid aside the sponge and rammer, but not before. We were bound to have the last word.

In this connection, I must relate another of Lieut. Garretson's experiences. One night, the date I can not recall, the enemy opened fire on the fort at 12:30 A. M., and kept it up for about two hours. They repeated this action on each of the two succeeding nights. The fourth night the question arose, "What will they do to-night?" All wondered if they would let us have one night's sleep out of four. I told Lieut. Garretson to get all the sleep he could this night, as he had had none for the past three nights, and that I would take his place. I also told him I would notify him if the rebels disturbed us too much. In answer, he said, "You know what Dr. McDonald told you to-day," (I had been badly wounded July 9th), "about doing more than you ought to." "That is all right," I replied, "but three nights' vigil is enough for any one. Now go and do as I say, and I will take charge of your guns for the night."

Garretson then called Sergeant John Starkins and told him, "I will lie down on the platform alongside your gun, and, if any disturbance arises, call me and don't let the Captain come out." He then lay down on the gun platform, just a little in rear of the muzzle of the piece, so that the gun could be discharged with safety to himself, and was soon fast asleep. Shortly after, Sergeant Starkins turned over the command to the gun-corporal. A little after midnight the enemy's batteries opened fire. The sentry at Post No. 1 called out, "Corporal of the guard, Post No. 1. Is the Lieutenant asleep?" We soon found that he was, and so I would not allow him to be disturbed. I got my crutches and told the corporal I would go with him. I then called for Sergeant Starkins, but he was not about. Then the piece was made ready and fired. Just as it recoiled, Sergeant Starkins crawled out from under the gun carriage; the discharge of the gun had evidently waked him up. The gun was reloaded, after the cannoneers had been cautioned to avoid stepping on Lieut. Garretson, as it was very dark. Three rounds were fired by this gun, yet the Lieutenant slept on oblivious of everything. He had been completely exhausted by his previous three nights' work.

The next morning the duty of making out the morning report of the preceding twenty-four hours' occurrences, fell to him. In this report, he had to record the number of shots fired, as well as all general notes. With his blank before him, and before he began to write, he said, "I thank God, Captain, that we have to report that no shots were fired during the night by our battery." In reply, I said, "We fired three shots, between 12 and 1 last night." He started and said, "Captain, you must be mistaken." I repeated my statement. "You don't mean to say," he answered, "you fired three shots without their being heard by me, sleeping as I did on the platform?" My story was corroborated by the statements of the sergeant, corporal, and cannoneers who had charge of the piece, and did the firing, but even then he could not be made to comprehend how it could happen. He put it down on the report that three rounds had been fired by the battery, but in his mind he doubted it.

To water the horses, they had to be led around to a point where the enemy had a direct range upon them as they passed in column, and, therefore, early in July, it was decided to dig a well. A site for it was selected on a slope running southwest and northeast, where, it was thought, plenty of water would surely be obtained. The necessary tools, spades, pickaxes, windlass, buckets, ropes, etc., were procured, and the men began to dig. They went down forty-seven feet, through stiff clay, and struck real creek mud. They dug through this seven feet, and in it were found many fine scallop shells, some of which I still possess.

The well was now fifty-four feet deep, but, as neither water nor any signs of water were found, and, furthermore, as it had become dangerous for the men to continue digging without blocking, it was given up.

Somebody told us that if we should take a peach-tree crotch, with the green leaves left upon it, keep it balanced in both hands, with the ends of the crotch pointing front, and give it a chance to work, it would point to water. Having procured the peach-tree twig, I went southwest from the well already dug. The ground over which I walked sloped upward at an angle of about forty degrees. I kept on my course until I had gone ninety paces, when I noticed some change in the position of the peach twig which now began to sway. I marked this spot and went on farther, but the limb remained quiet. I then retraced my steps, and when I reached the marked spot, the peach limb was affected as before, and there it was decided to dig.

The men all had something to say about the peach limb, but as they knew we must have water near by, if we did not want the horses to be targets for the enemy every time they went to water, they went to work with a will. After digging several feet, they came to a quicksand, and then it was predicted they would strike water within the next eight feet. After digging only six feet deeper, or ten feet in all, water make its appearance. After going a foot deeper the flow of water became so great that the men could not use their shovels. I then sent some men for buckets. To hurry up the matter, I told the men who were in the hole digging, I would give them a bottle of the best whiskey to be had, if, in thirty minutes by my watch, they would deepen the hole by another two feet.

As soon as the men arrived with the buckets, I set them to work bailing out the well, but, although the buckets fairly flew up and down, there remained constantly a depth of four feet of water of splendid quality. The top of the well was then covered with logs, except the central part, in which was placed a cracker box, minus its top and bottom boards. Two pine logs, each twenty-two feet long, and two-and-one-half feet in diameter, were obtained and hollowed out into splendid watering troughs, at which all the horses could be watered at the same time, and with safety from the enemy's fire.

The large fort in the enemy's lines, near Cemetery Hill, was about the most prominent one on their front from the Appomattox River to Fort Mahone, and was directly opposite Forts Willcox and Morton, in our lines. The distance between our lines and the enemy's, at this point, was about one thousand yards. In front of Fort Willcox, was a deep ravine running for a little distance, nearly east and west, but just beyond Fort Willcox, on the right, it turned sharply to the northeast, and thus gave the enemy an advantage over our troops.

The enemy's fort at the end of the ravine had an elevation of thirty or forty feet. Lieut.-Col. Henry Pleasants, of the 48th Pennsylvania Volunteers, which regiment had been recruited among the miners of the upper Schuylkill coal regions, obtained permission to run a mine under the above mentioned fort, and began the work on June 25th. A carefully conducted preliminary survey had shown him that he would have to dig a tunnel 510 feet long to place the mine directly under the fort, and thirty feet below it. The whole of the earth taken from the mine was brought out in cracker boxes. It took from the 25th of June to the 23d of July to complete the work, and everything was done quietly and with the utmost secrecy. All officers who knew of it, were cautioned to observe absolute silence regarding it.

At 9 P. M., July 29th, orders came for all batteries and regiments to be prepared to march out at a moment's notice. Early in the morning of the 30th (3:30), the troops of the Ninth Corps were massed in the immediate front of Forts Willcox and Morton. The First Division (Ledlie's) was to lead the advance, and was to be followed by the Third Division (Willcox's) to protect the left flank of the First, and the Second (Potter's) was to go to the right of the First. The Fifth Corps (Warren) and the Eighteenth (Smith) were to advance as soon as the Ninth was out of the way. Everything was now ready for lighting the fuse that should ignite the 8,000 pounds of powder placed in the mine. At 4 A. M. every artilleryman was at his post; the guns were all loaded; and the lanyards, in hand, ready to be pulled. The signal was given; the fuse was lighted; but the mine failed to explode. This caused a delay of nearly an hour, during which time, Sergeant Henry Rees and Lieut. Jacob Douty, of the 48th Pennsylvania Volunteers, re-entered the mine, repaired and relighted the fuse. At nearly 5 A. M. the mine exploded. Then followed a heavy shock as of an earthquake, and a tremendous upheaval of earth. As the earth opened all around, and an immense cloud of smoke and dust arose in the air, the view became entirely obliterated for a while, and the damage that had been done could not be estimated. The earth seemed to fly into the air, and, assuming the form of a waterspout as seen at sea, rose to a height of about forty feet, while the smoke and dust rolled up in a cloud to the height of seventy-five or a hundred feet.

When the smoke and dust had cleared away, we could see what effect had been produced by the explosion. Masses of earth twenty or more feet in thickness had been hurled out as if they had been merely pebbles. Where the ground sloped down in the direction of Fort Willcox, the heaving of the earth was very plainly perceptible, and one of the bronze guns that had been in the blown-up fort, had been thrown down the hill in the direction of our fort, some fifty or sixty yards beyond the earth thrown out. One of the enemy, who, as he explained the matter to us afterward, was standing on the top of the fort when the explosion took place, said, that when he felt the ground give way, he did not know what could be the matter, but when the immense quantity of smoke burst forth, he thought it best to leave, and at once did so, though not through his own exertions, and landed within our lines, a prisoner of war.

Immediately after the explosion, two hundred cannon in our lines opened fire causing the very earth to tremble with their thunder. About ten minutes after the explosion, the First Division of the Ninth Corps (Ledlie's), was ordered to advance to attack the enemy and take possession of the crater. This was followed by the Second Division (Potter's) and later still by the Third (Willcox's). Finally at 7 a. m., two hours after the explosion, the Fourth Division (colored) commanded by Gen. Ferrero, was ordered to advance and charge on the crater and the rebel works to the right and left of it. At the time of the explosion, all the rebels in our immediate front left their works in great haste running in the direction of Petersburg, but were soon brought back, and advanced to the attack on our Ninth Corps troops crowded together in the crater. The Fifth and Eighteenth Corps remained inert doing nothing to support the Ninth Corps.

All the movements of our own troops, and the greater part of those of the rebels, could be distinctly seen from our fort owing to its peculiar position. In consequence, seven general officers were assembled in the fort to observe them. Soon after the advance of the Ninth Corps, Lieut. Garretson asked permission to go down into the ravine where the troops were massed. I granted his request and added. "If you can do anything to help the matter along, do so." The battle was now at a fever heat, and the excitement of the troops was most intense, as cannon and musketry were pouring in their deadly fire on the men in the crater with the greatest rapidity. Just then, Lieut. Garretson returned fairly quivering with intense excitement.

"Captain," said he, "I am afraid the game is up, but if you and I had each a regiment of infantry, we could yet capture the Appomattox bridge." It is no wonder we were all thoroughly excited, for, being where we could distinctly observe all the movements of both sides around the crater, when we saw our columns did not advance as was ordered and expected, we began to fear that this action, upon which so much depended, was going to be a stupendous failure. This contest for the supremacy had brought on extremely hard fighting. Very heavy reinforcements were brought up from Petersburg, in addition to those who had abandoned the lines at the time of the explosion, and been driven back by their officers with drawn swords. The fire of the Union artillery upon them was exceedingly severe, yet their advance was not checked.

It was now 8 A. M. and the contest had been steadily increasing in severity for three hours, as the mine was exploded at 5 A. M. It was now learned that the enemy were collecting reinforcements from all points possible, and even from points on their lines twelve miles north of the Appomattox, which latter they were hurrying down across the bridge through Petersburg and out to Cemetery Hill with all possible speed. Most of the reinforcements were perfectly fresh troops. Hundreds of men were now cooped up in the crater, where, for a time, they found shelter from the enemy's fire, but could not advance as they had been ordered to do.

The enemy now brought up mortars of all sizes and, proceeded to make it as uncomfortable as they possibly could for the men in the crater. The result of their endeavors was this, that as soon as any one tried to climb out he was at once picked off. Capt. Brackett, A. A. G. to Gen. Willcox, had to clamber over the huge masses of earth thrown out by the explosion while carrying to our troops the orders directing them what to do. Three times did he have to climb up and over the same masses of earth in the performance of this work. During a battle, a general's aides must, no matter how heavy the firing may be, carry the orders to the points designated.

It was not long before the enemy had re-established their lines again both on the right and on the left of the crater, and had planted their mortars along their rear line, from which they opened fire upon the men still in the crater. As their shells exploded in that hole fifteen or twenty feet deep, we could see men blown to pieces many of which were sent flying through the air. It was a most horrible sight to behold. We in Fort Willcox did everything in our power to sustain our troops in the crater, as well as protect those whose mission it was to carry succor and relief to those troops. Our guns were trained on every point where we could do anything to benefit our troops and punish the enemy. Although we knew by this time that the game was lost for our side, we, nevertheless, did all we could.

Late in the afternoon a truce was arranged. Gen. Willcox was one of the commissioners During this, our dead were buried and our wounded cared for. After Gen. Willcox returned, he told me he was asked by a rebel Major, and Chief of the rebel artillery in our front, if the battery in front of the fort that was blown up was under his command. Gen. Willcox replied that it was, and that it was Capt. Roemer's Battery. "Well, General," the major continued, "that Battery did our troops more damage than all the other batteries in your front combined."

Thus ended the Battle of the Petersburg Crater, July 30th, 1864. "The four divisions of the Ninth Corps lost 52 officers and 376 men killed; 105 officers and 1,556 men wounded; and 87 officers and 1,652 men captured, total, 3,828."* A

---

* Battles and Leaders of the Civil War, Vol. 4, p. 559, Maj. W. H. Powell, U. S. A.

further result was, "on August 13th Gen. Burnside was granted a leave of absence and Gen. John G. Parke was assigned to the command of the Ninth Corps. Gen. Burnside resigned April 15th, 1865."† All this occurred because Gen. Burnside had not been supported as he believed he should have been.

---

† Battles and Leaders of the Civil War. Vol. 4, p. 572. (Foot note by Editors.)

CHAPTER XV.

SIEGE OF PETERSBURG CONTINUED.   AUGUST 1, 1864 TO DECEMBER 31ST, 1864.

After the Battle of the Crater, the same rivalry that had existed previous to it, still continued and the firing was constant on both sides, until August 25th, on which date the First Division of the Ninth Corps, consisting of the 51st N. Y., 51st Pa., the 2d, 8th, 17th and 22d Mich., and the 34th N. Y Battery* was ordered to go to Hatcher's Run to support Gen. Hancock and his Pennsylvania Bucktails of the Second Corps. The latter had had that day a hard contest with the enemy who had been too much for them. The Battery arrived at night and threw up breastworks, for shelter, after going into position. The following morning, the battle opened with a hot attack on our lines, but the rebels soon learned that some of the Ninth Corps were behind the Bucktails, and this fact appeared to satisfy them, as they did not venture far, being evidently afraid they might get in return what they had given the Bucktails the day before. One section of the Battery was then placed in Redoubt No. 1, while the other was sent to the Aiken House

The next day, August 27th, the Battery moved to the Jones House, where one section was put in position, and

---

* The 34th N. Y. Battery had up to this time occupied Fort Willcox, or Battery XVI, for about seven weeks, or since July 4th, 1864.

J. ROEMER.

earthworks thrown up at once. On the 30th I was severely wounded by a cut across the knee cap. This wound nearly cost me my life, for it soon became so inflamed that an amputation of the leg was determined upon, but I stoutly refused to permit it. On this account, the Battery was withdrawn and sent to the Aiken House, about five miles south of Petersburg, where it remained until September 28th, meanwhile constructing earthworks in front.

Then the Battery moved over to the Pegram House where a battle occurred on September 30th. This was short but severe. The artillery was all misplaced, and for this reason the Battery lost a number of good men killed and wounded, and was unable to do itself any good or properly protect and support our infantry. It really looked as if the officer who ordered the Battery into position in front of the picket line, was either ignorant of the proper way of handling artillery, or was determined to sacrifice the Battery to gratify some personal feeling. During the whole existence of the Battery from muster-in to muster-out, both as Battery L, 2d N. Y. Art., and as the 34th N. Y. Independent Battery, it had been obliged in many engagements to change its position to avoid capture by the enemy, but in this engagement, it had been the narrowest escape of all. Had not Lieuts. Garretson and Johnston possessed the courage, coolness, and presence of mind to do what they did in that emergency, the Battery, as well as other troops, would have been lost. It was wholly due to these officers that the Battery was saved from capture by the enemy, and I here record my appreciation of their bravery and skill. They had had scarcely time to fire three rounds before the loss of life among the members of the Battery had exceeded that incurred in any previous engagement.

I was not present with the Battery during this engagement, because I had gone home to Flushing shortly after I was wounded on August 30th, on sick leave for twenty days. On the 28th of September, shortly before the expiration of my leave, I had telegraphed to Gen. Willcox for a ten days' extension of my leave. In reply to this I received a telegram which said, "Come on at once." I immediately started for the front, where I arrived at 11.50 P. M. October 6th. The next morning, Gen. Willcox came to my tent and asked me if I could ride a horse. I asked him why. He answered by saying he wanted me to go with him over the battlefield of September 30th. I replied, "All right. I guess I can ride sideways." After viewing the field I asked him how many batteries were on the field during the battle. He replied, "Yours was the only one." I then told him I was very sorry the Battery had suffered such losses in killed and wounded, and then asked him why two batteries had not been placed north of the Pegram House and two south of it, for I saw that four batteries thus placed, could have swept the battlefield from end to end, as the height of the hill would have enabled the artillery to fire over our infantry with safety, thus protecting their advance, or sheltering them if they had been compelled to fall back. In the latter case, the enemy would not have been able to drive our men from their splendid position. "Well, Captain," Gen-Willcox replied, "it's all over now and he wears a stove-pipe." (Meaning by this expression that the Chief of Artillery, who had ordered the Battery into the position it had occupied, had been dismissed from the army.)

In this engagement Private S. Brunnemer was killed, Private Edward Ebell mortally wounded (dying October 6th at Beverly Hospital, R. I.), and Privates James Baine, William Berndt, H. Kasemeyer and Patrick Kiernan, more or less severely wounded. Besides these, three horses were killed and five wounded. All these casualties occurred within ten minutes. This position was afterward strongly fortified by us with redoubts and breastworks ; the latter were held by our infantry. The Pegram House was afterward burned, either by our own fire or that of the enemy. On the day preceding my return to the front, the enemy made an attack on our lines in the course of which the Battery fired ten rounds. One section was ordered to take position in Redoubt No. 2, to maintain a vigilant watch on the enemy's line.

October 12th the left section was in position in Redoubt No. 1, and the right section in Redoubt No. 2, and both sections fired occasionally during the day. The Battery remained here in position until November 1st, when it went into camp at Poplar Spring Church, and enjoyed a little rest. The 8th was spent in overhauling everything, men's quarters, gun-carriages, caissons, harness, etc., and, in what might be called a thorough "house cleaning." Two days later one section was drilled mounted, and one day later, both sections were thus drilled. On the 13th the Battery was inspected, and afterward there was a mounted drill in all the maneuvers likely to be required on the battlefield.

The Battery remained here until November 29th, and, meantime, the men were allowed to have some change of occupation.

On the 29th the Battery was ordered to go to the right some seven miles, to the Friend House, in rear of our main line fronting Petersburg. On the 1st of December, the guns were placed in position in Fort Friend, while the caissons went into camp still farther to the rear, near Meade Station on the U. S. Military Railroad. Both men and horses were, at this time, pretty well used up. I reported this state of affairs to Gen. Willcox, who said in reply, he had already considered our case, and had, for the very reason I had mentioned, ordered the Battery to Fort Friend, where both men and horses could rest comfortably, because that fort was one of the rear ones, and, consequently, the men would have little or nothing to do during the winter, beyond the routine work necessary to keep them in condition for instant service, and I would be allowed to give the men all the liberty and privileges I had at my disposal. Gen. Willcox said further, "I know your Battery has undergone very arduous service since the Battle of the Wilderness, May 5th. You will now be near my headquarters, and if I can aid you in making your men more comfortable just let me know." I thoroughly appreciated Gen. Willcox's kindness.

The Battery was now directly in front of Petersburg, but in the rear line, and the "Johnnies" could not peek at us so well as before, when their southern blood was up. Whenever they tried to do so, we gave them a good dose of northern pills to cool them off, and, according to their own acknowledgment, our medicine was, in most cases, very effective.

On December 2, 1864, the following order was issued to the Battery:

> HEADQUARTERS 34th N. Y. INDEP. V. V. LIGHT BATTERY,
> FORT FRIEND, before Petersburg, Dec. 2, 1864.

C. O. No. 19.

Winter quarters will be constructed for both men and horses. The Battery's guns will be parked facing south. The officers' quarters will be erected in rear of the guns, and the men's quarters on the right and left. The stables will be south of the fort, facing east and west, and will be 100 feet long by 50 feet wide. The hospital stables will be 25 feet by 25 feet. All fencing shall be 12 feet high. Log houses for the men shall be each 8 feet by 10 feet, and $4\frac{1}{2}$ feet high, and covered with shelter tents. All crevices must be filled with clay.   By order of

CAPT. JACOB ROEMER,
Commanding Battery.

John H. Starkins, First Sergeant.

The log houses constructed in compliance with the foregoing order accommodated four men each, comfortably. It took fully three weeks to complete the houses and stables, although all worked very hard early and late. Still all felt well repaid for their labor, and were very proud of their quarters, which were greatly praised by all who saw them. While at Vicksburg in 1863, I made the acquaintance of a Lieut. Graves, commanding a U. S. Battery. He and three other officers called on me soon after the camp was completed. After mutual greetings had been exchanged, Lieut. Graves said to me, "Roemer, just after our arrival from the Shenandoah Valley we heard that you had one of the finest camps around here. If you don't mind, I would like to inspect it and your stables." I acceded to his wish. After the inspection was over, he said, "Roemer, without any flattery, you have the very best constructed camp and stables of any battery in the field, regular or volunteer, and in this my three friends here agree with me." In reply, I told him I had not traveled for three years with regular batteries without learning something.

During all this time the Battery had fired an occasional shot at the enemy across the Appomattox, and had also had, at irregular intervals, mounted drills both by sections and by battery. When the houses were finished it received orders to fix up and paint the gun-carriages and caissons. This being finished, the Battery was inspected by Maj. Miller, Asst. Insp. Gen. First Div., Ninth Corps.

December 14, 1864, I received my commission as Brevet-Major U. S. V., from President Lincoln, for meritorious services in the field from the Wilderness to Petersburg, and particularly for services rendered at Spottsylvania Court House, on May 12, 1864. It was brought to me by Capt. Brackett, of Gen. Willcox's staff. Handing it to me he said, "Captain Roemer, I have the honor of presenting to you your commission as Brevet-Major of U. S. Volunteers, given you by President Lincoln for meritorious services rendered on many battlefields. This is one of the proudest moments of my life, for I also have one as Brevet-Major, dated the same day as yours (Dec. 2, 1864), from our noble President, Abraham Lincoln." We embraced each other, as was natural, and did what men do not generally do, hugged and kissed each other.

We had been constantly together during the campaign from the Wilderness to Petersburg, under most trying and dangerous circumstances, and on all the other battlefields as well as on that famous field at Spottsylvania Court House on that memorable 12th of May, 1864. Captain and Brevet, Major Brackett was one of my chief advisers and companions during the campaign, and it was but natural that we should be much attached to each other. In this campaign so far, the 34th New York Battery had thrown, by actual computation, 10,450 pounds of iron into the enemy's lines, in its endeavors to break the force of the terrible charges made by them upon our lines.

By Christmas, everything in and around Fort Friend had been put in perfect order,—camp, stables, etc., were all complete. Even Christmas trees had been planted in the little park in front of the tents. Looking at these, one would think it was June, rather than December. The holly bushes obtained from the Virginia woods, with their dark green glossy leaves and scarlet berries peeping out from among them, presented a picture well worth seeing. At a distance the holly berries might easily be mistaken for cherries, and, in fact, were by some of our distinguished visitors.

On Christmas morning we received the season's compliments from our numerous friends and visitors. This ancient holiday is greatly enjoyed every year by all living in Christian countries, but this particular Christmas was especially enjoyed by the true soldier in the field. His thoughts naturally turned to the dear ones at home assembled around the fireside, and, although he could not attend church, yet he could be as truly devout and worship God as sincerely out there in the field amid the beauties of nature as in the grandest church. I have commanded one hundred and fifty men constantly for four long years, have studied their natures, and have learned to know just how their thoughts will run at times, and also what constitutes a thoroughly good soldier. Such a one makes a good citizen, a faithful husband and a loving father. I have watched my men, not alone while they were under my command in the field, but ever since they received their discharge from the army, now thirty-one years ago, and I find that the opinions I then formed of them as to character, have remained unchanged.

Christmas presents were exchanged by the members of the Battery among one another, and I came in for my full share of them. I must mention one of them, it was so unique. It was a wreath representing a company of soldiers gathered around their commander on the battlefield. It was composed of one hundred and eighty pieces of wood obtained from the forests around us, carved and fashioned with an ordinary pocket-knife, and so fitted together that one single piece held the whole number in place, without the use of any nails, screws, or glue. It was a finished piece of work, and I still cherish it as a sacred emblem of my men's love for me, their commander.

During the month of July, my men had collected some fifteen pounds of rebel bullets picked up in and around Fort Willcox. These were taken by some men of the 48th Pa. Vols., (Engineers) melted and cast into the form of a miniature 10-inch mortar. This I still have in my possession and, on every recurring Fourth of July I salute the national flag with it, firing the requisite number of rounds—one for every star in the flag. Very many souvenirs of the war were made of these leaden missiles picked up inside of our lines, and to make them in the designs adopted, required talent and skill in workmanship of no mean order, but of these there was an abundance among the members of the Battery.

I have always felt a certain degree of contempt for the professional opinions of a certain high officer of the British army (Lord Wolsely) who has stated as his belief, that the Union Army of 1861-1865 was nothing but an "organized mob." However, every man who considers the subject candidly, thinks very differently, for he knows what arduous services that army performed on hundreds of battlefields from the First Battle at Bull Run to the Surrender at Appomattox Court House. In addition to their abilities as tireless fighters, the soldiers of that army were capable of performing any service whatever, from fastening a horseshoe to building a bridge either on pontoons or on piers, or repairing a locomotive. The troops of the Army of the Potomac were under fire day by day from the Wilderness May 5th to Petersburg, June 18th, a period of fifty-four days during which they practically fought all day and marched all night and had very little rest, and were seldom out of the range of rebel bullets.

CHAPTER XVI.

SIEGE OF PETESBURG CONCLUDED. CAPTURE AND RECAPTURE OF FORT STEDMAN. SURRENDER OF PETERSBURG.

New Year's Day, 1865, was formally opened with calls made on us by many officers who came to present their congratulations and wish us "A Happy New Year." One and all spoke of their hopes and longings for a speedy termination of the war. Dr. McDonald in particular, made a personal call, and then inspected our stables, officially, to ascertain their sanitary condition. While we were going through the stables he fell in love with a beautiful gray horse that had been severely wounded June 2, 1864, by a bullet striking him in the left fore shoulder. I had thought at the time we would have to shoot him, but when we were about to do so he looked at me so pitifully that I had not the heart to give the order to fire. I ordered the men to give him twenty-four hours more of grace. At the end of that time he had so far recovered as to be able to rise to his feet. A few weeks later he became fit to be ridden. Just before New Year's Day, however, he fell lame again. Dr. McDonald examined him and found the bullet had lodged in the left breast, where it interfered greatly with the movements of the muscles. The next day the doctor came again and extracted the bullet, and then said, "I have done this for my own satisfaction, but I did not think I should have to cut so deep as I did—three inches." He showed me the bullet, which had been so flattened out that it resembled a half dollar more than it did a bullet. After this operation the gray rapidly improved, and in a short time became the pride of the Battery. In June, 1865, he was turned over to the government in good condition.

First Sergeant Johnston, who had been acting second lieutenant since October 14, 1864, was mustered in as second lieutenant, to rank from January 1, 1865, and Sergeant William E. Balkie was also mustered in as second lieutenant, to rank from January 14, 1865.

The Battery passed the time it was in Fort Friend doing garrison duty and in drilling. An occasional shot was fired into the enemy's lines or at their baggage trains across the Appomattox. This manner of life continued until the 24th of March, when an order, Special Order No. 5, Headquarters, Artillery Brigade, Ninth Corps, came for the 34th N. Y. Battery and the 46th N. Y. Infantry, as the Battery's support, to proceed at once to Fort McGilvery and relieve Capt. Rhoad's Battery D, Pa. Art. (late Durell's). This fort was on the right and on the front line of our works about a quarter of a mile south of the Appomattox. The troops moved up to the fort at 9 P. M. and took possession of it. The guns were placed in position, and the infantry posted at once. I then examined the magazine, the ditch in front, the port holes, etc., very carefully, and made everything ready to meet any possible attack during the night. As we were all perfect strangers to this new position, and as there is nothing like getting used to new surroundings in war as quickly as possible, this careful inspection of these quarters was absolutely necessary. The fort was one of the strongest of the three large forts in our front line. Confronting it, was a very strong work of the enemy's not over nine hundred yards distant. When I took charge of the fort, I was charged to guard it most rigidly and vigorously, and therefore, in making our arrangements, I instructed the Sergeant commanding the guard, to keep one gun loaded ready for firing in case of an attack, and, in such a case, to call me if he should have time, but if not, to fire the gun which would be a signal for every man to be at his post without waiting for orders. No one was allowed to undress for the night.

At half-past eleven I took my blanket and lay down to sleep in temporary quarters provided by my servant, who then, wrapped in his blanket, lay down by my side. I slept lightly until about 3:30 on the morning of the 25th, at which hour Sergeant Rossbach, sergeant of the guard, awoke me and said, "Captain, there is some disturbance on our left in the direction of Fort Stedman, but I cannot make out what it is." I arose immediately and, with the sergeant went to the rear and left of the fort, and very soon saw there was trouble of some sort at Fort Stedman. We heard musketry firing. Some twenty or thirty shots were fired and then it ceased, but soon began again. I now ordered Sergeant Rossbach to send his corporal, with my compliments, to Lieut.-Col. Ely, commanding Second Brigade, First Division, Ninth Corps, to tell him I wished to see him at once in Fort McGilvery on important business concerning this musketry fire. Col. Ely soon came with his orderly. As he entered the fort, he inquired, "Roemer, what's the matter?" I explained the matter to him, and at the moment I had finished I saw one of the guns of Roger's Nineteenth New York Battery, stationed in Fort Stedman, fire a shot to the rear. At this I turned to Col. Ely and said, "Colonel, the Johnnies have taken Fort Stedman." This occurred at 4 A. M. while it was still quite dark. "What makes you think so?" he inquired. "Well, Colonel," I replied, "the gun just discharged would have been fired west if our troops had possession of the fort, but as it fired east, that makes me think the enemy have gained possession of the fort and turned

Rogers' guns on our men to drive them to the rear." I could not see, but I could hear, and while I was standing there pointing with my sabre in the direction of Fort Stedman, another of the fort's guns thundered to the rear. This startled Col. Ely, and he at once said, "Roemer, you are right." "Now, Colonel," I asked, "what are your orders?" He answered, "Captain, I will give you no orders. Exercise your best judgment in using your guns and the muskets of the 46th New York." "Then, Colonel," said I, "please order Lieut.-Col. Becker of the 46th, to open the three left port holes, and I will open fire at once on Fort Stedman with percussion shell." In half an hour the port holes were open and three guns in position at them, ready to throw shell into the fort which had been the position of Rogers' 19th New York Battery and rout out the enemy.

The growing light of the dawn in the east had now become sufficient for me to discern objects and to direct our shells so as to be effective in checking the enemy's progress. From our fort we could see the enemy's advancing lines, now but about four hundred yards distant from the Union lines, on ground rising some twenty or twenty-five feet up to Fort Stedman. Through my glass I could see some passing and repassing along the lines, looking, from my position, like sticks, though they were, in reality, the enemy's soldiers. All this time I did not notice the firing of a single shot at them from the guns, either of Fort Stedman or Fort Haskell. Our guns in Fort McGilvery fired some thirty or more shots before any others of our Union artillery opened fire.

It was now clearly evident that the enemy had broken through our lines and were in full possession of Fort Stedman. At this moment all the guns and mortars in the rebel lines from Cemetery Hill to the forts north of the Appomattox, opened fire on Fort McGilvery, for that fort was now, for them, the most important point to gain next, because it commanded the road to City Point on the James River, the base of supplies for both the Army of the Potomac and the Army of the James. Their lines of fire upon us in Fort McGilvery formed the radii of a complete half circle, of which our fort was the center or focus. They had full sweep upon us, and the air was filled with flying shot and shell. Several of their mortar shells entered the fort. One of these struck the ground near where my servant was lying asleep, and exploded, throwing a cart load of earth over him, and, of course, waking him up. He scrambled out and rushed over to where I was standing, a most thoroughly frightened boy. As soon as I saw who it was, I asked him, "Frank, what is the matter with you?" He then told me about the explosion, and added that he thought his last minute had come. I told him to go back, but he refused to stir an inch, saying, "Captain, I won't leave you, for wherever you are there is luck," and go back he did not, but always kept close at my heels or clung to my coat.

Everything was now hurried to head off the enemy's advance. Gen. Hartranft was among the first to advance against the enemy with his Pennsylvania Reserves of the Third Division, Ninth Corps, and close up on them. I saw that the enemy had secured two of the 19th New York's guns and several Coehorn mortars and taken them out in front of Fort Stedman ready to run them back into their lines. I called Sergeant Rossbach and asked him to tell me what he could see. He said he could see quite a group of men gathered around the guns and mortars. He then returned to his piece, and with the aid of my glass aimed it at the group of men who were struggling hard to take the guns away. Two shrapnel from Rossbach's guns frightened them terribly, and they ran away leaving the guns behind. The guns were, however, soon after retaken by our troops and brought back within our lines.

In the meantime the three guns in the left port holes of Fort McGilvery had been doing good work, but now the ammunition was running low. To obtain more I sent off two horsemen, one to artillery headquarters and the other to the Battery's caisson camp, with orders to get 200 rounds each. I thought that, perhaps, the one sent to artillery brigade headquarters might be captured, and, for that reason had sent the other as I did. The latter I told to go to the rear and far enough to the east to gain a deep gully, which would protect him, and bring back word whether the Battery's wagons had arrived at the place to which I had ordered them to go. The first horseman was captured as I had feared. The other returned in safety and said the wagons had arrived. I immediately sent him back to bring up the ammunition through the gully above mentioned.

The rebels had now reached ground fully one mile to the rear of our lines. We, in Fort McGilvery, were firing round after round and things were becoming very lively on our left, when I noticed a column of the enemy advancing on the rear and left of the fort along the Norfolk road at a point where there was a deep cut through a hill. As there were no port holes in the rear parapet of Fort McGilvery, no guns could be brought to bear on this column in the regular way, but as this advancing column was placing our infantry at the enemy's mercy, it had become a matter of the highest importance to check it, if possible, and very quickly, too. Our guns must be brought somehow to bear upon this column as it came through and out of the cut. I ordered gun No. 5, commanded by Sergeant A. Townsend to be pushed up the rear traverse and put on the parapet of the fort. It was done successfully but it took ten strong men to do it. Corporal Wm. Rierson was the gunner in charge of the piece. The Battery's beautiful guidon was planted beside this gun. Then were heard the cheers of the infantry when they saw gun and guidon on top of the parapet. All the infantry in our front and on our right were composed of some of our best troops. They were the 2d, 8th, 17th and 27th Michigan, the 51st New York, the 51st Pennsylvania, and the 21st and 36th Massachusetts Volunteers, besides others that were old stand-bys. When the officers saw our gun and guidon, they called out to the men, "Courage, boys, Roemer will take care of us."

This was a very trying time; events were occurring more rapidly than I can recount them. The situation was very critical. There, in our left rear, was the advancing rebel column; here, on the rear parapet of Fort McGilvery, were we with but one gun bearing upon the column. But as this column was very compact in the cut, we felt we could do pretty good execution. I set to work with this one gun and nine men to do all that could be done. I charged the gunner to fire low. Three shots were fired but all were too high, going over their heads. The column still advanced. I then stepped up and took charge of the gun, and said, "We must do better or we are gone." I also knew that the ammunition was running very low, and I thought, "What then?" Just at this supremely critical moment, when we had but seven rounds left in the fort, Mr. Cryder, sutler of the 51st New York, who had been sent to help get the ammunition wagon up through the gully, drove up into the fort at a gallop with it, and thus saved the day for us.

After firing a fourth shot, we, at last, obtained the proper range, and the next three shells went just where I wanted them to go, for they struck the ground about four yards in front of the advancing column and there exploded right in the faces of the head of the column, doing great execution. The eighth shell produced a like effect. Just as I was about to utter the command, "Fire," for the ninth round, I was struck on the right shoulder by a piece of shell which also struck John Bauer, No. 3 of the gun squad, and nearly cut him in two, thus killing him instantly. After eleven shells more had been fired by this single gun on Fort McGilvery's rear parapet, the enemy surrendered in a body. They lost 127 killed and wounded, besides those prisoners who surrendered. One of the prisoners told us that the Battery's seventh shot killed eleven men and wounded twenty-two. The casualties among the gun squad working this gun on the parapet were one man, John Bauer, killed, and three men, Corporal Rierson, Privates T. S. Griffin and Patrick Kiernan, wounded, besides myself. My wound was very serious; I was kept under the influence of morphine for three days and three nights after the battle, and I may say I suffer from it to this day.

By 8 A. M., Fort Stedman had been re-taken and our lines re-established by the troops of the Ninth Corps. Two thousand prisoners and about sixteen hundred small arms were captured by the Ninth Corps. Requests for assistance were telegraphed to General Humphreys, commanding the Second Corps, but it arrived too late to be of service. General Hartranft, who had entered the battle as a brigadier-general, had become, at the close of the engagement at sundown, a major-general of United States Volunteers, for having brought up his Pennsylvania Reserves so hurriedly into action and having therewith checked the onslaught of the enemy and also for having given efficient aid in re-taking Fort Stedman. The guns of the 34th New York Battery, that were in action during this engagement, fired in all 465 rounds of ammunition. I had in Fort McGilvery four of my own guns and two belonging to United States (regular) Batteries, besides two pieces in Battery V near Appomattox River.

A heavy attack was made on our lines on March 29th by the enemy with both artillery and muskets. The enemy charged on our lines but were not successful, as the elements interfered; a heavy rain-storm put an end to all fighting for the day. Our supporting regiment, the 46th New York Volunteers, lost three men killed and ten wounded. The 34th New York Battery had two men wounded and fired 281 rounds.

March 30th, it rained all day, still the enemy were engaged in massing troops in our front and evidently preparing for another attack, but all our commands were fully aware of their movements and entirely ready to meet it. All had an abundant supply of pills, both large and small, for use as occasion might require. Those that had been administered since the morning of March 25th, had proved very effective. At 10 A. M., the enemy were observed massing troops at the Crater. All our troops were at their posts and the order was given to each command to be on the alert and ready for any emergency that might arise. Sleep was dispensed with unless it could be secured with one eye and one ear open. The excitement everywhere was most intense.

Friday, March 31st, was a day full of conundrums. Something was going on that could not be clearly explained. My own mind was so charged with the idea that a great storm was brewing, that would scatter the chaff in our front to the four quarters of the earth, that I could think of nothing else. During the day, artillery attacks were made by the enemy occasionally at various points along our entire line from the extreme right to the extreme left. At about 10 P.M., a heavy artillery fire was opened by the enemy upon the lines of the Ninth Corps, and at about the same time I received information from Colonel Ely commanding 2d Brigade 1st Division Ninth Corps, that two men representing themselves to be members of the 34th New York Battery had come across the Appomattox River.

I, at once, left the work upon which I was engaged at the time outside of the fort, returned to the fort and ordered the guards at the magazine to be doubled, taking for this purpose some of the men belonging to the 5th United States Artillery, one section of which was in position in the fort. These guards were instructed to allow no men not on duty to pass the magazine guard, and, under no circumstances, to allow any one not authorized, to enter it, and, furthermore, to keep a sharp lookout for spies and to guard against any mishap. The 34th's four guns kept up a continuous fire for two hours, and even then the enemy's fire was still very rapid. I now ordered thirty rounds of fuse shell with fifteen-second fuses to be prepared for use as hand-grenades to be thrown over the parapet if the enemy should charge on the fort and succeed in getting into the ditch in front.

This artillery fire on our lines continued from 10 P. M., March 31st, till nearly daylight on the morning of April 1st. To the 46th New York Infantry, the Battery's support in the fort, great credit is due for their hearty co-operation with the Battery. Every one had the greatest confidence in the ability of Fort McGilvery's garrison to take care of the fort if the enemy should charge upon it.

Although the next day, Saturday, April 1st, was "All Fools' Day," the men in Fort McGilvery hoped they would not be fooled by the enemy. I thought and felt it was a good day for "cleaning house," and the actions of the rebels seemed to indicate that they had the same feeling, and had determined to clear their forts of all the ammunition they contained, so that when we moved in we should not be encumbered with any old iron. So anxious were they to rid themselves of their ammunition that they threw their shot and shell around very promiscuously among our troops, and this brought on severe fighting and plenty of it on both sides, and for both, the day proved to be a most fearful one.

As the day passed, death and destruction were dealt out on all sides, and the air was fairly filled with shrieking rifles and hissing mortar shells (I can hear them yet). These dropped all around and among us in Fort McGilvery, regardless of life and limb. The fighting was almost as severe as it had been on the 25th of March, but it was not at such close quarters as it was then, around the forts and trenches, yet it was close enough for comfort. Around Fort McGilvery it seemed as if an upheaval of the earth, of some sort, was going on, by the way the earth was torn up and regular gullies dug out where their shells had exploded. For hundreds of yards around just outside the fort, in our front, the ground looked as if droves of hungry hogs had been rooting in it. Some of the mortar shells penetrated the earth to a depth of from three to six feet, and then exploded, making holes large enough to bury horses in. The largest of these holes were made by the 100-pounders. One can readily imagine how great must have been the force that hurled these missiles forth to perform their work of destruction.

This firing continued throughout the whole day, and when night came on it did not cease, but was kept up until the next morning, Sunday, April 2d. In fact, between the hours of 11 P. M., April 1st, and 2 A. M., April 2d, the firing was greater than it had been during the preceding day. It had been constant for twenty-one hours out of the twenty-four, and this had been the case every day since the 25th of March. Although every one was worn out, yet all were ready for work, no matter how fatiguing it might be, if duty called them. All in Fort McGilvery were at their posts ready to act when the command was given, whatever the emergency might be. Cannoneers rested beside their guns whenever opportunity offered, and the infantry with muskets firmly grasped lay down and slept for a while whenever there was a lull in the enemy's fire, as best they could.

These were the soldiers of whom our country ought to be proud, for no one can fight as they did unless actuated by a sincere love for his country and its glorious flag. I do not think there was one of the 34th, officer or man, who had his clothes off between March 25th and April 4th. The Battery's four guns in Fort McGilvery fired 480 rounds between Saturday morning, April 1st, and Sunday morning, April 2d, and to do this, as may be readily understood, required very hard work. The two pieces in Battery V. fired sixty rounds. Our only casualties were Corporals T. S. Griffin and Fuller wounded. At 10 P. M. I was ordered to report at headquarters artillery brigade, and did so at 11 P. M., and then received orders to be prepared for any emergency, also to be ready to move with the troops to any point.

Just at daylight on Sunday morning, April 2d, we observed that the enemy were making some unusual movements along their lines and within their works. These movements seemed to indicate that they were reinforcing certain points. At 8 A. M. we saw what was thought to be a large fire in the city of Petersburg. They were bringing in troops from their outer lines and seemed to be preparing to attack our lines. While this was going on the fire in the city appeared to be spreading, as the volume of smoke was growing more dense. By noon it appeared to us that Petersburg was doomed to be completely destroyed. We conjectured that they must be burning some materials or stores. Standing upon the rampart of the fort, I could look with my glass, directly into the great market-place in the heart of the city. I saw that a great fire was raging there, and that a great concourse of people had gathered around it and were looking on. I thought this was a good opportunity for us to open fire. Acting upon this thought I sent an orderly to Gen. Willcox with a note asking permission to open fire upon this point. Gen. Willcox wrote upon the back of my note his reply in these words, "Yes, Major, open fire upon the city and help the fire along," and sent it back to me post haste. It did not take long to get the guns ready; in fact, they were ready before the reply came, I was so certain what its tenor would be.

The first four or five shots directed upon this point caused a great scattering of the people gathered around the fire. The Battery's fire appeared to be effective and it was kept up during the whole afternoon. The movements of the enemy's troops continued during the entire day, and among our own troops there were all sorts of conjectures as to what these movements meant and also much wonderment regarding the next act in this great drama of war, to be played on this magnificent stage. All were waiting anxiously for the curtain to rise and every eye was strained to see what the rising of the curtain would disclose. Some said Grant was like the great Napoleon at Jena or the Katzbach; we knew it could not be a Waterloo for Lee had no Blucher.

All along the Union lines the troops were waiting and watching everything closely, entirely ready for the tiger to jump and firmly determined to throttle him then and there. We were becoming impatient and desirous of a little active excitement to relieve the strain. By 3 P. M., seven different attacks had been made on as many different parts of our lines, but what the final result would be, could not be clearly defined. We believed, however, that it would soon be revealed, for the enemy appeared to be equally as determined as we, to have the thing settled speedily. The enemy's troops could still be seen marching here and there, placing batteries in position and arranging other details of their plans. We concluded that soon we should either come into close quarters in a most desperate conflict, or be at their heels. The glorious sun was sinking in the west, but what the prospect would be when it rose again, God alone knew. Our boys were hoping and praying—hoping that the war would soon end; praying that it might, for they could not stand the strain much longer.

During this Sunday, April 2d, between sunrise and sunset the Battery fired seventy-three rounds and suffered no casualties.

At 10 P. M., Sunday, April 2d, orders were received to the effect that at 1 A. M., April 3d, the Second Brigade of the First Division of the Ninth Corps was to advance under the command of Colonel Ralph Ely from Fort McGilvery against the enemy's lines under cover of the fire of Major Roemer's guns in the fort. This fire was to continue until the first hurrah was heard from the troops covered by it, when it was to cease. This brigade was composed mainly of Michigan, New York and Pennsylvania troops, which occupied the Union lines in front of Fort McGilvery, and on its right and left flanks. These regiments were all old "stand-bys" of the Battery, and had gone with it through many a "valley of the shadow of death." The 46th New York, the Battery's support in the fort, was also to go with the brigade.

Precisely at 1 A. M., Monday, April 3d, the Second Brigade marched out, and when the troops were two hundred yards away, the 34th New York Battery opened on the rebel lines, firing over the heads of the advancing troops while they were feeling their way toward the enemy's lines, where they would either drive out the enemy or be captured themselves by the rebels. Such chances must be taken, at times, in order to accomplish something definite. The Battery continued firing until 2 A. M. when, after a brief pause, the firing was resumed and continued until 3, but even then no answering "hurrah" reached our ears, and we began to think the rebels had taken down the telegraph poles, or the message expected had not reached headquarters, yet we were sure the message must come. We could not even think of the word "defeat," so confident were we that our cause must win.

At exactly twenty minutes past 3 A. M. on that memorable Monday, the electrifying cheer reached us, "Hurrah! Hurrah! Hurrah!" and it was as if a galvanic battery had sent an electric shock through every man. All were on the *qui vive*. I then gave the order "Cease firing," and asked if all the guns were empty. Sergeant Townsend said, "My gun is still loaded." This gun was fired, and that shot was the last one fired into Petersburg, and was also, for the 34th New York Battery, the last shot of the war. I looked at my watch and noted the time: it was 3:40 A. M. As the echoes of this last shot died away, I shouted, "Petersburg is ours; the war is over; and to-day is my 47th birthday. Boys, you have done nobly." Can any one who was not in active service during the late war imagine the scene in the fort that followed my remark, or the time the boys made about it? After four long years of hard service in the field, all my boys, the bravest of the brave, were now gathered around me, grasping my hand and offering congratulations that I knew were honest and heartfelt. There were genuine tears in many eyes as the boys grasped my hand, and some were wholly unable to utter a word.

When we knew that all was quiet along the lines, and when the congratulations were over, I said, "Boys, you have done nobly for Uncle Sam, and he, in turn, appreciates you, and has provided some 'commissary' as a tonic for your worn-out nerves." There was a wild cheer for Uncle Sam. The "commissary" disappeared rapidly, for the boys drank heartily and, furthermore, I was repeatedly called out and my health drank.

All day long there was universal rejoicing along the entire line among the troops that had not as yet been ordered forward, for all now knew they would soon return to their beloved homes and families. No matter which way one turned and met another, whether soldier or officer, there was a hearty clasping of hands accompanied with a fervent expression of thanksgiving. The usual remark was, "Petersburg is ours, and our strife is over." As soon as it became known that Petersburg had fallen, and was really in our possession, all that could obtain leave were off to the city to see the sights and secure trophies as mementos, but a more permanent memento was engraved on the heart of every soldier who served before Petersburg, for the memory of the hardships they had there endured could never be effaced, but for the moment, all that was forgotten. The first thing all sought to obtain was tobacco, for they had been on a short allowance of that article for months.

In the previous June, I had bought $200 worth of tobacco and had since that time dealt it out very sparingly, to make the supply hold out. It acted like a charm; whenever the men were sick and not able to tell what ailed them, I gave them some tobacco, and, presto! all ailments were forgotten. This tobacco bought in June and some in addition bought from the Battery's sutler was placed under the charge of the quartermaster sergeant, who distributed it weekly in small quantities, but the supply was now giving out, and this prospect of obtaining more was hailed with joy and delight. Hearing that tobacco could be had in abundance in Petersburg, I started out at daylight on the 4th of April with four men and rode directly into the city, where I could see things in it without the aid of my glass. What we had strained our eyes to see the day before, was now right before us. We reined up in front of a large tobacco warehouse and saw that all were helping themselves liberally, and at that same moment two cavalrymen came out bringing with them a case of tobacco weighing two hundred pounds.

I, at once, seized the case for my men, broke it open, divided it into four parts weighing fifty pounds each, and gave one to each of my men to carry back to Fort McGilvery. The cavalrymen strongly objected to this procedure, but I told them they were privates and had no right to take it from the warehouse; I said, furthermore, that cavalrymen are always taking all the chickens and ducks, while we, artillery men, have to be satisfied with the feathers. I sent my men back to the fort; I knew, without going back with them, how much my men would appreciate what I had sent them.

I now had an opportunity of seeing at close range the result of what we had witnessed at a distance the preceding Sunday — the great fire. I learned that, on that day, four million dollars worth of tobacco had been burned by order of General Lee. It was no wonder then that there had been such an immense volume of smoke. Riding around the various parts of the city, I saw where buildings had been burned and also others that were still burning which had been fired by the enemy just previous to the evacuation of the city, so that we should not reap the fullest benefit of the capture. Those of our troops that first entered the city, did their utmost to extinguish the fires.

After my return to Fort McGilvery, I found that my ride into and through the city had been injurious to me as I had not yet fully recovered from the wound received on March 25th. I was seized with an internal hemorrhage, and my boys were greatly frightened. The surgeon was called, and I was ordered to keep very quiet. I felt that I could now do so, for I had had the satisfaction of procuring some tobacco for the men which I knew afforded them much gratification. "A contended mind is a continual feast," and that feast I had as I lay there in my bunk.

It was a general holiday for most of the troops lying before Petersburg; such a holiday as we had never had since the war began. My young son, Louis H. Roemer, and Mr. L. Budenbender, our worthy Battery sutler, came up from our caisson camp to congratulate the boys of the 34th on their successful fight and the capture of Petersburg. The news appeared to electrify every one. "How must our folks at home feel at this news since we ourselves feel so happy over it?" inquired our worthy sutler.

CHAPTER XVII.

RETURN FROM PETERSBURG TO WASHINGTON. THE GRAND REVIEW.

WHILE in Petersburg on the morning of April 4th, I learned that the 46th New York Infantry and the 1st Michigan Sharpshooters were the regiments that had charged and carried the fort in front of Fort McGilvery on the morning of April 3d. The 46th was a fighting regiment, and I remember that when, on the night of March 24th, the 46th Infantry and the 34th Battery were on the road to Fort McGilvery, and were passing some regiment or battery, the latter would sing out, "Roemer, where are you going with your Battery?" and I would answer, "To Fort McGilvery." Then they would ask, "Who are your supports?" and the answer would be, "The 46th New York," and to this they would respond, "Then we will have a fight by G—." It had usually happened that whenever the 46th New York Infantry and the 34th New York Battery went out together on the skirmish line or, in fact, anywhere, it was considered a foregone conclusion that a fight was at hand. This had been generally remarked all along the lines, and thus the reputation of the two organizations had become well established in the Ninth Corps and also in other Corps.

The 34th New York Battery had been, at different times, christened with quite odd names, both by our own troops and by rebel regiments; at Spottsylvania, where our black pills proved too effective to suit the rebels, the latter shook their fists and shouted, "You red-whiskered devil, if we catch you, we will have you drawn and quartered with four yoke of oxen." Such threats naturally made us very much afraid of them, for we did not want to experience such treatment at their hands, but we consoled ourselves with the reflection that they were not at all likely to capture us.

This same day, April 4th, all the troops then in front of Petersburg were ordered to march out and join in the pursuit of Lee and his army, which was then retreating on the road to Danville.

The 34th New York Battery (Brevet-Major Roemer), the 7th Maine Battery (Capt. Twitchell), and the 14th Massachusetts Battery (Capt. Wright) were ordered to remain where they were and await further orders. These three batteries were placed under my command. We did not go with the other troops in pursuit of Lee because of my wound received on March 25th. We were to do "Home Guard" duty, as it were, and look after the Confederate artillery and ammunition captured by the Ninth Corps when it took the rebel works in its front. I was ordered to make a careful inspection of them, classify them, and then turn the whole over to the ordnance officer of the Ninth Corps. The captured artillery comprised three batteries—one of six-pounder Parrot rifles, much the worse for wear, a second, of six-pounder bronze smooth-bore Napoleons, and a third of twelve-pounder bronze smooth-bore Napoleons, that had never been in use—two ten-inch mortars loaded and ready to be fired, and 3,200 rounds of shot and shell. The new bronze battery was one that had been cast in Richmond, and had many defects in the way of pits or sand-blasts in the bore of every piece. Some of these pits were so deep that I could very easily detect them with my mirrors, as they were from one-fifth to one-fourth of an inch deep. These defects I reported to the ordnance officer when I turned the guns over to him.

I received orders on April 5th to take my three batteries and two others to City Point, Va. We arrived there at 5 P. M., and went into camp on the north side of the road. The ground was totally unfit for an artillery camp, but as the weather was fine we did not mind the ground so much. My son, Louis, and Mr. Budenbender, our Battery sutler, went with us. The next day, April 6th, I suffered much from my wound in consequence of this ten-mile march, because I had ridden the whole distance on my horse, and thus had overworked myself. The surgeon told me very plainly I must keep quiet, very quiet, indeed, or he would not be answerable for my life. I was thereupon relieved from duty, the command being temporarily assigned to Lieut. J. J. Johnston. My wound was very painful and I was very glad indeed, of the rest that relief from active duty afforded.

On the 7th the Battery changed position to better ground outside the works, in the direction of Petersburg. At 2 P. M., while lying in my bunk, almost unable to move, word came for all guards to turn out, as President Lincoln was passing through City Point on his way from Richmond to take the boat for Washington, accompanied by Gen. Willcox and attended by a numerous staff. As I greatly desired to see our illustrious President once more, I called my servant, and with his help, I rose up sufficiently to look out through the front of my tent, which was thrown wide open. As the head of the column reached the front of my tent, which stood close to the road, I saw Gen. Willcox speak to the President, who was riding between Gen. Willcox and another general, whose name I do not remember. The President drew nearer to my tent and greeted me with a pleasant smile, at the same time raising his hat to me as I lay on my couch. I shall never forget that smile, for it is too deeply engraven upon my memory for time to efface. His face seemed to be illumined with something unearthly. He was on his way to the nation's capital, whence he would soon announce to the world that what had been was now past—four long years of strife. His pure soul shone through his eyes, and as one looked at them, he would feel convinced that President Lincoln had, nearest his heart, the welfare and glory of his country.

The next day I was busy the whole day making out, with the help of the battery clerk, the quarterly ordnance returns for the first quarter of 1865, and the monthly quartermaster, animal, and forage returns for the previous month, March, 1865. In the afternoon of April 9th, a telegram was received at City Point from Gen. Grant's headquarters, announcing that Gen. R. E. Lee and his Army of Northern Virginia, had surrendered at Appomattox Court House, to Lieut.-Gen. U. S. Grant, commanding the armies of the United States. This put the finishing touch to the glorification begun with the fall of Petersburg and Richmond, formed the last of a series of brilliant victories gained for the union by the Army of the Potomac and the Army of the James, and heralded the return of permanent peace throughout our glorious country. It seemed almost too good to be true, that the contest was really at an end, and that soon we should return to our homes laden with honors.

I transmitted my ordnance and quartermaster's returns to the War Department, Washington, the next day, April 10th, by mail. The following day, news came that all the rebel troops in Lynchburg, Va., had surrendered. This occasioned renewed gratification. The 12th was spent in writing out a history of the 34th New York Independent V. V. Light Battery, to be sent to His Excellency Governor E. D. Morgan, of New York, as a part of the history of all the batteries of artillery sent out from that State. It rained the whole morning, and when it rains in Virginia, it rains, as the darkies say, "for fair." On the 13th, warrants for the non-commissioned officers were made out. Rain again fell heavily. On the 14th, was celebrated the anniversary of the surrender of Fort Sumter. At that place the flag that was lowered April 14, 1861, was again raised over it, April 14, 1865, by the same hands that lowered it, Gen. Robert Anderson, in the presence of a most distinguished company. This day the rain was still heavy and the weather very cold, for April, in Virginia.

April 15th, 1865. How can I describe this day! This day it was reported that President Lincoln had been assassinated in his box at Ford's Theater in Washington, by John Wilkes Booth, during the evening of April 14, 1865. Hardly had the face of our beloved President faded from our view, when we received this terrible news. The news spread like wild-fire among the troops, and every one was horror-stricken. "Oh, for the fiend that did the deed," was on every soldier's lip, and all were ready to tear him limb from limb. To think that only seven days before he had passed us with such brilliant prospects before him, with such bright hopes in his heart, and so beloved by every soldier that it was dangerous for any one to utter a harsh word against him in their presence, and now, to think that a cowardly assassin had put an end to his life, was almost too much for belief. At the City Point Hospital there were rebel patients as well as Union ones. When the news of Lincoln's assassination was received there, a rebel remarked that Lincoln was well out of the way; he was immediately attacked by the crippled Union soldiers with their crutches and, had the surgeons not interfered, would certainly have been killed.

This same day the Battery was to have been inspected, but, because of the heavy rains that had been falling the last few days, as well as because of the sad news received, the inspection was postponed till further orders. The next day, the 16th, I was confined to my cot all day, unable to move. The Battery changed camp on the 17th in obedience to orders requiring all the batteries of the Ninth Corps to be massed preparatory to moving. All stores were also ordered to be drawn without delay. On the 18th Gen. Willcox and staff (including Major Brackett), besides other officers of the Ninth Corps, visited me in my tent. We talked over past events and discussed the possibility of our soon returning to our respective homes. On the 19th there was a battery drill with four pieces. Part of the day was spent in arranging the camp and putting everything in complete order. On the 20th the mess account of the men entitled to a commutation for rations while on their veteran furlough, was made out to be presented for payment. The number of men was forty-nine, each of whom would receive six dollars and thirty cents.

The Battery was inspected on the 21st by a lieutenant of the 5th U. S. Artillery, who found everything connected with the Battery to be in the best of order. The same day I received another visit from Gen. Willcox and staff and other Ninth Corps officers, all of whom expressed the hope I would be able to go with them when the order came to move. The next day orders came for the Battery to be ready to embark on a steamer at a moment's notice, with four days' forage and seven days' rations. On the morning of the 23d, the members of the Battery were paid by Major Wiley, and at 2 P. M. came an order to embark the 34th and 19th New York Batteries, and the 207th Pennsylvania Volunteers on the screw steamer, *Davis*, at 3 P. M. All were on board by 6 P. M.

The steamer left City Point at 4 A. M. on the 24th for Fort Monroe, and arrived there at 12:30 A. M. on the 25th. Here the steamer grounded, but after a few hours' delay floated off again, and at 5 A. M. started off and steamed up Chesapeake Bay and the Potomac River, and arrived at Alexandria at 5 P. M. on the 25th. Here the Battery landed the next day in pursuance of orders received through the captain of a gunboat, and went into camp for the night, two and one-half miles west of the city. The day was very warm. The grass in the field where the Battery encamped was fully twelve inches high, and the horses thoroughly appreciated it, especially as it was the first fresh grass they had had this season. I now reported to Col. Ely commanding 2d Brigade, First Division, Ninth Corps.

The next day, the 27th, orders came to make out the muster and pay rolls to April 30th. The same day the Battery was moved to Fort Ellsworth, on the road to Fairfax Court House, where was found fine grazing for the horses and good camp ground for artillery. The 19th New York (Captain Rogers), the 27th New York (Captain Easton), the 34th New York (Captain Roemer), and Battery D, Pennsylvania Artillery (Captain Rhoads), were encamped together. While here the Battery was visited by Captain Miller, A. A. Insp. Gen., Ninth Corps, who complimented us on the efficiency and trimness of the Battery. Here also we learned of the capture and death of John Wilkes Booth, the assassin of President Lincoln, in a barn near Port Royal, on the right or south bank of the Rappahannock River.

Copies of the muster and pay-roll of April 30th were sent to the Adjutant General U. S. A., at Washington, D. C., and to the Adjutant General of New York, at Albany, May 1st. The monthly quartermaster's returns of camp and garrison equipage, animals and forage, were also sent to Washington. On the 3d, the Battery's sutler, Mr. Budenbender, opened his booth for the accommodation of the men, as no passes were granted to cross Long Bridge to Washington. Orders came May 5th to draw twenty-eight horses and to put the Battery in complete order for active service. Two days later the history of the Battery, both as Battery L., 2d New York Artillery, and as the 34th New York Indep. V. V. Light Battery, from 1861 to 1865, was completed and sent by mail to Col. L. L. Doty, Chief of the Bureau of Military Statistics for the State of New York, at Albany, New York. On the 9th the Battery was inspected in mounted drill, preparatory to going to Texas. Two days later occurred the heaviest rain and hail storm I ever saw; the hailstones were often as large as pigeon's eggs, and greatly damaged the trees and growing crops of all kinds.

On the 12th, the Second and Fifth Corps arrived and passed us going into camp, near Alexandria, to prepare for the grand review. Later Sherman's army also passed and went into camp, near Alexandria, for the same purpose. When the news of the surrender of Kirby Smith's forces was received in camp, the boys were happy, because the trip to Texas was thus made no longer necessary, and a speedy return home was now sure. For this reason also, mounted drills were discontinued.

My wife, two daughters, Louise and Clara, and one son, Louis H. Roemer, my wife's sister, Mrs. Budenbender, wife of our sutler, and her son, George, were visiting me at Mount Eagle Farm, near Fort Ellsworth. They had the pleasure of seeing Gen. Sherman's army pass by. Such a sight as that army presented, I do not think was ever presented before. Many of the men were shoeless; very many were coatless; and many were also even hatless. Some carried frying-pans while others carried tin cups, and there were some who wore pieces and rags of blankets strapped on their backs. All, however, were so happy at seeing the ladies that they cheered the latter most heartily. My wife said to them, "You are all good and brave boys," and then the cheers were renewed; all the country round echoed and re-echoed with the shouts of the boys who had done so much for their country.

I was very glad that so many of my family were enabled to witness these sights as well as the grand review, which taken all in all, is the grandest recorded in history. We, of the 34th New York Battery, were now also permitted to take part in this review through Kirby Smith's surrender. On the 22d orders came to march to Washington and go into camp on Capitol Hill, then an open field, and prepare for the great review. All the troops were assigned to their camps in such a way that they could fall into line for this review without interfering one with the other. Our friends soon learned that the Battery had arrived in Washington, and they quickly found their way to our camp. During the evening of May 22d a large number of friends visited us, among whom was a fellow-townsman, Joseph Bedell.

Mrs. Kimball, our Sanitary Commission friend, also found us and claimed the honor of decorating the Battery for the morrow's parade. She was on hand the next morning, bright and early, accompanied by a corps of assistants bearing wreaths of laurel and bouquets of flowers. They placed the wreaths upon the muzzles of the guns and gave the bouquets to the officers and men. When the decoration of the guns was completed, Mrs. Kimball came to me and said, "Major Roemer, I am thankful for this privilege, for I can thus, in a measure, repay you and your men for your kindnesses to me and my associates during our visits to you and your boys in front of Petersburg in the summer of 1864." It was to be a proud and joyous day for us all, and it was eminently fitting that our guns and caissons should be in gala dress on this festive occasion, and particularly because they had performed their full duty in the late conflict.

The morning of May 23d dawned bright and clear. Everybody in the camps of the Army of the Potomac that extended from Capitol Hill to the Navy Yard, a distance of two miles or more, and were occupied by a mighty number of men and a great mass of implements of war, was actively engaged in preparing for the grand march past the highest officers of the National Government. But through all this joyful excitement there ran a vein of sadness, for, after this day, those who had been close associates for months and years, were to part, never to meet again, perhaps, this side of eternity. Only old soldiers can know what close attachments may be formed on the battlefield, and how strong and enduring such attachments are.

At 10 A. M., came the order to be ready to march. Soon the head of the column started; the grand review had begun. The glitter of the bayonets as the bright rays of the sun fell upon them was almost enough to blind those who observed it. Such a magnificent sight had never been witnessed before. There is no record of so large an army being massed in so small a space even in the time of the great Napoleon. Where have we read of the assembling of one-fifth of a million soldiers, a body, whose camps covered nearly four square miles and composed, too, of the flower of the land? These men had fought on hundreds of battlefields and hundreds of miles apart; had marched miles and miles along rough and broken roads, through miry swamps, across deep and dangerous rivers, over steep mountains, and through narrow valleys, working and fighting night and day as they went on; and had, at last, achieved a victory over all obstacles and every foe.

To show what distances were frequently traversed by various commands in the Union army, a single instance will suffice. Our battery—then Battery L. 2d New York Artillery—left Falmouth, Va., Feb. 5, 1863, for the west with the Ninth Corps detachment commanded by General John G. Parke, and arrived at Vicksburg, June 18th. During this time the number of miles passed over by the battery, would be, counting all marches made, not much less than twenty-five hundred miles.

But the reader may be becoming impatient to learn of the grand review as we of the Battery saw it and took part in it. At 10:30 A. M., we were on the march and just entering Pennsylvania Avenue from the eastern side of the Capitol. The battery had been assigned to the first battery position behind General Parke and staff at the head of the Ninth Corps column, and we felt our importance mightily. We marched battery front; our line stretched from curb to curb, along which, on either side, cavalry were posted to keep back the immense throng of people. There were twenty-seven horses abreast in the front line of pieces, and allowing three and one-half feet to each horse and rider, one can easily calculate the space covered. It was in what might be called a solid column closely packed. The whole column was equally solid throughout its entire length. One can easily imagine it must have been, when informed, that sixty-four thousand men passed the reviewing stand inside of four hours.

As the Battery wheeled to the right into Fifteenth Street at the Treasury Building, I had for the first time an opportunity to look back towards the Capitol at the marching column, and what a sea of heads and what a forest of bayonets were behind us. While passing the Treasury the cannoners of the Battery, sitting erect on the limber and caisson chests with folded arms, looked like so many statues. Then the Battery wheeled to the left into Pennsylvania Avenue again and advanced to pass the grand reviewing stand at the White House. At this point were assembled the highest officers of the government, both civil and military, President Andrew Johnson, Lieutenant-General Grant, Major-General Sherman and very many others. The absence of President Lincoln caused sadness in every heart, and Major-General Sheridan was also missed. Each officer saluted in passing, and in turn received a salute from the reviewing officers. As soon as the Battery had passed the reviewing stand it was dismissed from the parade, and then returned to its former camp ground at Fort Ellsworth, on the Virginia side of the Potomac, while the troops composing the armies of Gen. Sherman, which were to be reviewed the next day, the 24th, took our places on Capitol Hill to be ready for the march. The troops reviewed the first day were those belonging to the Ninth Corps under Maj.-Gen. Parke, the Fifth under Maj.-Gen. Griffin, and the Second, under Maj.-Gen. Humphreys, with Sheridan's Cavalry Corps under Maj.-Gen. Merritt, in the lead, while Maj.-Gen. Meade headed the column.

Upon reaching the bridge to cross the Potomac, I turned the command over to Lieut. Heasley, and returned to Pennsylvania Avenue to call on Mr. Riggs, then the chief banker in Washington, at his establishment opposite the Treasury Building. When we met, he said, "Major Roemer, allow me to congratulate you and your command on the magnificent showing you made to-day. That 'left wheel' you made opposite my door here was a credit to you, your command, and the Nation. In fact, it was the finest Battery wheel made by any battery that passed. As your Battery was the first to march past, I particularly observed it, and determined to watch the others and compare them with yours. Your line was so straight and compact that I could not count the horses, and so must ask you how many you had in the front line." I replied that there were twenty-seven. He then continued: "They were certainly well trained or they could never have performed the part they did this day. I really saw the fire fly as their hoofs struck the pavement. How those on the outside flank going at a gallop could keep the straight line they did during the wheel, seems to me to be something marvelous. Had I not seen it myself, I could not believe it to be possible, that such a feat could be accomplished by an animal." After some further conversation, I bade Mr. Riggs good-by and rode off down the avenue to meet my wife and daughters and the friends who were waiting for me. In company with them, I found Major Miller, Acting Inspector of the Ninth Corps, who was congratulating them on the splendid behavior and fine appearance of the Battery during the review. When I had come up and dismounted, the major seized me by the hand and said, "Major, we ought to be proud of a country that can show such soldiers as passed in review to-day. Just think of it, only the Army of the Potomac was reviewed to-day, and yet there were nearly 75,000 men in line." So ended the first day of the grand review.*

The next day, the 24th, I had an opportunity of beholding the mighty columns of Gen. Sherman's armies as they passed in review. These columns were composed of the Army of the Tennessee, commanded by Gen. John A. Logan, consisting of the Fifteenth Corps, under Gen. Hazen, and the Seventeenth Corps, under Gen. F. P. Blair, and the Army of Georgia, commanded by Gen. H. W. Slocum, consisting of the Fourteenth Corps, under Gen. J. C. Davis, and the Twentieth Corps under Gen. Mower. (The Army of the Cumberland was not present). These armies passed in review in just the same way they marched through Georgia, South Carolina, North Carolina and Virginia, carrying the camp

---

*I will here mention that I still have in my possession, one of the laurel wreaths with which the Battery's guns were decorated during the review, and that I cherish it as a most valued trophy of the occasion, and as a memento of the many kindnesses shown to the Battery by Mrs. Kimball and the other ladies who prepared the decorations.

and field equipments they had brought from Georgia, or had picked up during their march thence to Washington. These equipments were of all sorts, shapes and sizes. Following the troops were the infantry, cavalry and artillery baggage wagons, in or on which were carried goats, ducks, chickens, pigs, dogs, opossums, raccoons, monkeys, parrots, canary birds and eagles. All these had been so tamed and trained that they kept their places as the soldiers did theirs. There were also negro boys and girls occupying the places assigned them in this grand review. Each brigade was followed by its company of "bummers" or foragers, dressed in the strange, fantastic and ragged garb they had worn on the march through Georgia and the Carolinas. The sights presented were, at times, very amusing and quite mirth-provoking, but when one looked at the soldiers themselves, he could see by their bearing that they were thorough soldiers.

The men in these armies had not had any opportunity of fixing up, to any extent, for they had arrived near Washington from their long march through North Carolina and Virginia only a day or two before the grand review. To me it was a grand sight, and such a spectacle, I do not believe, was ever seen before, or will ever be seen again, it was too unique.

The behavior of the animals, the pets of the different regiments, was truly wonderful. Nothing seemed to frighten them in the least. They looked around as unconcernedly as if they were in camp in their usual quarters, and seemed to feel perfectly at home. They had been carried by the boys for hundreds, perhaps, thousands of miles, and formed a very peculiar and distinctive feature of the parade, and some of them were roundly applauded by the spectators. Whether the horses or mules walked or trotted made no difference to them; they looked around at the sights and appeared as deeply interested in the show as were many of the country folks present. The only difference lay in this, that they were perfectly familiar with the different divisions of the Armies, while the country folks were not.

As an illustration of the familiarity with the troops, guns, etc., I will relate the career of a pet belonging to the Battery. While the Battery was in Kentucky early in 1863, the boys found a young crow and raised it. When able to fly it would hunt out its master in camp wherever he might be, and soon became acquainted with the entire command. Any one in the Battery could handle him, but he had to be treated just so ; if any one ill-treated him, he was no longer regarded as a friend. His "post of honor" was the limber chest whereon his master sat when on the march. If this man was not at his post, the bird would occupy the seat and await his coming. The cannoneers belonging to a gun detachment are numbered from one to eight. The crow's master was No. 6, and whenever the bird saw that everything was ready for a march, he would fly to No. 6's place, and sit there as if awaiting orders.

It was emphatically an artillery bird through and through, for he never made friends with a soldier belonging to the infantry or the cavalry; he was always perfectly at home with the Battery boys. This crow went from Kentucky to Vicksburg, with the Battery, went through the Siege of Vicksburg, thence to Jackson, and back to Vicksburg, and up the Missisippi on the steamer. On this boat with us was a regiment of infantry. While it was approaching Memphis, an infantry soldier passed the limber chest whereon the crow was sitting, and scared him. He flopped off the chest on the port side of the boat, and before he could recover himself fell into the water. Precisely at that moment, another steamer going up the river, as we were ourselves, against the current, passed close to our boat, and the surge from the steamer's wheel kept the bird down and engulfed him ;

and then, our precious crow was gone. Naturally, the boys felt the loss keenly, for it had been with them so long, and had helped to pass in fun many an otherwise dreary hour in camp. I also felt the loss greatly. If the Colonel of the regiment and I had not interfered, the poor infantryman, who had been the cause of the loss, would have fared very badly at the hands of the boys of the Battery.

The keeping of such pets was generally allowed and often encouraged by commanding officers, for it tended to promote harmony among the men. Isolated, as they were, from all domestic life, they seemed to need something upon which to lavish their affections, and with which they could amuse themselves when off duty.

The Battery boys used also to engage in various outdoor games, and often came to my tent to ask the quartermaster and myself to join them in these games. We generally acceded to their requests and took part with them, for we knew it would please them, and that it tended to make them feel more contented. Furthermore, this action of ours made stubborn and morose men more tractable and obedient, when they saw that their officers were in sympathy with them. These games frequently dispelled gloomy thoughts and feelings of home sickness.

But to return to the review of Sherman's armies; they made a most excellent showing, that reflected great credit upon themselves, their great commander and the Nation. Thus ended the second and last day of the grand review. The world has never before seen and, in all probability, will never again see, such a review so unique in so many respects.

We, of the 34th, saw these troops of Sherman's armies again as they returned from the review and passed our camp near Mount Eagle Farm, on their way to their camps, happy in the thought that the time when they should return to their homes was rapidly drawing near.

Here I would like to speak of one feature of Sherman's army that, I think, is not generally rightly understood, and has been the cause of many slurs cast upon that magnificent army by hostile critics, and that feature is the so-called "Bummers' Brigade." In the march from Atlanta to the sea, the "bummers" or rather "foragers" always marched in front of the army and on its flanks, and kept their weather eye open for any and everything in the shape of food and incidentally for other things and not the least of all, for all movements of the enemy's troops and were often the ones who gave the first warnings of the approach of the enemy to the commanding officers. It is a certain fact that the army was at times almost wholly dependent upon these foragers for its means of subsistence.

I should judge from their appearance that everybody and everything would certainly give way to them and deliver to them whatever was demanded, without a single thought of resistance, for they had the determined look of men who were bound to have whatever they undertook to obtain. They wore broad-brimmed slouch hats of the Mexican "greaser" style, that gave them a genuine dare-devil look. When smoke-houses well filled with hams and bacon, or chicken coops well stocked with fowls, came in their way, the contents thereof were confiscated without any particular ceremony. Even barns and corn cribs were far from safe from their visits, for, as they had horses and mules, hay, oats, corn and other cereals, had to suffer with the rest. If their arms were not long enough to secure what they wanted without trouble, they called in strategy to assist them in obtaining it. If it happened that the supplies found were too abundant for their means of transportation, and these were always limited, and there would be no chance for going back for them, they carried off what they could and made a bonfire of the remainder. As the section of country through which Sherman's army marched, had long been and still was, the granary of the Confederacy, and thus had supplied the southern armies with the sinews of war, it was sound policy to take or destroy.

Sheridan's cavalry corps, which was reviewed in connection with the army of the Potomac, as previously stated, was a splendid body of men, which had performed most valuable services during the last year of the war. This arm of this service was, as is well known, sadly neglected in the northern armies at the beginning of the war, and in this respect the Confederates had a very great advantage over us. Our troops were not adepts in fighting cavalry and had much to learn in this particular. It was soon discovered that it helped matters wonderfully to have cavalry as well as infantry supports for the artillery. Napoleon is said to have remarked on one occasion, that "Providence was on the side of the heaviest battalions," and I can vouch for the truth of his remark so far as it applies to artillery. Well served cannon form an all-powerful factor on the battlefield.

My experience during the war taught me that thousands of shots were fired to no purpose whatever, as they went too high to do good execution. Against an infantry charge, they more often flew over the heads of the charging columns than not. Low firing in such a case, with the fire directed at the feet of the charging line, would be far more likely to break the force of the charge, than when the fire is otherwise directed. In attempting to break the force of a cavalry charge, I found it particularly effective to fire quite low so as to strike the horses' legs, for, when a cavalry man loses his horse in a charge, he is, for the time, as much disabled as if he were wounded, and is, furthermore, liable to be ridden down, and either killed or injured by the onward rush of the charging column. Thereafter, I always ordered the gunners to aim at the feet of the men in an infantry charge, and at the legs of the horses in a cavalry charge. After adopting this plan, the Battery never failed in breaking a charge with from two to five rounds by battery fire, and I am convinced that if the enemy had used this same plan at all such times, our losses on many battlefields would have been fully three times as great as they actually were.

The Battery has often maintained its position on the battlefield with six pieces against ten, and at Manassas, August 29th, 1862, it had but three guns with which to fight ten of the enemy, and yet it maintained its position there from 3 to 7 P. M., and not only did that but also had, by the latter hour, silenced all but one of the rebel ten, and their men, horses and guns had become so thoroughly disabled that the batteries had to yield to the inevitable and give up the fight. Battery L, as it was then named, on the contrary, had neither man nor horse so disabled as to be unfit for duty. I have always regarded this battle as affording conclusive evidence of the truth of my opinion that firing low is the more effective method. I also recognize the hand of Providence in it, that Battery L was preserved from injury in that most disastrous battle.

CHAPTER XVIII.

HOMEWARD BOUND. THE BATTERY MUSTERED OUT.

Immediately after the grand review, all organizations, regiments, batteries, troops, etc., of the volunteers, in the several armies collected in and around Washington began preparing for their muster-out and return to their respective homes. Those belonging to Sherman's armies were sent to Capitol Hill, there to remain until the final ceremony of muster-out took place, as they were to be the first ones mustered out, and then those of the Army of the Potomac would go there in their turn for the same purpose. The "Flushing Battery" would then be transported back to its birthplace for the final separation of its members. All felt that the sooner the order came to return home the better it would be for every one.

With the assistance of my officers and clerk, I now set to work to prepare the muster-out rolls and all the other necessary returns that must be made and transmitted to the War Department at Washington, D. C., and to the Adjutant General's Office of New York, at Albany. Complete and accurate returns of all government property in their possession must be made by all officers responsible for such property, after the property has been properly turned over to the representatives of the Ordnance and Quartermaster-General's Bureaus, and these returns, accompanied by the necessary vouchers, must be approved before such officers can be relieved of their responsibility and receive a discharge and full pay without any deductions.

At that time much was said in the newspapers concerning the indebtedness of officers, and very many read these accounts without understanding how such indebtedness could arise, and wondered at it. I do not know that this matter was ever fully explained in print, and I will here show how it could happen.

A captain or other officer commanding a battery of artillery, a company of infantry, or a troop of cavalry, obtains the proper amount of government property necessary for the use of his command by making a requisition for such property upon the officer in charge of it. When these supplies, arms, ammunition, camp and garrison equipage, etc., are received by such commanding officer, the officer issuing them gives duplicate invoices, while the officer receiving them gives duplicate receipts to the other. Returns of property, for which an officer is responsible, must be made monthly, bi-monthly, or quarterly, as required by Army Regulations, to the Quartermaster-General, Chief of Ordnance, etc., giving an accurate account of the property under his control. With these returns must be sent a complete set of vouchers, showing how and from whom the different articles were received, and to whom and why transferred, how they were expended, or how they were otherwise disposed of. These returns must account for every single article received, transferred, issued, expended, lost, or destroyed, and the sum total of articles on hand, and expended, etc., must exactly correspond with the sum total of articles on hand at date of last report and since received. If, now, any officer responsible for government property loses any of his vouchers, or omits to account on his return for any single article, the value thereof, as fixed by the government, is charged against his pay account, and the value of the whole amount of property in his possession is charged against the same account if he fails to make the returns called for; and if he cannot properly explain the matter or account for the missing articles, their value is deducted from the pay due him, and if there is not enough pay due him to square the account, he will be compelled to pay it out of any other resources he may happen to have, or submit to the sentence that will surely be imposed upon him.

When, therefore, an officer has completed his term of service and desires to secure a settlement of his accounts, if he has been negligent in any way respecting his returns, and has, through carelessness lost any of his vouchers, or failed to account properly for all the property that has been under his control, he will find all this brought up against him at the final settlement, and he may find himself in debt to the government, although he may have been strictly honest and thoroughly honorable. As an illustration of this, I will cite the case of a Pennsylvania captain of artillery, on duty before Petersburg, in 1864. His three years of service ended in the summer of that year. At the expiration of his term of service he forwarded his final returns to the War Department, and, according to his own calculation, about $800 was due him for pay.

His account was returned to him from the War Department, together with an account, which showed that he, himself, was, on the contrary, indebted to the government to the tune of $1,500. Thus, it will be seen at once that "Uncle Sam" has a way of keeping his officers straight. Now, in reality, this officer did not owe the government one dollar. This apparent deficit arose as a result of his carelessness in the keeping of his accounts; he had neglected to send the proper vouchers or had failed to account properly for articles drawn upon requisition. To clear himself, to obtain an honorable discharge, and to secure the pay really due him, he was compelled to go down on his knees before Gens. Burnside and Willcox, and solemnly declare on oath, that he was not a defaulter, but had been guilty of the grossest carelessness in the keeping of his accounts.

On the 31st of May I received orders to turn over at once to the proper officers at the Washington Arsenal, all the property for which I was responsible, with the exception of such tents as would be necessary for use in sheltering officers and men on our homeward march, and to be ready to proceed to Hart's Island, New York Harbor, State of New York, there to be mustered out of the United States service. I proceeded immediately to comply with the requirements of this order, but, as the first of June had been set apart as a day of thanksgiving and prayer to God for His goodness to the country, in pursuance of orders dated May 31st, 1865, War Department, U. S. A., the Battery waited until June 2d, when it crossed from Alexandria to Washington, arriving at 9 A. M. All the government property under my control, except the tents above mentioned, one ambulance and one baggage wagon, were turned over to the Ordnance Officer and the Quartermaster on duty at the Arsenal. After this was done the Battery returned to Alexandria, while I, myself, remained in Washington till the next day, staying at Erhurt's Hotel in Eleventh street, for the night. By 6 P. M., of June 2d, all my reports were finished, signed, and left with the proper officers for their examination and approval. The property turned over consisted of:

Four 3-inch rifled cannon and carriages.

Six caissons complete with 1,098 rounds of shot and shell.

One battery wagon and one forge—turned over to the Ordnance Officer—ninety-nine artillery horses with the same number of sets of harness, eight baggage wagon horses and one baggage wagon to Quartermaster Capt. Carl Pearce, of the Ninth Corps.

All my returns and reports were approved on June 3d. The next day, June 4th, were received General Orders No. 17, dated, Headquarters Artillery Brigade, June 4, 1865, and Special Order No. 34, dated Headquarters Ninth Army Corps, June 4th, 1865, to be ready to march to Washington, D. C., the next day, June 5th, *en route* for Hart's Island, New York harbor, and home. The Battery left Alexandria for Washington on the morning of June 5th, and after the baggage had been left at the Baltimore and Ohio Railroad Station, I proceeded to the Arsenal and turned over all the property over which I had control, except the tents, before mentioned, which would be turned over at Hart's Island. By 4 P. M., all these matters were settled, and at 6 P. M. the Battery, consisting of five officers, 119 enlisted men, four servants and one laundress, 129 persons in all, left Washington for Baltimore, where it arrived at 11 P. M. It passed Havre de Grace at 6 A. M., June 6th, and arrived at Philadelphia at 4 P. M., where it found awaiting it at the famous "Cooper Shop," a fine dinner, to which, I need not tell our Flushing friends, the Battery boys, did full justice. Many were the blessings bestowed by the men upon the good Philadelphians, who had contributed so freely to feed the hungry soldier boys. The men were on their good behavior and I was proud of them. But having gone so far on our homeward journey, anxiety to reach home as soon as possible overmastered all other desires. Home! How good that word sounded to us, that had braved the hardships of the march and the battle field for four long years!

We left Philadelphia soon after and arrived at Pier No. 1, North River, New York, at 11:45 P. M., June 6th. Leaving the Battery, which was provided with quarters at the "Battery Barracks" in charge of Senior First Lieutenant Heasley, I went on to Flushing, where I arrived at 5.40

A. M., June 7th, to give the people timely notice of the Battery's arrival. I took breakfast that morning by invitation with our patriotic townsman and the Battery's treasurer during the war, Mr. Henry Clement. Lieutenant J. J. Johnston and Ex-Lieutenant Alonzo Garretson were dispatched to New York City to escort the Battery to Flushing. The Battery, under the command of Lieutenant Heasley, reached Flushing at 3 P. M., June 7th.

The reception, given to the Battery by the citizens of Flushing, was an overwhelming one, and, doubtless, there are many still living in the village who will remember that joyful day. I can yet see the crowds filling the street and cheering at the top of their voices as the brave boys of the 34th New York Battery entered the village. Then, indeed, I felt proud of my men; all the hardships we had undergone seemed as nothing in view of this most hearty welcome home given us by the citizens of my adopted town. I know we marched down Main Street to the hotel where a splendid dinner was waiting for us, but how I reached the place I hardly know. Conducted by Mr. C. R. Lincoln, who took me by the arm, we marched through what seemed to me, a sea of faces on either side, while the assembled multitude shouted, hurrahed and showered us with flowers. We finally reached the hotel and were put in charge of my beloved pastor, the Rev. Dr. J. Carpenter Smith. He led me to the head of the table in the dining room, and then, in behalf of the citizens of Flushing, bade my command and myself partake of what they had provided for Flushing's heroes.

When I beheld that table so bountifully laden with all the delicacies of the season, my feelings quite overcame me, for I could not help recalling how often my brave boys, now seated before me, would have been glad to have a crust of bread to eat and a glass of water to moisten their parched lips and quench their burning thirst, and as I looked at the well filled table before them, it did not seem to be real. However, I soon collected my wandering thoughts, and on looking around recognized the familiar faces of many of the good ladies of Flushing and many of her most prominent citizens. There I saw Luther C. Carter, Edward E. Mitchell, General and Colonel McDonald, Rev. Dr. J. C. Smith, R. C. Embree, Garrett Van Sielen, Captain George B. Roe, Professors E. A. Fairchild and A. P. Northrop, Henry Clement, Wm. R. Prince, W. K. Murray, J. K Murray, Charles R. Lincoln, Wm. Phillips, G. R. Garretson and many others whose names I cannot now recall.

It greatly rejoiced my heart as I looked upon the bronzed faces of my men gathered around me, to see they were thoroughly enjoying the feast that had been prepared for them. They were war veterans, indeed, of four years' standing, and I know that history records no better fighting than that done by the Flushing Battery. Near the close of the banquet, the following brief resume of the Battery's doings was given: "This Battery has taken part in 57 different engagements, has marched 18,758 miles, and thrown from its guns during this time over 56 tons of iron. The whole number of enlisted men that have belonged to it during its four years' career is 271, of whom 19 yielded up their lives in the service of their beloved country and 47 have been discharged for disabilities incurred in the field, through wounds or disease. Such" said I in conclusion, "is the record of "Flushing Battery," which was organized four years ago through the liberality of the citizens of Flushing to go into the field and assist in suppressing a most, if not the most gigantic rebellion." I think that those good and patriotic people of Flushing, who, with their beloved pastor at their head, so splendidly banqueted their country's defenders as represented by the 34th New York Independent

Veteran Volunteers Light Battery* in such a grand and noble style, must even now feel proud of their kind and generous actions at that time, and must truly believe that the members of that Battery fully appreciated the honor conferred upon them.

As soon as the banquet was over, the members of the Battery were furloughed to visit their friends, with orders to report at 10 A. M., June 9th, at the College Point Dock, to take the steamer for Hart's Island, to prepare for the final muster out. At 11 A. M. on that date, the Battery left College Point and arrived at Hart's Island at 12 o'clock noon. Here the men were quartered in the government barracks and the work of making out the muster-out and pay-rolls was begun without delay. I returned to Flushing the next day, Saturday, June 10th, to pay some bills incurred in behalf of the Battery and to spend Sunday with my family. Many friends from New York and Flushing called on me that Saturday evening to pay their respects. I had sixty callers in all. It made me feel very happy to be once more with the folks at home and see how much I was thought of by them.

On the 12th, I returned to the Island and found that no progress had been made in the muster-out rolls, as all but one of the lieutenants had taken leave of absence. Lieuts. Johnston and Balkie had gone away leaving Lieut. Durfee in command. I forthwith called in an extra clerk to hasten matters. June 13th was one of the hottest days I ever experienced, and being quite unwell with a fever hanging over me, I thought I could not possibly go through the day. I sent my son, Alexander, who was staying with me on the Island, to Flushing for his mother and sister. This day the first copy of the muster-out roll was finished and found to need but little correction.

* The only organized body of soldiers that went out from Flushing.

At noon of the 14th, quite a party of ladies landed upon the Island. Among them were my wife and daughter, Mrs. Miller and Mrs. Hamilton. They were shown all through the barracks and the officers' quarters and then escorted down to the rebel prison pen where 273 rebel prisoners of war were confined. All these were dressed in rebel gray uniforms or what was left of them, and some were literally in rags, and very many looked as if a little soap and water would be beneficial to both faces and clothes. Many of them had made little trinkets of wood they had obtained, and when the ladies passed by they asked the ladies to buy these trinkets. No one passed without either buying something or giving them some small sum of money. When my wife passed them with me, one of them asked her for a five-cent stamp, and she took out her purse to give him one. This was a signal for about fifty of them to come crowding about the ladies and saying, "Good lady, give me a five-cent stamp to buy some tobacco." Having visited them myself previously and learned their tricks, I had advised the ladies, before going to the prison, to provide themselves with small change. To see the eager faces light up when they had received their gifts made it a pleasure to the visitors to contribute these trifling sums, although they were "giving aid and comfort to the enemy."

These prisoners were served with the same kind of rations that were dealt out to our own soldiers, and here, at least, they did not die of hunger, as thousands of our poor fellows did at Andersonville. The prison camp was at the north end of Hart's Island where they had a fine view of Long Island Sound. The prison camp was separated from our Union camp by a very strong twelve-foot fence. The entrance to the prison camp was through a very strong and massive door or gate. The whole camp was most strongly guarded by numerous sentries on land and by patrol boats on the water, and it was thus quite impossible for any one to escape from the island.

At the south end of the island were the recruiting stations where the majority of all the New York Volunteers were mustered into the service. There were also a number of barrack buildings and officers' quarters fitted up with every convenience for men, and officers and all had a very pleasant time during their short sojourn in these fine quarters. Numbers of ladies and gentlemen visited the island daily and all points of interest were shown to all who came. The rebel prisoners were the greatest attraction, and they were always glad to see visitors for they had learned to know that the liberal hearts of northerners would respond to their appeals. One of them remarked to me once, "Your people are very kind to us."

The muster-out rolls were completed at 1 P. M., June 16th and at once sent to the mustering officer. The next day was passed in making out discharge papers for all officers, non-commissioned officers and privates, (128 in all), except Private James D. Sprong, who had still to make up time lost by desertion. I was sick all day on the 18th and confined to my quarters with a fever; I was therefore unable to go to Flushing as I had promised. On the 20th the last ordnance returns for this command were made out; this was a very easy matter as nearly everything had been turned over to the proper authorities at Washington on the 3d of June. At 4 P. M., June 21st, 1865, the members of the 34th New York Independent Veteran Volunteer Light Battery were mustered out of the service of the United States by the mustering officer, Lieutenant Dolan, 2d United States Infantry, and on the 24th all were paid off except the commanding officer. The members of the Battery now separated to go to their respective homes, and thus the military service of the Battery came to an end.

I was not paid off with the men because my accounts had not yet been audited at Washington, and it was not until the latter part of August that I received a notice from Washington that they had been passed and found correct. With this notice I also received an order to go to the paymaster's office in Bleecker street, New York city, and receive my final payment. I went as directed, and when I presented my order to the paymaster, he remarked, "I see, Major Roemer, you are one of the lucky ones, for, according to this order, your accounts are all straight." He then paid me the sum due.

When the paymaster pronounced my name, several gentlemen came to me from the other side of the room, and one of them inquired, "Major Roemer, are you the same Roemer who was the captain of a battery before Fredericksburg, in December, 1862?" "Yes," I replied. "Well, Major," he continued, "do you remember that very stormy day and night when my regiment came five miles from the rear to support your Battery during the night? We had been on picket duty before the city, and when we arrived at your position we were wet to the skin. You and your men immediately set to work, although it was 9 o'clock at night, made, and served out to us several kettles full of good hot coffee. Your extreme kindness to us on that occasion has never been forgotten, but has been referred to a thousand times by the officers and men of my regiment. All of them agreed that coffee never tasted better than on that stormy night before Fredericksburg. I am very glad to have the opportunity and honor of again thanking you for your kindness to us."

I then learned that they had just discovered something. They had obtained rations from the Commissary, in 1862, while before Fredericksburg, and had had them charged to their account. Since that time they had drawn their pay regularly, but had not paid the Commissary, and had, doubtless, thought the government had forgotten their indebtedness to it. The Colonel told me he had had no idea that the Commissary's account still stood against him, and would be deducted from his pay. Yet here were the accounts of the Commissary showing what these officers had received and had not paid for. The result was that each had to pay his proper share of these subsistence accounts.

I never had any subsistence stores charged to my account, but have, at times, had to borrow money to pay for them. I remember that after my return from the war, many a one said to me, from time to time, "Well, Roemer, I suppose you made plenty of money while off to the war?" This often made me very indignant, but when I reflected that they did not know how exceedingly difficult it was for an officer to make any money beyond his pay, I let the matter pass.

APPENDIX.

REGISTER OF COMMISSIONED OFFICERS.

BATTERY L 2D N. Y. ART. AND 34TH N. Y. V. V. IND. LT. BATTERY.

*Mustered out with Battery, June 21st, 1865, per S. O. No. 34, H'd'q'rs Army of the Potomac, dated June 4, 1865.

Names.	Date of Commission.	Remarks.
Captains.		
T. L. Robinson.	Dec. 4, '61.	Dismissed U. S. service, May 23, '62, to date Mar. 4, '62.
*Jacob Roemer.	Mar. 4, '62.	Prom. from 1st Lieut., Commissioned Bvt Maj. Dec. 2, '64.
First Lieutenants.		
Jacob Roemer.	Dec. 4, '61.	Prom. Captain, to date from Mar. 4, '62.
H. J. Standish.	June 6, '62.	Resigned, Oct. 25, '62.
Wm. C. Rawolle.	June 6, '62.	App. A.D.C. to Gen. Sturgis, June 3, '62. Resigned from Battery, June 4, '62.
Moses E. Brush.	Oct. 25, '63.	Prom. from 2d Lieut. Resigned, Nov. 8, '63.
*Thomas Heasley.	Feb. 26, '64.	Prom. from 2d Lieut., A. A. A. G., Art. Brig., Oct. 3, '64, to May 23, '65.
Second Lieutenants.		
Wm. H. Hamilton.	Dec. 4, '61.	Resigned, Jan. 11, '62.
Wm. C. Rawolle.	Dec. 4, '61.	Prom. 1st Lieut., May 23, '62, to date Mar. 4, '62.
Wm. Cooper.	June 6, '62.	Prom. from 1st Sergt. May 23, '62. Resigned, Oct. 8, '62.
J. Van Nostrand.	June 6, '62.	Prom. from Sergt. May 23, '62. Resigned, Oct. 8, '62.
Moses E. Brush.	Nov. 29, '62.	Prom. from 1st Sergt, Oct. 8, '62. Prom. 1st Lieut., Oct. 25, '63.
Thomas Heasley.	Oct. 25, '63.	Prom. from 1st Sergt, Oct. 25, '63. Prom 1st Lieut., Jan. 1, '64.
Charles R. Lincoln.	Feb. 26, '64.	Joined as 2d Lieut. from civil life. Resigned, May 31, '64.
Alonzo Garretson.	May 3, '64.	Prom. from 165th N. Y. Vol Resigned, Jan. 26, '65. Disability.
*J. J. Johnston.	Nov. 16, '64.	Prom. from 1st Sergt, to date Jan. 1, '65.
*Wm. E. Balkie.	Dec. 22, '64.	Prom. from Q. M. Sergt, to date Jan. 14, '65.
*George H. Durfee.	April 22, '65.	Prom. from 14th N. Y., H. A. Never mustered.

APPENDIX.

REGISTER OF MEMBERS

OF BATTERY L. 2D N. Y. ART. AND 34TH N. Y. V. V. IND.
LIGHT BATTERY 1861-1865.

R stands for re-enlisted in veteran organization, Nov. 15th, 1863.
* marks those mustered out with the Battery, June 21st, 1865.

NAMES.	MUSTERED INTO SERVICE.	REMARKS.
*Adams, Edward	Nov. 16, '64.	
*Baine, James	Mar. 15, '64.	Wounded Sept. 30, '64.
*Baird, Robert	Apr. 13, '64.	
*Balkie, Wm. E.	Nov. 26, '61.	R. Prom. Corp'l and Q. M. Serg't and 2d Lieut.. (See Com. Off.)
*Barnes, Wm. H.	Mar. 25, '64.	Wounded June 20, '64.
Bauer, John B.	Oct. 26, '61.	R. Killed at Fort McGilvery, Mar. 25, '65.
*Baumann, John	Oct. 23, '61.	R.
*Baxter, Chas. W.	Oct. 9, '61.	R.
*Beary, Lorenzo	Mar. 5, '64.	Prom. Corp'l Jan. 1, '65 and Serg't Feb. 25, '65.
*Beck, Wm.	Oct. 1, '61.	R. Disch. in '63 on account of wounds. Re-enlisted Feb 27, '64.
Becker, Ludwig	Oct. 1, '61.	Deserted June 4, '62.
*Beddes, Richard	Aug. 27, '61.	R.
*Bell, James M.	Oct. 9, '61.	R. Prom. Serg't April 1, '64.
Bennett, Alonzo	Oct. 1, '61.	Deserted May 29, '62.
*Bennett, John J.	Feb. 29, '64.	
*Berndt, Wm.	Oct. 1, '61.	R. Wounded Sept. 30, '64.
*Bernstrube, Fred.	Feb. 20, '64.	
*Boehnlein, John	Oct. 29, '61.	R.
Bohleyer, David	Oct. 23, '61.	Deserted June 9, '62.
Boland, Andrew	Oct. 29, '64.	Deserted. Never reported for duty.
*Boulanger, John	Oct. 23, '61.	R.
Boyd, John T.	Oct. 23, '61.	Discharged for disability, July 2, '62.
Bracken, John	Oct. 1, '61.	R. Transf from 2d N. Y. Art., Aug. 18, '62. Deserted Dec. 31, '64.
*Brewster, Wm.	Nov. 16, '64.	
Briggs, Samuel		Drafted. Joined July 18, '64. Sent to Hosp., Aug. 20, '64.
Brill, Christ, Jr.	Oct. 1, '61.	Discharged Sept. 30, '64. Expiration of service.
Brill, Christ, Sr.	Oct. 1, '61.	Discharged Sept. 30, '64. Expiration of service.
Brister, Randolph	Sept. 6, '64.	Discharged at hospital Apr. 28, '65.
Brown, James	Nov. 16, '64.	Deserted. Never reported for duty. Not on M. O. roll.
Brunnemer, Louis	Oct. 1, '61.	R. Killed, Pegram Farm, Sept. 30, '64.
Brush, Moses E.	Aug. 27, '61.	Prom. 1st Serg't. May 23, '62, 2d Lieut, Oct. 8, '63, (See Com. Off.)

Names.	Mustered into Service.	Remarks.
Burger, Dominicus	Aug. 29, '61.	Deserted Sept. 29, '61.
Burke, Patrick	May 3, '64.	Deserted. Never reported for duty.
*Burke, Richard	Oct. 1, '61.	R Transf. from 2d N. Y. Art. Aug. 18, '62.
*Cahill, John	Oct. 24, '64.	
*Campbell, Wm. F.	Mar. 12, '64.	Wounded slightly July 26, '64.
Carpenter, Stephen	Oct. 1, '61.	Discharged for disability July 2, '62.
*Carr, Geo. H.	Mar. 29, '63.	R. App. Artificer, April 1, '64.
Case, John	Oct. 9, '61.	Deserted May 29, '62.
*Cavanagh, James	June 30, '62.	R.
Charlie, Joseph	Oct. 1, '61.	Deserted June 4, '62.
Chatterson, Jesse	Oct. 16, '61.	Discharged Mar., '65, after release as prisoner of war.
*Cochard, Oscar	June 26, '62.	R.
Collinge, John	Oct. 9, '61.	Deserted May 29, '62.
Cork, Wm.	Oct. 2, '61.	Discharged at Washington. Cause and date unknown.
Cooper, Wm.	Oct. 1, '61.	1st Serg't from muster in. Prom. 2d Lieut., May 23, '62, (See Com. Off.)
*Cornell, Jas. C.	Aug. 27, '61.	R. Prom. Corp'l April 1, '64. Serg't Jan. 1, '65. Wounded Aug. 30, '62.
Covert, Benj. C.	Oct. 1, '61.	Died at Falmouth, Va., Nov. 26, '62. Heart disease.
*Cox, Usa! M.	Mar. 29, '64.	Wounded slightly June 19, '64.
Davis John	Mar. 28, '64.	Deserted. Never reported for duty.
*Danner, John M.	Oct. 1, '61.	R.
*Davis, John	Sept. 2, '64.	Transf. from 24th N. Y. Indep. Battery, Feb. 4, '65.
Dehne, Fritz	Aug. 27, '61.	Discharged Aug. 26, '64. Expiration of service.
*Deckers, Andrew	Mar. 5, '64.	Wounded May 12, '64
*Dersch, John	Aug. 27, '61.	R.
Devany, John	Oct. 16, '61.	Deserted July 9, '62.
Diebold, Andrew	Sept. 10, '61.	Deserted Sept. 23, '61.
*Dingman, Sylvester	Sept. 6, '64.	Transf. from 24th N. Y. Indep. Battery.
*Doherty, Thos.	Mar. 26, '64.	
*Doremus, Francis M.	Oct. 29, '61.	R.
Doremus, Wm. H.	Oct. 8, '61.	Deserted June 17, '62. Not on M. O. roll.
*Doughty, John	Oct. 1, '63.	R.
*Douglass, Jas.	Oct. 5, '64.	
Douglass, Chas.	Mar. 22, '64.	Deserted. Never reported for duty.
Dubbert, Fred.	Oct. 26, '61.	Deserted June 9, '62.
*Duerer, Henry	Oct. 1, '61.	R.
Ebell, Edward	Feb. 26, '64.	Wounded Sept. 30, '64. Died Oct. 6, '64.
Ellis, Wm.	Oct. 1, '61.	Deserted Sept. '62.
Everwahn, Emil	June 20, '62.	R. Deserted Mar. 24, '64.
Farrington, Chas. W.	Oct. 16, '61.	Deserted May 25, '62.
Ferster, John	Aug. 27, '61.	Discharged from hosp., cause and date unknown.
Fessenden, Asa D.	Aug. 30, '64.	Discharged Apr. 28, '65.

NAMES.	MUSTERED INTO SERVICE.	REMARKS.
*Fessenden, Jas. B.	Aug. 2, '64.	
Fitzmaurice, Henry	Mar. 28, '64.	Deserted. Never reported for duty.
*Fogarty, Michael	Oct. 1, '61.	R. Wounded slightly Aug. 7, '64.
Foster, Chas.	April 30, '63.	Deserted Aug. 31, '63.
Foster, Samuel	Aug. 27, '61.	R. Discharged May 2, '64 to accept 2d Lieut. in 4th N. Y. H. A.
Francis, Geo. R.	Mar. 15, '64.	Deserted April 2, '64.
Frank, Louis	Oct. 1, '61.	Prom. Act. Serg't Jan. 5, '63. Discharged Sept. 30, '64.
Freundle, Jacob	Oct. 23, '61.	Died. Heart disease at Falmouth, Va., Dec. 6, '62.
*Frey, Joseph	Oct. 1, '61.	R. Prom. Corp'l Nov. 1, '65. Serg't April 2, '62.
*Fuller, Decatur	Mar. 9, '64.	Prom. Corp'l Jan. 1, '65. Wounded Mar. 29, '65 and Apr. 2, '65.
Funk, Simon	June 14, '64.	Died Jan. 15, '65.
*Gaffney, Thos.	Mar. 31, '64.	Wounded July 5, '64.
*Garland, Brien		R. Transf. to Battery L., Aug. 6, '62. Taken prisoner Aug. 9, '62.
Garretson, Alonzo	Dec. 17, '63.	Prom. 2d Lieut. from Private 165th N. Y. V., May 3, '64. (See Com. Off.)
*Gerbe, Henry	Oct. 1, '61.	R. Wounded July 7, '64.
Getz, Joseph	Aug. 27, '61.	Deserted Sept. 22, '61.
*Gibbons, Francis	April 6, '64.	
Gilbert, Lewis	Oct. 2, '61.	Died Mar. 30, '63.
*Glasser, Andrew	Oct. 29, '61.	R.
Gordon, Geo. H.	Mar. 22, '64.	Deserted. Never reported for duty.
*Graham, Alex	Feb. 29, '64.	
*Graham, Hugh F.	Feb. 27, '64.	
Green, Anderson	April 8, '63.	R. Deserted Jan. 19, '64.
Green, John	Oct. 1, '61.	R. Deserted Apr. 1, '64.
Grisel, Joseph	April 16, '63.	Deserted Aug. 31, '63.
*Griffin, Albert	Oct. 9, '61.	R. Prom. Corp'l Sept. 18, '63. Serg't Nov. 13, '64.
*Griffin, Thos. S.	May 4, '64.	Prom. Corp'l Jan. 1, '65. Wounded Mar. 25 and Apr. 2, '65, T. G. Sutton.
Griffin, Wm.	Oct. 1, '61.	Died Aug 27, '63.
*Grithman, John	June 27, '62.	R.
Hall, Thorn	Oct. 1, '61.	Deserted May 29, '62.
Hamilton, Wm. H.	Oct. 1, '61.	Prom. 2d Lieut. Resigned Jan. 11, '62. (See Com. Off.)
*Harris, Chas. H.	Mar. 12, '64.	
Harris, Henry A.	Oct. 9, '61.	Deserted June 25, '62.
*Hayden, Alfred A.	Feb. 26, '64.	
*Hayden, Wm. H.	Feb. 26, '64.	
*Heasley, Thos.	Oct. 16, '61.	R. Prom. Corp'l, '61 Serg't, 1st Serg't Oct.8, '62, 2d Lieut. '62, (See Com. Off.)
Heilman, Peter	Oct. 16, '61.	Deserted June 19, '62.
Herbert, Philip	Aug. 27, '61.	Discharged. Hernia. May 26, '62.
Herr, Franklin L.	Feb. 29, '64.	Taken prisoner May, '64. Exchanged Dec., '64. Not on M. O. roll.
Hewlett, Nathan	Oct. 1, '61.	Deserted Sept. 6, '62.

APPENDIX.   313

Names.	Mustered into Service.	Remarks.
*Hubbard, Taylor	Sept. 2, '64.	
Hodges, John	Oct. 1, '61.	Died, Chronic diarrhoea, Jan. 5, '63
*Hoffman, Fred.	Feb. 27, '64.	
Hoffman, John	Oct. 1, '61.	Deserted June 19, '62.
*Holcomb, Russell	July 23, '64.	
*Howard, Wm. J.	Oct. 16, '61.	R.
Hubble, Geo.	Oct. 1, '61.	Deserted May 29, '62.
*Huber, Joseph	Mar. 21, '64.	
*Illerd, Dennis	Oct. 1, '61.	R. Wounded Aug. 30, '62.
Jacobs, Peter	Oct. 16, '61.	Deserted May 29, '62.
Jacques, Chas.	Mar. 26, '64.	Supposed to have died Aug. 1, '64 from wounds June 12, '64.
Janoschofsky, H.	April 19, '63.	R. Deserted Mar. 14, '64.
Johnson, Samuel	Oct. 1, '61.	Deserted May 29, '62.
*Johnson, Wm. J.	Mar. 15, '64.	
*Johnston, D. S., Jr.	Oct. 9, '61.	Taken prisoner Oct. 31, '63.
Johnston, D. S., Sr.	Oct. 23, '61.	Discharged, Rheumatism, May 30, '62
*Johnston, J. J.	Oct. 9, '61.	Prom. Corp'l Oct. 9 '61, 1st Serg't Jan. 5, '63 2d Lieut., (See Com. Off.)
Johnston, Wm. E.	Oct. 9, '61.	Prom. Corp'l Nov., 1861. Died, Chronic diar., Aug. 28, '63.
*Jones, Thomas	Aug. 16, '64.	
*Kasemeyer, H. A.	Oct. 23, '61.	R. Wounded Sept. 30, '64.
*Kaufman, John	Aug. 27, '61.	R. Prom. Corp'l Oct., '61, Serg't Jan. 1, '62, Q. M. Serg't Jan. 1, '65.
*Keene, John	April 6, '64.	
Kelly, John	April 11, '64.	Deserted '64. Never reported for duty.
Kiernan, John	Oct. 1, '61.	Deserted April 3, '63.
*Kiernan, Patrick	Oct. 16, '61.	R. Prom. Corp'l Nov. 18, '64. Wounded Sept. 30, '64, Mar. 25, '65.
Kierstead, Jos.	Oct. 1, '61.	Died, Chronic diar., Dec. 13, '62.
Kimmeler, Peter	Oct. 1, '61.	Died, Chronic diar., Dec. 30, '62.
Kliegel, Benj.	Oct. 1, '61.	Prom. Corp'l Nov., '61. Taken prisoner, exchanged and deserted. Not on M. O. roll.
*Klinger, Pius	April 12, '64.	
Koch, Simon	Nov. 26, '61.	Deserted June 25, '62.
Koelling, Wm.	June 20, '62.	Deserted Mar. 29, '63.
*Kohler, John	Mar. 26, '64.	
*Konstanzer, Konrad	June 27, '62.	R.
Kraft, Joseph	Oct. 1, '61.	Deserted July 9, '62.
*Krouse, Edward	Mar. 10, '64.	
Leich, John J.	Oct. 2, '61.	Discharged Sept. 9, '64. Expiration of service.
Lester, John D.	Feb. 25, '64.	Discharged, Disability, Dec. 16, '64.
Lincoln, Chas. R.		Appointed 2d Lieut. Resigned May 31, '64. (See Com. Off.)
*Ludwig, Carl	Oct. 1, '61.	R. Wounded June 22, '64.
*Ludwig, Wm.	Oct. 1, '61.	R. Wounded May 12, '64. Prom. Corp'l Jan. 1, '65.
Link, Gottfreid	Oct. 1, '61.	Discharged, Disability, Feb. 13, '63.
*Mack, John G.	Oct. 1, '61.	R. Prom. Corp'l April 30, '64.

Names.	Mustered into Service.	Remarks.
Mahony, Michael	Oct. 1, '61.	Discharged, Disability, May 30, '62.
*Markland, Wm.	Oct. 16, '61.	R. Wounded Nov. 16, '63, June 18, '64.
Marshall, Thos.	Aug. 31, '61.	Deserted Sept. 22, '61.
*Mattern, Jacob	May 29, '64.	
McCan, Edward	Mar. 17, '64.	Deserted April 2, '64.
Meehan, John	Oct. 1, '61.	Discharged, Disability, Aug. 29, '63.
Mellen, Geo. W.	Oct. 16, '61.	Deserted June 17, '62.
*Melsom, John	Oct. 1, '61.	R.
*Merithew, S. R.	Mar. 29, '64.	
*Mesaros, Joseph	Oct. 1, '61.	R.
Meyer, Conrad	April 6, '64.	Wounded June 19, '64. Deserted Nov. 12, '64 from Hosp.
Meyer, Joseph	April 7, '64.	Deserted. Never reported for duty.
Miller, Chas. H.	Oct. 1, '61.	R. Q. M. Serg't. Discharged. Disability, Feb. 25, '65.
*Miller, Louis	Oct. 1, '61.	R. Prom. Corp'l April 1, '64.
Molony, Daniel	Oct. 9, '61.	Discharged Dec. 12, '63.
*Morton, Simeoe	Sept. 29, '64.	True name, P. S. M. Munro.
*Mosser, John N.	Oct. 2, '61.	R.
Muller, John Jacob	June 25, '62.	R. Wounded June 18, '64, Disch., Disability, Feb. 25, '65.
Muldoon, John	Oct. 16, '61.	Deserted May 29, '62.
Murray, Thos.	Nov. 6, '61.	Deserted Nov. 30, '61.
*Nau, Michael	Oct. 26, '61.	R.
*Nestman, Geo.	June 20, '62.	R.
Nulty, Michael	April 20, '64.	Deserted. Never reported for duty.
*O'Brien, Daniel	Mar. 30, '64.	
O'Brien, Dennis	Oct. 1, '61.	Captured Aug. 30, '62. Disch. from Hosp. Feb. 24, '63.
Osborn, Geo. C.	Mar. 9, '64.	Discharged, Disability, May 8, '65.
*Oswald, Joseph	Nov. 26, '61.	R.
*Paar, Stephen F.	Feb. 16, '64.	Wounded June 7, '64.
*Paine, Ezra	Feb. 25, '64.	
Palfrey, Frank	April 6, '64.	Wounded June 3, '64. Died in Hosp. June 5, '64.
Palmer, Samuel	Oct. 1, '61.	Discharged Sept. 30, '64. Expiration of service.
Parg, John C.	Oct. 2, '61.	Discharged Jan. 31, '63.
Pearsall, John	Oct. 1, '61.	Deserted May 29 '62.
Pettit, David	Oct. 16, '61.	Disch. Oct. 7, '64. Exp. of service.
*Pifer, Jacob N.	Mar. 12, '64.	Prom. Corp'l April 30, '64. Wounded June 19, '64.
*Quigley, John	Feb. 15, '64.	Injured Sept. 9, '64 by fall of a tree.
*Quis, John A.	Oct. 1, '61.	R. Prom. Corp'l April 30, '64.
*Ratcliffe, Henry	Oct. 1, '61.	R. Wounded Aug. 2, '62.
Rawolle, Wm. C.	Oct. 26, '61.	2d Lieut. Oct. 26, '61, (See Com. Off.)
Read, James	April 12, '64.	Deserted. Never reported for duty.
*Reed, John	Feb. 27, '64.	
*Reim, John	Oct. 1, '61.	R.
Reinheimer, Daniel	Oct. 1, '61.	Discharged, Hernia, June 10, '62.
Rierson, Stephen J.	Oct. 2, '61.	Deserted May 30, '62.
*Rierson, Wm. J.	Oct. 1, '61.	R. Prom. Corp'l Feb., '62. Wounded Mar. 25, '65.

APPENDIX. 315

NAMES.	MUSTERED INTO SERVICE.	REMARKS.
Richards, Geo.	Oct. 1, '61.	Discharged Sept. 30, '64. Expiration of service.
*Rinchel, Geo.	Aug. 27, '61.	R.
Riniker, Frederick	Oct. 1, '61.	Died, Chronic Diar., Sept. 5, '63.
Robinson, Chris. D.	Aug. 27, '61.	Discharged May 23, '62.
Robinson, Thos. L.	Oct. 1, '61.	Captain Oct. 1, '61. Dismissed May 23, '62, (See Com. Off.)
*Roemer, Jacob	Oct. 1, '61.	1st Lieut. Prom. Captain May 23, '62, (See Com. Off.)
*Ross, Leander	Sept. 8, '64.	
*Rossbach, Valentine	Oct. 9, '61.	R. Prom. Corp'l Serg't Oct. 17, '63.
Roth, Geo.	Nov. 6, '61.	R. Prisoner of war May, '64. Not on M. O. roll.
Schaefer, Peter A.	Oct. 1, '61.	Discharged, Disability. Mar. 10, '62.
*Schafer, Nicholas	July 12, '64.	
Schultz, James J.	Oct. 26, '61.	Prom. Corp'l Nov. 1, '61, Disch. Disab., April 27, '63.
*Schumacher, Fred.	Aug. 27, '61.	R. Bugler from first enlistment.
Scoutan, Jerry	Oct. 2, '61.	Deserted July 27, '62.
*Shannon, Jas.	Mar. 3, '64.	
*Shaw, Adelbert A.	Mar. 15, '64.	
*Simpson, Joseph	Mar. 18, '64.	
Smith, Chas.	Mar. 24, '61.	Deserted. Never reported for duty.
*Smith, Douglass	Feb. 26, '64.	
Smith, Epenetus	Aug. 27, '61.	Deserted May 29, '62.
Smith, John	Aug. 28, '61.	Deserted Sept. 22, '62.
*Sparrow, John W.	Feb. 9, '64.	
*Spring, Frank	Mar. 12, '64.	
*Sproll, Wm. J.	Mar. 18, '64.	
*Sprong, Jas. D.	Oct. 29, '61.	
Stamford, Wm.	Oct. 1, '61.	Discharged Sept. 30, '64. Expiration of service.
Standish, H. J.	Oct. 16, '61.	1st Lieut, (See Com. Off.)
*Stanley, Geo.	Oct. 1, '61.	R.
Stapleton, Nicholas	Sept. 6, '61.	Deserted Sept. 22, '61.
*Starkins, John H.	Sept. 6, '61.	R. Prom. Corp'l '62, Serg't Oct., '63, 1st Serg't Jan. 1, '65.
Starkins, Joseph	Oct. 1, '61.	Deserted May 29, '62, Joined Navy, Charge of Desertion removed.
*Starkins, Sam. S.	Feb. 27, '64.	Wounded July 11, '64.
*Stauder, Geo.	Oct. 1, '61.	R.
Steinbrecher, John	Oct. 1, '61.	Deserted June 25, '62.
*Steinbrook, Wm.	Mar. 18, '64.	
Stern, Henry	Oct. 29, '61.	Discharged, Disability, June 10, '62.
*Sternberg, Casper	Oct. 1, '61	R. Bugler from Nov., '62.
Sternberg, Jurgon	Oct. 1, '61.	Discharged Sept. 30, '64. Expiration of service.
Story, Alex	Apr. 6, '64.	Deserted. Never reported for duty.
Strickland, Henry	Oct. 16, '61.	Deserted Sept. 6, '62.
Sturtevant, Lewis	Oct. 1, '61.	Deserted May 29, '62.
*Sutorius, Jacob	Oct. 1, '61.	R.
*Tacey, Joseph	April 2, '64.	
Teme, John J.	Oct. 1, '61.	Disch. Aug. 26. Exp. of service.

Names.	Mustered into Service.	Remarks.
*Townsend, Albert	Aug. 27, '61.	R. Wounded Aug. 30, '62. Prom. Corp'l Nov. 1, '62, Serg't Nov. 13, '64.
Troy, John	Sept. 9, '64.	Deserted Sept. 22, '64.
Truck, Joseph	Oct. 1, '61.	Deserted June 13, '62.
Van Nostrand, J'ome	Sept. 23, '61.	Prom. Serg't Oct. 1, '64, 2d Lieut. May 23, '62. (See Com. Off.)
*Vogt, Jurgon	Oct. 1, '61.	R. Wounded Aug. 12, '64.
*Wallace, Thos.	Oct. 1, '61.	R.
Weisgaber, Geo.	Feb. 29, '64.	Deserted April 8, '64.
*Wellington, Wm.	Feb. 26, '64.	Farrier Jan. 1, '65.
Welsh, Lawrence	Oct. 16, '61.	Deserted Sept. 6, '62.
Wenzler, Leopold	Feb. 27, '64.	Died, Chronic Diar., Sept. 1, '64.
Werner, Fred.	Oct. 1, '61.	Died, Typhoid fever, Dec. 12, '63.
*Wetzel, Peter	Aug. 27, '64.	R.
*Wheeler, Ferd. A.	May 9, '64.	
White, Patrick	Mar. 12, '64.	Deserted March 26, '64.
*White, Thos.	Oct. 1, '61.	R.
Wiedemann, Chas. J.	Oct. 9, '61.	Died, Heart disease, Nov. 22, '62.
*Weidemann, Chris.	Oct. 1, '61.	R.
Wiessner, Valentine	Oct. 1, '61.	Deserted June 25, '62 and May 26, '64.
Wilhelm, John	Oct. 1, '61.	Transf. to V. R. C. Not on M. O. roll.
*Williams, Rodney	July 28, '64.	
*Wilson, Jas.	Mar. 14, '64.	
Winter, John A.	Aug. 27, '61.	Discharged, Disability, Mar. 4, '63.
Wirth, Adam	Oct. 1, '61.	Prom. Corp'l '61, Serg't '62. Wounded Aug. 30, '62. Died Sept. 25, '62.
Woener, John J.	Oct. 2, '62.	Discharged, Disability, May 26, '62.
Woodrow, John	Oct. 16, '61.	Deserted May 29, '62.
Zuberbier, Otto	Oct. 1, '61.	Deserted Oct. 11, '62.
*Zuger, Joseph	Oct. 16, '61.	R. Wounded severely, July 12, '64.
*Durfee, Geo. H.	Aug. 29, '63.	Joined battery Oct. 23, '64. Received com. 2d Lieut. Not mustered.

RECAPITULATION.

The battery left Flushing, Dec. 1, 1861 with   155
Number of deserters prior to Dec. 1, 1861   8

Total enlisted prior to Dec. 1, 1861   163
Number of recruits received subsequent to Dec. 1, 1861   108

Total number recorded on the rolls   271

Number mustered out per M. O. roll June 21, 1865   129
Number discharged prior to June 21, 1865   47
Number of deaths from wounds or disease   19
Number of deserters prior to June 21, 1865   69
Number of men not accounted for on M. O. roll   6
Detail from 14 N. Y. H. A. borne on battery roll   1

Total membership   271

Horses lost in action or died of wounds afterwards   101
Horses died of fatigue and various diseases   64
Horses turned over to the Government at various dates   230

Total number of horses drawn from the government   395

Rounds fired of canister, shrapnel, fuse and percussion
    shell, and solid shot   9,780
  Total weight of iron, lead and powder at 11 lbs. per shot 107,580
No. of miles traveled on foot, horse, rail and boat   18,758

www.ingramcontent.com/pod-product-compliance
Lightning Source LLC
Chambersburg PA
CBHW022022240426
43667CB00042B/1056